MsAdventures

"Women you know Sir are
considered as Domestick Beings,
and altho they inherit an Eaquel
Share of curiosity with the
other Sex . . . the Natural tenderness
and Delicacy of our Constitutions,
added to the many dangers we are
subject too from your Sex,
renders it almost impossible for
a Single Lady to travel without
injury to her character."
Abigail Adams

MsAdventures

Worldwide Travelguide for Independent Women

By Gail Rubin Bereny

Chronicle Books San Francisco

To My Family.

Cover photography by Baron Wolman.
The Bed and Breakfast Inn, Robert and Marilyn Kavanaugh, Proprietors.
British cab courtesy of Susan McBride of Grubb and Ellis.
Cover personalities, Jane Vandenburgh and Jack Jensen.
Book and cover design by Bob Harriman.
Composition by Hansen & Associates Graphics.

Special thanks to Dick Schuettge who had faith in the idea, Susan Harper, who
did such a super editing job, and to Jane Vandenburgh, who solved numerous
literary traumas.

Library of Congress Cataloging in Publication Data

Bereny, Gail Rubin.
    Ms adventures

    1. Travel.   I. Title.
G151.B47   910'.2'4042   77-18228
ISBN 0-87701-106-0

Chronicle Books
870 Market Street
San Francisco, CA 94102

CONTENTS

Don't Listen to Your Mother: Talk to Strangers

Getting Down to Basics: Food and Shelter

Money Matters: Getting It and Spending It

About How To Get About

Business Business

The Fine Art of Staying Out of the Slammer

MsCellaneous

RAMBLINGS OF AN OPEN MIND

A lot of my travel ideas are unorthodox, but if I had nothing new to offer, you wouldn't need me! There are already plenty of conservative books telling you to pack with tissue paper and bring travel irons and sturdy walking shoes—none of which I recommend. Nor is this a typical travel book telling you which hotel costs how much or how old the ruins in Delphi are or where you can find a three-star restaurant. Rather, it's a personal travel guide to more fun and less hysteria.

Don't let other people (including me) dictate your trip. Glean advice from people who have tastes and budgets like yours, but ultimately go where and do what you want and can afford. Be true to your real self—it's your time and money. If you huff and puff after walking from a cab to the curb, you're hardly a candidate for a backpacking trip through Nepal. If you don't like museums at all here, why go to them somewhere else? No one is going to grade you when you get back. If you do like art, history, or politics, but don't *love* them, there's still no need to see *every* museum, ruin, or government capital. Just pick representative places, the high spots. Anyway, if it's a really good trip, you'll recall people more than places!

Above all, remember that the most important thing you can take anywhere is not a Gucci bag or French-cut jeans; it's an open mind. Don't leave home with preconceived ideas about *any* country. Every place is different—or else why would you want to go? America itself is made up of many "countries"—although that thought doesn't prevent you from crossing state lines. Attitude, speech, and clothes differ as much from New York to Peoria as they do from Chicago to London.

You will not bring back fond memories if you approach your trip like a job—something to be done from 9 to 5 (unless it's 9 PM to 5 AM!). And speaking of memories, don't compare this trip to a trip you took with a former loved one. It won't be the same—nothing ever is. Enjoy the difference. Don't live in the past.

Keep things on your trip in perspective, and you'll be amazed at the perspective you'll gain on things back home while you're away. When you're involved with different people in different places, questions of whether Elliott still loves you or Sally is jealous or your apartment needs painting become miniscule problems. I know I've always come back less fearful, more aggressive. One's little world is put into perspective by the bigger world out there.

Stay loose everywhere. Don't be fussy or rigid. Roll with the punches to soften them. If your coffee tastes bitter or room service takes forever, it cannot be the end of the world. Believe me, these things happen right in your hometown.

People's customs vary about as much and as little as people do. Since you are expected to conform to *their* ways, notice how they behave in public. Do they run like crazy for buses, pushing and shoving their way ahead Mediterranean style, or do they queue up in orderly Japanese fashion? Do they check their coats? Do they stand for their national anthem? Do women shake hands? Keep in mind that *you* are the foreigner. *Their* language, currency, and customs are the standard. So don't be frustrated because they don't all trade in dollars, eat with a knife and fork, or speak English. How is your Japanese?

One last bit of advice: go where you are wanted. Life has enough aggravations without your wandering into an anti-American country. (But remember, many people love us even when their politicos don't.) The English, Israelis, Fijians, and Italians (for starters) welcome us with the proverbial open arms, while the Russians, Albanians, and Bahamians (again, for starters) make things as difficult as possible. So work *with* the odds!

Excuse the lecture.

"... the most important thing you can take with you anywhere is not a Gucci bag or French-cut jeans; it's an open mind."

Unraveling Travel

TRIPPING OUT

BEFORE YOU GO Don't just say "I'd like information about France." Tell your source of information that you want to know about charming little hotels in the bohemian district of Paris or deluxe quarters near the fine shops in Nice.

1

When you pore over travel brochures from *anybody*, take them with a grain of salt: the pictures are glossy and the adjectives glowing. But keep reminding yourself that nouns mean more than adjectives—"mountains" and "beaches" tell you more than "romantic tour." And pictures are not always worth a thousand *honest* words. I've been in hotels I certainly wouldn't recognize from the brochure pictures—they must have moved the best furniture from the owner's suite into their "average" room and placed every handsome waiter in a tux on the dance floor so they could snap a picture of their "glamourous crowd."

Plan your trip realistically for the amount of time you can spend and the most suitable season for your kind of vacation. April in Paris is colder than it is romantic and August in Acapulco is more torpid than torrid.

When you're ad-libbing your trip, do arrange in advance for special events or sights you're dying to see. Don't just arrive and then find that the world famous Casals concert in Puerto Rico is sold out, or the Prado Museum is closed the only day you'll be in Madrid. Indeed, you can pre-plan and pre-pay as many or as few things as you wish, from theater tickets to hotel reservations, even if you are not going on a tour.

If you want to make all the arrangements yourself, you'll need a computer timetable for a brain to figure the quickest and/or cheapest way to get anywhere, what with constant schedule and tariff revisions. So use a good travel agent whether you're looking for a deluxe tour or a budget one, a swinging singles' resort, a ranch for a wholesome vacation, a cruise, a round-the-world tour, an off-beat destination, or some other adventure. A good travel agent is as important as a good doctor or hair colorist. The less you have traveled in the past, the more you need the help of a good travel agent. Whatever, whenever: you do what *you* want—the agent only suggests, but it's *your* decision because it's *your* money. Women have often been conditioned to let "experts" decide things for them, but don't simply accept the agent's word as IT.

Here's what you should tell a travel agent in order to get the trip most suitable for you:

1. Mention *what* you want to do *when* and for how long. The agent should then be able to tell you weather conditions for that particular time of year, the most economical means of travel; and whether or not your prospective itinerary is feasible.
2. Tell him/her your total budget, including souvenir shopping, cocktails, and other personal expenses. This way the agent can figure out how much should be spent for various components of the trip.
3. Tell him/her why you are taking the trip. Do you want to meet people? Soak up the local culture at museums, opera houses, and cathedrals? Shop? Pursue a hobby? These personal tidbits help your agent arrange things to meet your interests. Romance is up to you, but he/she can at least point you in the right direction.
4. Tell the agent if this will be your only trip to that area. If so, perhaps there are outstanding things which you shouldn't miss but which you don't know about. I confess that I flew over one of the great wonders of the world, Ankor Wat, in what was then Cambodia, because I didn't know it was there!

Your trusty agent can also tell you what kind of clothes to take, all about travel documents such as passports and visas, what inoculations you'll need, super shopping specials, and so on.

How do you find such a gem? Check to see if your company uses a travel agent—and use the same one; you'll get preferential service. Or go to an agent who belongs to ASTA (American Society of Travel Agents). Agents usually advertise their ASTA association in their yellow pages ads or have a sticker on their window. If not, ask. And check with the Better Business Bureau.

What does it cost to use an agent? Nothing, unless you ask for special services. It's usually the airlines (et al) who pay the commission. You'll generally pay the same price whether you buy your ticket from an agent or directly from an airline or cruise company. You will be paying more if you need a custom-made itinerary or book hotel reservations for stays of only one or two nights.

What to look out for? An agent who is pushing anything that doesn't meet your desires: that means he is getting a hefty commission on the package; and values that more than your enjoyment. Also beware of any travel agent or tour guide who tries to give you an 18-year-old's youth discount when you're 33; if he's dishonest in one area, he's probably dishonest in others. If you're offered any special-for-you-honey deals, be wary: you will probably get what you've paid for—a round trip to Peoria! Be careful of people selling you seats for an affinity group of which you aren't even a member. Double check sellers of unwanted extras such as nightclub tours or side trips. Beware of outlandish claims such as a promise of the best view in the best hotel on short notice during the height of the season. Never offer to buy someone else's ticket, even though it may be offered at a cut rate: in this day of tight security checks, if your passport and ticket don't match, you'll have a lot of explaining to do.

$ It'll cost you proportionally less the more you prearrange. The more the gypsy leaves your soul, the more the money stays in your pocket. Flexibility and independence cost money.
$ Book as far in advance as possible, since the good deals go first. But if you can't, wait for the *last* minute—sometimes cancellations are good bets.
$ Plan your trip for the "low season" when prices may be 50% less than "high season" prices. High and low seasons differ among countries and climates: winter is Europe's low season, but it is the Caribbean's high season. Sometimes it's just a matter of postponing or speeding up your trip a few days.

$ Check into special deals offered by different countries. Some have special packages if you'll study there for the summer.

$ Buy special tickets here, like Italian museum tickets or Swiss Holiday tickets for railroads.

$ See how friendly your friendly bank really is. Some are connected with "savers' clubs" offering sightseeing, restaurant, car rental, and resort discounts.

$ Maybe your boss will pick up part of the tab if you go to a convention or seminar which you can convincingly state is vital to your work. See if a trip is tax-deductible.

$ Which are the cheapest and most expensive countries today? It's usually a matter of country versus city, rather than whole country versus whole country. A small town in Louisiana is certainly cheaper than Chicago, just as accommodations in the English countryside are cheaper than those in London. But in general, your dollars will disappear faster in Tokyo (probably the most expensive city in the world), Stockholm, and Paris than in Lisbon, Madrid, Bombay, or Dublin. All countries are beset by inflation, so gone are the days when you could live like a rajah on a few dollars a day. For some reason, warmer countries are usually cheaper than cold countries. Spain is cheaper than Belgium, Portugal less costly than England. Of course, there are exceptions, but it does appear to be a general rule.

$ There are certain countries such as Switzerland and the Scandinavian quadruplets that are so clean you can use third class restaurants, trains, and hotels with great security.

$ Get free information from tourist information offices. (The addresses are listed below.) Or get free information through your library's travel section. Or sift through other people's opinions, student publications, and the travel sections of women's magazines. If you'll be traveling in America, get free facts from the Department of Tourism of any state you plan to visit.

Visitors information bureaus are fonts of free, objective information. I say "objective" because while they do glorify the entire country, they won't rave about a commercial establishment as part of a pay-off. They simply aren't paid by individual enterprises. I'll list the main offices so that you can write for information before

"If you're offered any
special-for-you-honey deals,
be wary: you will probably
get the excitement of the
vacation you've paid for—
a round trip to Peoria!"

you leave, but there are often branches at airports and railroad stations in other countries, as well as a local branch here and there.

The information available at the centers covers tourist resorts, travel and sightseeing facilities, annual events, theater programs, other day and night entertainment, motoring, shopping, factory inspection tours, etc.

Arab Republic of Egypt Tourist Administration, 630 Fifth Avenue, N.Y. 10020
Australian Tourist Commission, 1270 Avenue of the Americas, New York, N.Y. 10020
Austrian National Tourist Office, 545 Fifth Ave., New York, N.Y. 10017
Bahama Islands Tourist Office, 30 Rockefeller Plaza, New York, N.Y. 10020
Belgian National Tourist Office, 720 Fifth Ave., New York, N.Y. 10019
Brazilian Government Trade Bureau, 551 Fifth Ave., New York, N.Y. 10017
Bulgarian Tourist Office, 50 E. 42nd St., New York, N.Y. 10017
Colombia Government Tourist Office, 140 East 57th Street, New York, N.Y. 10022
Czechoslovakia Travel Bureau, 10 E. 40th St., New York, N.Y. 10016
Danish National Tourist Office, 75 Rockefeller Plaza, New York, N.Y. 10020
Dominican Republic Tourist Office, 64 W. 50th Street, New York, N.Y. 10020
Finnish National Tourist Office, 75 Rockefeller Plaza, New York, N.Y. 10020
French Government Tourist Office, 610 Fifth Ave., New York, N.Y. 10020
German National Tourist Office, 630 Fifth Avenue, New York, N.Y. 10020
Great Britain (England and Scotland) Tourist Authority, 680 Fifth Ave., New York, N.Y. 10017
Greek National Tourist Office, 601 Fifth Avenue, New York, N.Y. 10017
Hong Kong Tourist Association, 548 Fifth Ave., New York, N.Y. 10036
Hungarian Embassy, 2437 15th Street NW, Washington, D.C.
India Tourist Office, 30 Rockefeller Plaza, New York, N.Y. 10020
Indonesian Director General of Tourism, 5 E. 68th St., New York, N.Y. 10021
Irish Tourist Board, 590 Fifth Ave., New York, N.Y. 10036
Israel Government Tourist Office, 488 Madison Ave., New York, N.Y. 10022
Italian Government Travel Office, 630 Fifth Ave., New York, N.Y. 10020
Jamaica Tourist Board, Suite 254, Pan American Building, 200 Park Ave., New York, N.Y. 10017
Japan National Tourist Organization, 45 Rockefeller Plaza, New York, N.Y. 10021
Kenya Tourist Board, 15 E. 51st St., New York, N.Y. 10022
Korea (South) National Tourism Corporation, 460 Park Avenue, New York, N.Y. 10022
Malaysian Tourist Information Centre, Transamerica Pyramid Building, 600 Montgomery Street, San Francisco, Ca. 94117
Mexican National Tourist Council, 677 Fifth Ave., New York, N.Y. 10022

Netherlands National Tourist Office, 576 Fifth Avenue, New York, N.Y. 10036
Nigerian Mission to the UN, 757 Third Avenue, New York, N.Y. 10017
Norway National Tourist Office, 75 Rockefeller Plaza, New York, N.Y. 10019
Pacific Area Travel Association, 228 Grant Street, San Francisco, Ca. 94108
Panama Tourist Office, 630 Fifth Avenue, New York, N.Y. 10020
Portugal (Casa de), 570 Fifth Ave., New York, N.Y. 10022
Puerto Rico Tourism Development Company, 1290 Avenue of the Americas, New
   York, N.Y. 10019
Romanian National Tourist Office, 500 Fifth Ave., New York, N.Y. 10036
South African Tourist Corporation, 610 Fifth Ave., New York, N.Y. 10020
Spanish National Tourist Office, 122 E. 42nd St., New York, N.Y. 10017
Swedish National Tourist Office, 75 Rockefeller Plaza, New York, N.Y. 10019
Tahiti Tourist Board, 6290 Sunset Blvd., Los Angeles, Ca. 90028
Thailand Tourist Organization, 20 E. 82nd St., New York, N.Y. 10028
Turkish Tourism and Information Bureau, 500 Fifth Avenue, New York, N.Y.
   10036
U.S.S.R. (Intourist) Tourist Organization, 45 E. 49th S., New York, N.Y. 10017
Venezuelan Tourist Office, 485 Madison Ave., New York, N.Y. 10022
Virgin Islands Department of Commerce, 16 W. 49th St., New York, N.Y. 10020
Yugoslav State Tourist Office, 630 Fifth Ave., New York, N.Y. 10020

THE GETAWAY! Single women are notorious for leaving last minute chores until the very last minute, probably because there's nobody to nag them about niggling details. So I suggest you make a detailed list of all the things you must do before takeoff time.

1. *Make sure your passport and health card are in good order.*
2. *Consider your luggage. Does it need repair? Are there good identifying tags? Have the old destination tags been removed?*
3. *Make certain you have appropriate clothes in good repair. Trial pack.*
4. *Make duplicate lists of your travelers' checks and credit card numbers. Put one copy in your suitcase, the other in your purse (though not right with the stealable item). Also record insurance information (i.d. number and how to reach your insurance representative) and your social security number.*
5. *Check into special trip insurance for your body, your valuables, your vacant home, your car (if driving abroad). I've*

discussed health, baggage, and car insurance in detail in the obvious chapters, but this is the place to read about protecting your home, valuables, and children. Make sure all clauses in your homeowner or renter policies will be in effect while you're away. Many such policies negate certain areas of coverage if your home is vacant for a specified period. See what protection in your homeowner's policy you might already have for the valuables you'll be carrying with you; you might need extra coverage for expensive items such as cameras or jewelry. If you're leaving your car at home, see if you can suspend liability and collision coverage and get a refund on part of the premium. If you're the breadwinner in the family, make certain that you have insurance to take care of your children should anything happen to you. If you aren't otherwise covered, take out such insurance at the special counters at the airport.

6. Hunt through your papers for receipts or insurance policies on any new foreign-made equipment, like cameras and watches, or register the items with U.S. Customs before you leave.

7. Arrange to have your pets cared for.

8. Buy a self-watering gadget for your plants or make plans with a friend to care for them.

9. Make arrangements to have your rugs cleaned while you're gone so they'll have plenty of time to dry before you traipse back through.

10. Leave an open container of baking soda in your refrigerator to freshen it.

11. Make sure that you've pulled out the plugs of all appliances. I once worried my way through Canada, thinking that I had left the iron on and that the house was in flames (I hadn't and it wasn't).

12. Turn off any gas jets and all water faucets.

13. Ask the police or your apartment security to check by for signs of any activity—and give them your itinerary so they can reach you in case of trouble.

14. *Put your valuables in a safe deposit box or leave them with a trusted friend.*

15. *Plan to have your vacant home look occupied. Use an automatic timing device to turn lights on and off to make it look like you're there when you aren't. Lock all doors and never, never leave a note pinned to the door—it just advertises the fact that you're away. If you live in a house, make certain grass is mowed or snow cleared while you're away so it won't be obvious there's no one there to take care of things. Have your mail and newspaper stopped.*

16. *Pay all bills—in advance if need be; so they won't disconnect your electricity while you're gone, or cancel your insurance or credit card use.*

17. *Tell the newspaper columnist about your trip after your trip, not before your departure.*

18. *Leave your itinerary with a friend so that you can be notified in an emergency.*

19. *After travel plans are made, confirm reservations before leaving.*

20. *Make arrangements to get to the airport, after checking the length of time it takes. But do call again before leaving home to be sure the plane is on schedule.*

21. *Try to get a good night's rest—but I never have!*

22. *Before leaving, make one last check around (under the bed, in closets, etc.) to make certain you haven't forgotten anything.*

Bon Voyage!

AFTER YOU'VE ARRIVED

$ The local chamber of commerce or visitors bureau can often tell you about free sightseeing opportunities such as plants and factories. (Some factories even give away free samples or sell heavily discounted products.) They can also sometimes help you if you've been foolish enough to arrive without a hotel room or have one but want another. They can tell you what freebies are available, like certain days at museums, etc.

$ Don't assume all long-hairs are drug-degenerate hippies; quite a few of them are professional people who have taken a year's sabbatical to roam the world. They are usually fonts of information about where to stay, eat, and sightsee cheaply.

$ Joining a guided tour—day or night—can be a big savings. In a day, you will cover all the main attractions of the city in the comfort of roomy tour buses, with the highlights of each stop explained in English by your tour guide. Hiring guides, paying admission fees, and paying for transportation would be much more expensive. There is the alternative of taking tour map and guide book in hand and getting about yourself, via public transportation, to those sights which hold particular interest for you.

$ A series of mini-walking tours is one way of getting a feel for your host city and, of course, it costs you nothing to walk and look.

$ Stay away from the areas frequented by tourists; if you live like the hosts and not the guests, you'll cut your costs considerably.

WINGING IT!

LET'S TAKE THIS from the beginning: *which* plane should you take? 2
You'll save money by asking your travel agent for the best deal
—it could be charter (you fly with a group on fixed dates), no-frills, economy class, special package (air/sea), excursion, or off-hour discount. There are so many different deals and they change so rapidly that it would be better for you to check with an agent than to read a list here which is out-dated before the ink is dry. But here are some tips to keep in mind.

PLANE CASH

$ For international travel, always determine what free stopovers you may be entitled to. Most airlines permit them on direct route to your destination; some permit stopovers at unexpected places, too.

$ Check to see if your airline provides free transportation between the domestic and international departure sections of the terminal.

$ Inquire about special intra-country one-shot travel tickets. (For example, for travel in Colombia you can buy a "Know Colombia" ticket for $75 which is valid for 30 days' unlimited travel within the country. Since this is only available outside Colombia, check on it—and other such deals—through the airline or national tourist office *here.*

$ Sometimes you save by buying tickets far in advance; occasionally you'll get a last-minute break. There are no firm rules, but *usually* earlier is cheaper.

$ Don't buy tickets at overcrowded counters—especially at airports—because the agent will be too busy to answer questions or take the time to work out the least expensive fare.

$ Don't choose an airline as a budget saver because it offers in-flight meals—big deal; almost all of them serve food if you're aloft more than five minutes.

$ All "name" airlines are pretty much the same, regardless of their claims. Movies may differ as do stewardess's costumes, but how important is that to you? Basic rates are similar—except for Icelandic and International Air Bahama, which really do offer cheaper fares and on-board liquor but, as in the case of most good deals, are usually booked months in advance. Remember, you'll only save by *types* of fares, not regular airline offerings, except for the new Laker Sky Train fares.

$ Stick with one airline per trip if possible. It's complicated enough for a ticket agent to be familiar with the fare for his own airline, but if he has to quote you prices for another, you're less likely to get the best deal.

$ Once you've decided on a carrier, then changed your mind in favor of another one, go to the one you're switching *to*. They'll be *getting* a sale, not losing one, so you'll get much more cooperation in looking for money savers. (Be certain baggage tags have been altered correctly after such a ticket change.)

$ Keep baggage to a minimum to avoid overweight penalties and porters' fees.

$ Go with a group—and if it's a big one, see if you can all meet in one place and hire a special bus to get you to the airport.

$ You can get air fare refunder insurance for charter flights, paying you for a regular ticket home if illness prevents your return with the group.

$ If you can talk twenty people into taking a regular-fare trip, you'll get your trip free.

$ Buy a package; the more that is prearranged, the cheaper.

$ Check if you get a lower fare by traveling at a certain time of day or on a certain day of the week. But be sure you understand any restrictions. (Some fares aren't applicable during holidays and some family fares aren't good in the summer—when you need them!)

$ Just as you'll have a choice of flights, you may also have a choice of airports. So try to use the closest (you'll save money enroute), smallest (less terminal traffic hassle) airport.

$ Always check the cheapest, fastest way to and from the terminal —it's usually the airport bus or limo, but occasionally a taxi is cheaper, especially if you share it. The tourist office can give you advice on getting *to* the airport; your stewardess can tell you how to go *from* the plane. But be sure your hotel hasn't already sent someone for you.

$ Check on how long it should take you to go to and from the terminal. You might want to allow yourself extra time to be able to take advantage of the airport money-saving duty-free shops. (The best are in Shannon and Amsterdam.)

$ If you'll be gone for any length of time at all, it's usually not a good idea to drive to the airport and leave your car there. Not only are the rates often prohibitive, but there's also usually vandalism and inconvenience. (Long term parking facilities are always a long way from the terminal.)

$ Determine which departure *city* saves you money.

$ If your next flight is just a few hours off, check into a day room at an airport hotel when you can pay for just a short time and take a nap, shower and change clothes without schlepping to a hotel and back.

PLANE SENSE Deal only with reputable anybodys and anything. Unworthy charters have crashed because of sheer negligence, and tourists have been stranded abroad because of non-valid tickets from phony agents. So choose your charter and/or travel agent with care. *Know* who you're dealing with. Get *everything* spelled out in detail and in writing.

The *ways* to make reservations if you're going it alone depend upon how much time you have. Here they are in ascending amounts of hysteria:

1. *Discuss the ticket over the phone with your airline representative and have the airline send you the tickets by mail.*
2. *Have your travel agent arrange things. This doesn't cost you— they get their commission from the airlines.*
3. *Go to an airline ticket office as far in advance as possible.*
4. *Scurry to the airport ticket counter and pray that you can get through that line during rush hours—and forget a lengthy conference on how to get the best deal: you'll have to take what you can get.*

If you make reservations yourself, you'll need to specify where and when you want to go (and perhaps return), type of travel (first class or tourist), and how many are traveling. The following words and phrases may be of help.

WAIT LIST: Waiting list of names and phone numbers of persons who wish to reserve a seat on a flight that is already sold out. If a cancellation comes up, they'll call you. Even the wait list may be closed during heaviest traffic periods around major holidays.

STANDBY: When the flight you want is sold out, and even the wait list is closed, passengers may go to the airport departure lounge as standbys. If last-minute cancellations come up, or someone misses the flight, standbys are boarded just prior to takeoff.

TRANSFER: Ground transportation by bus, limousine or cab between airports and resorts or hotels, or between two airports. Vacations often include transfers, and certain resorts meet guests at the airport in your own "courtesy car."

RECONFIRMATION: A phone call to the airline several hours before flight time, stating that you will in fact be using your on-going or return flight reservation. Reconfirmation is not necessary at your initial starting point.

If you miss your flight and it's the airline's fault, they must arrange for your next flight out, even if it's on a different airline. They must also provide you with meals and hotel accommodations until you can get going. If your plane is delayed more than four hours, or canceled, and you're rerouted on a later flight, the airline must provide you with a hotel room if the delay is between 10 PM and 6 AM, meals at regular hours, one three-minute telephone call anywhere in the U.S. or a fifteen-word telegram, and money for transportation between the airport and hotel or home. And don't forget to have the carrier notify anyone who's expecting you—from a friend to your first hotel.

Get to the airport on time! Your space is subject to cancellation twenty minutes before the scheduled departure on international flights, five minutes for a domestic one. But you should allow much more time than that for pre-departure check-in, government requirements (if an international flight), and personal activities. Actually, "bumping" starts earlier than the airlines admit, so arrive at the airport early and board early to keep from being "replaced." Airlines do overbook and you can keep from being an innocent victim if you're on before the bumping starts. Another safeguard against this practice: check your ticket to make sure the clerk has written down the right day, time, and flight. If you are bumped, your airline must reschedule you on a flight that arrives within two hours of your scheduled flight (four hours if an international one). If the airline can't do this, you will get the price of your ticket back. You can only expect financial compensation on domestic flights, and when you accept it you forfeit further rights to sue the company or seek redress. If your ticket is without a U.S. point, you don't have any legal rights in this area. But the more of a fuss you make, the more help you'll get. Just to get rid of you, they'll usually up the ante. This is where your assertiveness training should come in handy.

If you don't have a ticket, you must go to the counter in the main terminal: no tickets are sold at the gates. And always find out if you can check your bags through right at the terminal curb, making certain the baggage tag he affixes is to the right destination.

One last thought before you leave. Don't encourage last-minute gifts—where are you going to put any last-minute items, when your hands and purse and tote bag are already overflowing? You can't refuse them, but you can avoid them in the first place by arranging to have bon voyage parties a few days in advance—not at the terminal.

Where to sit? Socially speaking, pick your seat this way. Arrive at the airport early. Go to the departure lounge and watch the arrivals. Then decide where and with whom you want to sit, and ask the agent for that particular seat.

Semi-socially speaking, when you're already traveling with someone and don't want to be split up, reserve the window and aisle seats when there are three seats across. Chances are no one will want the seat between you—and if someone has to take it because of a crowded flight, you can probably switch with the middle person and sit next to your companion. The stranger is not going to want to have you talk over him or her the whole flight.

For seating comfort, choose the no smoking section if it applies to you. And don't take a seat right by the galley or toilet where the traffic and commotion might bother you. The "J" section on a 747 has only two seats per row. Any big jet gives you more leg room in the front of the tourist section or by the emergency exit.

On board, you can use the time either going to the lounge to meet your *fellow* fliers, asking the stewardess for some cards and/or games and setting up a little of your own action, or simply chatting with that special person you cleverly arranged to sit next to. If all else fails, I hope you've brought along a paperback that you'll get so absorbed in, you won't care that you've picked the seat next to an 85-year-old grandfather of seventeen! Or you can sleep, using those mysterious black eye shades you've brought along for just such occasions. If you do want to sleep en route, keep your seat belt loosely fastened or the stewardess will awaken you to put it on if there's any turbulence. If you're not wearing airy, chic sandles, take off your shoes and put on those folding slippers you had in your tote. But ease your shoes on about an hour before landing, so your feet can shrink back down to size.

Here are some air chair exercises that Scandinavian Airlines has come up with. First, you can "warm up" by raising your heels alternately as high as possible. While kicking up your heels (so to speak), raise your arms in a bent position, rocking rhythmically forward and back. Do this for three minutes. Follow the jogging contortions with rising on your toes thirty times to improve blood circulation. Then roll your shoulders in large circles forward and backward; this stimulates the joints and relaxes muscles. If you have not been restrained by either a straight jacket or the glares of your fellow passengers, and wish to continue, here are some more exercises. Turning your head and nodding is good for the joint capsules and cartilage in the upper spinal column. Bend forward thirty times, with stomach sucked in and feet up; then relax both; this is supposed to be good for bowels and for blood circulation. Stimulate your wrists by turning hands from knuckles up to palms up. If you arrive *psychologically* intact after all these shenanigans, you should arrive fresh and alert. Need I mention that you do these with unfastened seat belts?

Walk up and down the aisle every hour or so to prevent muscle cramps—and while you're up, scout around for an attractive man with whom to share a taxi from the airport. Or if you're boxed into the window seat and have to climb over two irritable passengers just to get to the aisle, save your aisle trips for going to the john, and do isometric exercises in your seat.

When you leave the plane, check to make certain you haven't left anything behind. Each year passengers leave the damndest things—from address books to wooden legs! So check under, above and on your seat, and check the lavatory when you leave it.

There are some things that are just plane good manners. Here are some things that aren't: (1) trying to sneak on too much carry-on luggage, and making a scene when you are forced to obey regulations; (2) smoking pot in the lavatories or becoming high on alcohol during the flight; (3) letting your elbows dangle or feet rest in the aisles; (4) insisting on sitting next to someone when an adjacent seat just isn't available.

At your final destination, go directly to the baggage pick-up station, since some luggage areas aren't guarded and your bag may just disappear. When you do claim your bag, be sure to match the check stubs in your ticket envelope with those on the bag so you won't get to your hotel with a bag full of nun's habits. Strap on your collapsible luggage wheels and be off.

A final word (or two): if you have a fear of flying, rest assured that statistically flying is safer than driving. You just hear more about the few plane crashes since they're more spectacular. Actually, if there is the slightest suspicion that anything is wrong, the airline will not let the plane take off. And you might want to conquer your fear of flying through the "Fly Without Fear" organization. You can get further details by writing Travel and Fly Without Fear, Inc., 101 Park Avenue, New York, New York 10017. They may be able to tell you about similar organizations near you.

So up, up and away—and I hope you'll soon know what flying high really means!

ON BEING ABOVE BOARD

WHY FLY? Take a boat instead. You'll be more comfortable in transit, and you'll certainly have better meals and more of a choice of activities. You'll also pretty well know how much **3** the entire trip costs ahead of time, since just about everything is included except tips. And you won't have to worry about baggage and checking in and out of hotels. What's more, you'll arrive and return more refreshed than a plane traveler. Plus you can bring back the heaviest gifts you desire!

Well, since we know there's no nirvana, what are the cons? You may be the only person under 80 years old aboard, it's expensive, and it demands more time and fancy clothes than other means of getting about.

So that you won't stop reading after that deadly sentence about being "the only person under 80," I'll face the "meeting people" issue right here as well as in the "Meeting Your Knight in Shining Guccis" chapter.

Your chances of meeting younger, single people go up considerably if you take short (one-week) cruises to sunny places during summer or holiday periods. Older ships generally have more single cabins than newer ones. Don't take a cruise advertised for "swinging singles" unless the age limit is spelled out. And do choose a smallish (four hundred or so passengers) ship which gives you a lot of open public rooms for casual socializing. Choose a cruise geared to your particular interest (e.g., tennis or music), so you'll meet others more easily (you'll be thrown together at concerts or bridge matches) and have a good time even if you don't meet someone exciting.

Since so much cruise life revolves around eating, you might keep that in mind when booking a cruise. And ask to be seated at a large table, thus greatly increasing your contacts. While most ships have superlative food, some are not only better than others but might also be your ethnic preference. (Do you prefer Italian, French or Scandinavian edibles?)

Before picking a ship, visit different ones in port if you live in a

---

"While kicking up your heels (so to speak), raise your arms in a bent position, rocking rhythmically forward and back."

---

town where that's possible. Your newspaper or the ship's office can give you the schedule.

To make sure your bags get on board when you do, put stickers on them with your name and cabin number clearly printed. If it'll make it easier for you, bring your luggage to the ship the day before embarkation. Although there are no weight restrictions on cruise ships, keep in mind any other form of transportation you might be using later (like a car to tool around Europe, or a plane as part of a sea/air package).

CRUISING CASH

$ To save money, look into off-season cruises; they're as good a deal as off-season resort rates. But you may miss in the way of single men what you'll make up in saved money.

$ When you calculate cruise costs over costs of other types of travel, remember that your cruise expenses cover transportation, food, accommodations and entertainment. Since the least expensive cabins are the first to go, reserve early or take a chance on a last minute cancellation.

$ If you desire, cruise lines will try to team you up with a roommate. (Sorry, it must be the same sex.) You'll save a good amount sharing as opposed to the single rate.

$ Since everyone in each class gets to use the same facilities (dining room, pool, etc.), you might as well take the cheapest cabin you can find. But do study a diagram of the ship—cabins are noisy by the restrooms, pantry, linen closet, elevators, and public rooms. Cabins in the middle are the most stable. How important is an outside room to you? I think a porthole to look out of is very important —someone else might not. It's your vacation (and money). Cabins in the area right between First and Tourist Classes are usually similar—so ask for Tourist, pay Tourist but get close to First Class comfort.

Cargo ships carry from thirty to eighty passengers. The meals and entertainment are more lavish on these lines than on freighters, but the clothing is still casual.

Freighters are as different from luxury cruises as prop planes are from jumbo jets. You'll never have to dress up (indeed, you'll look ridiculous if you do) and there is no organized entertainment. And your time must be flexible, since freighter schedules change to fit the shipping company's needs, not yours. If you like a lot of action, you'd probably feel bored and hemmed-in on this type of ship. I personally love their informality and off-beat stops.

The main thing to note about freighters is that there are only twelve passengers, so you'd better check ahead as to who they're going to be. The purser or captain will probably help you, since he doesn't want unhappy passengers either. I once lucked out on a freighter from Tahiti to Fiji: there was a fascinating single male artist aboard and I was the only single woman. However, I've heard horror stories from female friends who were stuck on a boat with all couples.

Two final freighter notes: (1) Since these ships have no doctor aboard, and ports are few and far between, pregnant women are not allowed on many freighters; and (2) I've found that for freighters you either have to reserve very far in advance or try to get a last-minute cancellation.

Solo? Or No?

GOING IT ALONE

IF YOU LIVE ALONE and like it, you're sure to love traveling alone. If you have a roommate or roommates, try a short vacation alone to see if you're up to it. But if you think you can possibly do it, do it! I worked my way around the world by myself for ten months when I was 21! And I was no big city sophisticate, unless you consider Peoria (my home town) the Big Apple.

Need to know some advantages before you get up your courage and go it alone? Here they are.

1. *There's no question that it's easier to meet people when you're alone. Men are much more apt to strike up a conversation with you when you're alone than when you're with other women. And others will take you in hand—older couples will want to take care of you: you'll remind them of their daughter or neighbor, depending on your age—and theirs. Maybe not romantic, but an assurance that you won't be alone and a good entrée to being fixed up with an attractive man you may spy; you might feel less "aggressive" if you had them ask him to join you for a drink.*

2. *Singles are now welcome everywhere. More and more women are traveling on their own all over the world. If you do meet someone who feels gadding about alone is not a woman's place (whatever, wherever that is), feel it's his problem, not yours. You won't be looked on as an object of pity as you might have been even a few years ago: today the childless single woman is more often a target of envy than pity!*

3. *You'll feel free to people-watch, window shop, get lost in crowds, flirt outrageously, ignore people, become involved, or feel totally anonymous and in control.*

4. *It isn't better traveling with just anyone than by yourself.*

The most important thing about traveling alone is to realize that it doesn't really matter if you meet someone or not. You should be self-sufficient enough to enjoy your own company!

If you are going alone, I strongly suggest your first activity be a day or half-day tour of the city. It'll cover the real highlights and your guide will tell you everything you ever wanted to know. Then you can go back by yourself later to anything you wanted to see in more depth. But the important thing is that you'll be oriented! And such tours are terrific ways of meeting people—many a morning tour of a national monument has been the start of an evening tour of night spots!

If you don't want to go on an escorted tour, but don't want to ad-lib it as you go along, you can take the middle course by pre-planning your itinerary before you go alone—having reservations, some sightseeing junkets, and being met by some travel representatives in each city, yet not being bound to a group.

You can even have as many things pre-planned as on an escorted tour if that'll make you feel more secure and frugal. Make reservations either through a travel agent or on your own; see the "Winging It" and "Lodging Logic" chapters, to unsnarl the wonderful world of reservations. Or you may want to pre-plan the bare minimum—just transfers (getting to and from the airport, trains, etc.)—so while culture shock hits you, at least you won't have to worry about luggage and rupees.

If you go completely on your own, remember you'll pay a premium for your independence—you not only won't get the discounts big groups get, but you'll also usually have to pay about as much for a single room as doubles would (and *they* can *split* the tariff). But if you like to go with the wind and hate to be told what to do when, then go it alone. If this independence extends into no planning whatsoever, at least take the precaution of going off-season, off-main event (not during a main convention or fair), off the tourist track.

Don't be self-conscious—people never spend as much time thinking about you as you would think. They'll be too wrapped up in themselves to really care—and even if they do, you'll never see them again. I wasn't even self-conscious as the only woman in a large Turkish restaurant filled with leering men. I just figured their thoughts were their own, I wanted to enjoy my yogurt salad, and I couldn't possibly be raped in the presence of 150 people in a well-known public restaurant.

If you're dining alone, there may be a tendancy on the waiter's part to tuck you away out of sight, since for some reason a single woman eating alone signals to the *waiter* neither glamour nor romantic expectation, but rather one person's tips and tab versus two or more. But if you demand that you get good service and a pleasant table, you will. They'd rather give in than have you make a scene. Actually, a lone attractive woman has a good chance of having another single person ask to join her. You can help things along by asking the maitre d' to seat you next to an appealing man or alerting him that you would not mind sharing your table with an attractive diner should one come into the restaurant after you've been seated.

Other dining tips: you can take a book to a restaurant—look engrossed if there's a nebbish pestering you or put the book down if he's a doll! Don't go into an empty restaurant. That's as depressing as gaining ten pounds. Peek in and don't be embarrassed to leave if there's no one else there. And conversely, always call and reserve a table for yourself with a Dr. title in front of your name—they'll assume you're the secretary and reserve a better place (because they'll think it's for a man!). Anyway, do reserve in advance—it'll be even harder for anyone to *try* to turn you away.

For some reason, you'll feel easier about eating alone at a first class restaurant abroad than at home. I know, when you're alone at home it's tuna fish in front of the tube or a hamburger at a local coffee shop. But inhibitions seem to fly out the plane window, and you'll feel strangely *free*. Relax and have some wine!

Hotels may try to give you as bad a deal as restaurants. But if you again demand (with voice steadily rising) a better room, you'll probably get it. Always remember that a scene makes them more uncomfortable than it does you. Remember your assertiveness training!

TRAVELING WITH A MAN

FIRST AND FOREMOST you must agree beforehand as to who will pay for what. A remote country inn eighty miles from Tokyo is no place to discover that from there on out you will be expected to foot the whole bill! And if you're supposed to split the tab (which I think is fair), you should at least know in advance so that you can budget accordingly.

Another thing to establish before vacationing *à deux*: do you share the same interests? Some differences are fine and will bring added excitement to your trip when you've gone your separate ways for a day only to come back bursting with pleasure about your day. But if the two of you like totally different things—you want the seashore while he wants the mountains, he likes it (the climate) cold while you like it hot, you like spontaneous experiences while he is uncomfortable (not to mention irritable) if everything isn't planned and orderly—I suggest you go it alone or with someone else.

Are you both realistic? Travel ads aside, tans are sometimes burns (with an unromantic, no-touch aftermath), promised sunshine can become perpetual rain, and some candlelight dinners in exotic places will lead more readily to indigestion than to passion. Make sure you're *both* realistic and adaptable.

Just like the myth that a baby can hold together a faltering marriage, so too is it a fantasy that a vacation can bind up a splintering relationship. You'll simply be together *more*—so if you've been getting on each other's nerves at home, you'll only have more time to do it on vacation.

Even if you're wild about your traveling companion, don't be with him every second. Although you may always want to see the same things, see them separately occasionally. And don't eat every meal together—have other people join you once in awhile to keep your relationship from getting stale or confining. When you do dine together, make it special: have a picnic in an idyllic spot or a candlelight dinner in a charming bistro or a romantic meal on a floating barge.

Don't go anywhere one of you has already been *à deux*. If Paris is where he and his ex-wife spent their honeymoon or you and your ex-great passion had a fling, don't go again. Whichever one of you had the previous romantic experience will always be comparing the present trip to "when I was here with. . . ."

Investigate honeymoon packages even if you're not on your honeymoon . . . you'll not only save money, but you'll also probably get some extra goodies (like free champagne, fresh flowers, breakfast in bed).

If you are traveling by ship with a man and if the two of you wish to dine alone, reserve a table for two when you make your reservations since such tables are scarce.

Keep your hotel room clean. Unless you have a suite, the room is likely to be crowded and small, so you'll really get on each other's nerves if you have things strewn all over. Try to take care of your personal things when he isn't around for the horror show: set your hair when he's at the barber shop, give yourself a facial when he's out by the pool.

Check with your travel agent before you go as to whether or not unmarrieds can share a room. Some countries are still strait-laced about this sort of thing, even in this Age of Aquarius. The South American countries, Spain, Portugal, Ireland, and Russia are most uptight about unmarrieds sharing a room. In France, they'll probably be charmed by the whole thing. The Scandinavians couldn't care less. The English are iffy about it—you pays your money and you takes your chances. Actually, a lot of the hotel keepers don't care, but they have to protect themselves by following the law. When you register in *any* hotel in most areas (like Europe), you have to turn in your passport for police data. And your passports will show different names. One friend of mine got around the problem by writing up a marriage document (dated *after* the passport, of course) and placing it with his passport. You'll have fewer problems at the hotel desk when traveling with a group, since the tour leader collects all the passports and turns them in en masse; the only problem may be some of the small minds on your tour.

If you look "straight" (you're not an interracial couple, are nicely dressed, the man doesn't have long hair), you'll have much less trouble than you would otherwise. But if you feel "chicken" or beset by legalities, ask for adjoining rooms. (But you'll pay for two.)

THE BUDDY SYSTEM

6

INEXPERIENCED WOMEN TRAVELERS often assume they have to travel with a companion. Why? Most men don't travel on the buddy system. I think the only thing that could be worse would be traveling with *two* buddies. The one big advantage of traveling with another woman is that you split all the costs, which are often little more than one person alone would pay.

If you decide you must travel with a girlfriend, make sure you're compatible. Try a weekend together at a nearby resort as a test. Do you attract men while she turns them off? Is an evening of chamber music your idea of a rousing night out, while she wants to do the Hustle at a swinging disco? Are you a day person who's thinking of traveling with a night owl? Do you want to go first class while your prospective traveling companion is a real cheapie? Think again. Only with the opposite sex, do opposites attract.

Work things out in advance—shared expenses, who tips, what to do if an attractive man shows an interest in *one* of you.

Don't be inseparable. Take separate rooms occasionally, as well as separate day tours. Eat with others periodically, or even eat alone. Don't be inseparable or your trip will be unbearable!

There are some travel agencies who will try to find you a compatible companion. Ask your travel agent if he/she can do this or if he/she knows anyone who can. To show you how specialized the whole thing has become, there's even a Widows' Travel Club. For a $15 yearly membership fee, you are put in touch with other widows who want to travel and given a brochure describing trips, plus a questionnaire that tries to match personalities and travel preferences. Write Mrs. Beatrice Green, 17 East 45th St., New York, N.Y. 10017.

Cruise ships also will usually try to find someone with whom you can share a room. (But since you probably won't meet the person until sailing, you're really taking a chance.) And certain resorts will buddy you up. Clubs Meds will, among others. (See the "Meeting Your Knight in Shining Guccis" chapter.)

HUSBAND? NO. CHILDREN? YES.

YOU'RE A DIVORCEE or widow with children. Do you take them along? It's your decision, but you should be able to make a more intelligent choice after reading these pros and cons. **7**

Pros:
1. *Sometimes it's actually easier to meet people when you're with children, since people will warm up to the kids and then to you. Many men will start a conversation with you en famille because it seems less predatory than other conversation starters.*
2. *Your children will learn responsibility, adaptability and foreign facts.*
3. *Trips together help bring a family closer.*
4. *With children's transportation and hotel discounts, it's often cheaper to take the kids with you than to leave them at home with a paid sitter or to send them to camp.*
5. *You'll save long-distance worrying.*
6. *You'll get a new perspective by seeing things from a child's point of view.*

There are some cons, however, and they should be mentioned. Children are narrow-minded travelers who will want to order hamburgers and vanilla ice cream in a heavenly French restaurant famed for soufflés, will always have to go to the bathroom when there's not one around, would rather go swimming than sightseeing (unless *you'd* rather go swimming than sightseeing!), can last about ten minutes in a museum, will whine about missing their friends, and can put a crimp in your plans to have a date with a marvelous new man if you can't find a baby-sitter. Now that you've been both encouraged and forewarned, read on.

Since the major responsibility for getting a vacation together falls to you, pre-plan as much as possible and as far in advance as possible. February is not too early to begin laying groundwork for a summer holiday. Make written lists to cover what to pack for everyone and what else to do before leaving.

See that each family member has proper travel documents and vaccinations if these are required for your destination. At the time of inoculations—or by phone if no shots are needed—ask your physician any questions you have about food, beverages, vitamins, and medicines for the trip.

Give every family member above the toddler stage a voice in decision-making. Children have strong views about vacations and if you don't listen now, you'll be listening constantly later. And continue with this feeling of group participation by having older children read and report on travel books about the country you'll see and keep diaries of their own experiences. Younger children can collect free postcards from tourist spots and save them for a travel scrapbook. Let them feel "grown up" by being mainly responsible for their own suitcases and belongings.

Let a small child take along a favorite toy as a security blanket. Actually, you should have travel-sized games for all-aged children since English language ones are hard to find abroad and foreign language television usually means no television.

Pack sturdy drip-dry clothes, with an emphasis on things which don't show spots (such as plaids and small prints). But do carry proper city clothes for children—in other countries children are dressed more formally than here for restaurants and downtown sites. Children traveling on international flights at half-fare get the same luggage allowance as adults. Infants traveling at 10% fare get no allowance, but a portable cradle will be carried free.

Think about baby-sitting arrangements before you leave. Can you bring a mother's helper from home who is already acquainted with your kids? If not, when you're abroad look into baby-sitting services as recommended by your hotel or national tourist organization. Student organizations often have economical baby-sitting services. Or put your children in one of Europe's children's hotels —they'll be well taken care of in these established places. Some regular hotels have counselors and supervised activities for children, with "night patrols" to assure the safety of children while you're out in the evenings. Look for hotels with lifeguarded swimming pools and supervised playrooms and playgrounds.

A child under 2 usually fares best at a Canadian or Caribbean resort, where familiar food, reliable sitters, and attentive service are available. The same resort is fun for a child of kindergarten age, and he or she can also handle a bit of sightseeing. A grade-school child can appreciate many adult pleasures, though a morning of museums should be varied with a picnic lunch in a park or an afternoon at the zoo. Children's librarians can tell you about free or low cost children's programs such as story-reading hours and puppet shows. Safety at some of these is so good that you can leave the children and get what amounts to a free baby-sitter service.

Do what children like to do at home: visit zoos, planetariums, amusement parks, circuses, beaches, puppet shows. If you check into local folk festivals, you might find a child-oriented one such as Japan's Shichi-Go-San festival, where Japanese children under age 7 are taken to shrines in colorful kimonos. Older children can be entertained cheaply and wholesomely at folklore spots.

A good way to save money on lodging is to take advantage of hotel family rates if you share the room with your children. Most places let children under 12 share a room with a parent free; others extend it to 18 or under. Even though you'll usually get a substantial discount for the child's share of your room, it's good to have separate (but adjoining) rooms whenever the budget allows. Spend some time apart.

Another lodging tip: sometimes two divorcees or widows with children can share a rental home or apartment, and split costs and child care responsibilities.

When children are small, certain trips are guaranteed disasters. Such excursions are long, overland drives, rugged camping trips and whirlwind, multi-stop tours. A properly planned family vacation is something else again.

TRAINS AND PLANES AND KIDS   When you make plane or train reservations, state the ages and number of children you're bringing with you. Besides family discounts or child's fares, they'll furnish special children's meals, and most airlines will give you priority treatment, either providing you with a stroller or letting you on board first.

Plane rules for children flying within the U.S.A. are:
1. *One child under 2 years old not occupying a seat is free with each accompanying fare-paying adult passenger.*
2. *Children under 2 years occupying a seat, or over 2 and under 12 years, or more than one child under 2 years accompanying a passenger are each charged two-thirds of the normal adult fare.*
3. *Children under 5 years must be accompanied by a passenger at least 12 years old. Children between 5 and 12 may travel alone only by prior arrangement. Unaccompanied children between the ages of 5 and 12 will be charged the full adult fare.*

International rules are:
1. *A child under 2 years not occupying a seat will be carried at 10 % of the adult fare with each accompanying full fare adult passenger.*
2. *Children over 2 and under 12 years, a child under 2 occupying a seat, and more than one child accompanying a passenger are each charged one-half of the adult fare.*
3. *Children between the ages of 5 and 12 may travel alone (so that if they begin to drive you crazy, you can ship them back by the rules.) Another handy thing to keep in mind when planning a plane trip en famille: movies are most important when flying with children since those flickering screen gems can keep the kiddies from squirming for hours. So check ahead of time as to what's playing. It's even worth scheduling around the pictures.*

Flying with a baby? Pack in-flight necessities in a small carry-on bag—a change of clothing for the tot if your destination is in a different climate; formula if your baby is bottle-fed; bottled water if your doctor recommends it; disposable diapers; medicated baby powder; cleansing tissues; cotton balls and moist cleansing pads; and disposable bibs. Baby gear is not weighed. On board, a flight attendant will warm the baby's formula and food and supply you with disposable diapers should you run out.

Hold the baby during takeoff and landing, and whenever the "Fasten Seat Belt" sign is on. When the plane takes off and lands, the baby may cry because the change in air pressure bothers his ears. A few swallows of water will relieve the pressure.

There are some no-no's that sound so atrocious you'll think no one does them. Wrong. They have consistently been named as pet peeves by stewardesses I talked to. The gripes are: mothers changing their babys' diapers while nearby passengers are eating, or stuffing a used diaper in the pocket of the seat in front of them, or handing the stewardess a dirty diaper when she has her hands full passing out food trays. Less revolting but still annoying are unsupervised (by their parents) pre-schoolers who bother the other passengers by playing with their food or making too much noise.

Train (Amtrak) rules: unaccompanied children 8 through 11 years may travel alone on Amtrak trains if it is not an overnight trip and the child and parent have had a previous interview with the station manager. Children from 2 years up to 12 are charged one-half the adult fare (or family fare, whichever is applicable). One child under 2 years not occupying a separate seat may travel free with each person 12 years or older. Additional children under 2 are charged the fare for children from 2 years to 12 years of age.

CRUISING WITH KIDS   If you listen to the inviting travel folders from the steamship companies, you'll "bring the kids and have a fabulous time." Well, maybe. Remember that ship cabins are little bigger than walk-in closets, and a family sharing such tight quarters better be on very good terms and immune to seasickness. If you think it's bad being cooped up with a sick child at home, just picture said child throwing up in your little cabin on some bad night at sea.

While the last sentence does not invite this next train of thought, it's as good a time as any to mention food. Good news—ships are a child's version of an edible heaven. There are free hamburger stands, gooey desserts that would make your family dentist jump overboard, constant snacks, and buffets filled with all sorts of strange and wonderful things. As for regular meals, most ships either request or demand that children eat during the first shift (6:30 PM).

How will they be entertained when they aren't eating? There are big pool decks and small pools, the new electronic games (skeet shooting, paddle tennis, etc.) and often special Scrabble or backgammon lessons for the young. Many ships also have nurseries, teen rooms, craft centers, junior spas, and counselors for the kiddies. These counselors can sometimes be bribed to babysit. If they can't, beg your room steward or purser—but do remember that these are not kindly little old ladies who will teach your little ones the virtues of being good—they got their jobs aboard ship for other qualities (although some just may be good and pure and virtuous).

Some enlightened ships have special shore trips for youngsters. Others seem to have a knack for putting children and child-haters together on one bus for a day of unforgettable togetherness. And Bereny's Rule states that the children who did not get seasick, are the ones who will get bus sick.

DRIVING WITH CHILDREN Keep plenty of healthy snacks available so that you won't have to stop so frequently for food. And remember that if you give your youngsters a nibble just *before* you go to a restaurant, they won't be so famished that they'll be cranky until the meal arrives. Once you're in the restaurant, ask for a children's menu or request sharing privileges if you don't see children's portions on the regular menu.

To vary the restaurant syndrome, try picnics at *off-hours.* Actually, off-hour eating even in restaurants is good for children since service is usually much faster and there's less potential for childish fussing.

Carry a cooler in the car for ever-available cold liquids. For infants, use a bottle warmer device which plugs into the dashboard cigarette lighter. You can also use it to warm jars of baby food. Carry "The Wet Ones" (a more economical type of "Wash 'n Dri") or some other type of finger and face washer-upper such as washcloths dampened and kept in plastic bags. Have a blanket and pillow available for naps. Keep car doors locked.

Have plenty of games handy and stop either for a walk or for the evening *before* restlessness starts in. Have in mind games children can play without paraphernalia; if you've never heard the chaos that develops when the car makes a sudden stop, throwing Scrabble tiles all over the floor, then you have lived a very sheltered life. The following *materially* uncomplicated time-passers are therefore included for your very existence. One child counts the number of cows, telephone poles or whatever on one side of the road while the other counts those on the other side—the one who totals the most, wins. If there are more than two children, it can simply be a free-for-all! Or have them figure out what cars are from what countries by deciphering foreign license plates. Or let them play word games; while they're in a traveling mood, have one of them give the name of a location while the next must think of a place starting with the last letter of that word; for example, one child starts with Spain and the next says Nevada, the next uses Australia. Coloring books are good for times when you don't want to hear a word out of them (for a few minutes).

ON BEING A GROUPIE

8

FIRST OF ALL, why go on a group tour? I'll give you the negatives to begin with, and if you aren't turned off, then go ahead and take a tour after reading the warnings in this chapter.

1. *Don't take a tour if you're a swinger. Tour members are usually sedate, older couples or pairs of widows. And most of the couples will cleave together very biblically.*
2. *Don't take a tour if you're intolerant: you'll have to put up with people who would drive you crazy at home, and see places that interest the common denominator (but maybe not you).*
3. *Don't take a tour if you're a loner. "You'll Never Walk Alone" or do anything else alone except sleep alone (and that's if you pay a supplement).*
4. *Don't take a tour if you like impulsive, independent action. On tours everything is pre-planned and independence will either be impossible or costly.*

Now for the advantages.

1. *You're bound to find someone with whom to share your experiences: you'll never be lonely.*
2. *You'll have all the tedious pre-arrangements and actual trip details taken care of for you: plane reservations, bus seats, hotel rooms and dinner tables will always be guaranteed.*
3. *Packaged tours are always the cheapest way to go—the more prepackaged, the more you'll save. And except for personal items (shopping, laundry, drinks), you'll know the total cost in advance.*
4. *You'll never have to guess what to wear since your tour guide will tell everyone the same thing—so even if he's wrong, at least you won't be alone!*
5. *Since sightseeing is planned by pros, you won't be stranded at the Louvre the day it's closed; you'll have an expert guide to every place.*
6. *You won't have to worry about other languages (but you probably won't mix with the locals, either).*

Once you've decided to take a tour, how do you decide which one is for you? First you must pick one that has a good reputation, is within your budget and time allowance, and goes where you want to go and will show the things you want to see. Then you decide which airline you prefer—one that has a good reputation for comfort and security. You may also have a personal interest in the type of meals served on board and the quality of the inflight service.

Find out the quality of the hotels. Get the names (not just general terms like "you'll stay at first class hotels") and look them up in a guidebook for more objective descriptions. Or check their tour to a city you're familiar with, and if you agree with their taste there, chances are you can agree with it elsewhere. Taste is taste.

Are any meals included in the price? How many and what kind? On some tours, no meals are included. Others include "full American breakfasts" of bacon or ham and eggs, rather than the continental breakfast of rolls and coffee. When some lunches and/or dinners are included they usually refer to the Modified American Plan with a *table d'hôte* menu, a varied but limited selection. Often a tour will feature special dinners. In such cases, the menu is planned to include "native flavor" but has usually been heavily Americanized. These are costly banquets, so don't eat them on your own.

Does the tour have a "dine-around" option? This enables you to sample different restaurants: these are usually pre-selected and limited to table d'hôte menus, and include tax and service.

Many tours include special events in the tour price. Check to see which tours include which attractions, since tours can save you a lot of money compared to paying your own way—besides sparing you the frustration of missing things that aren't exactly around the corner for you to get back to.

Do you want a "fully-escorted" tour? That's with a tour director accompanying you every step of the way from the moment you take off until you return. Other tours include "local host" escort service to guide you during transfers and sightseeing tours and to provide you with helpful local information. Local hosts are experienced and always speak your language.

You can take tours once you've landed for as little or as long as you'd like—fly over by yourself and join a tour of one European country, for example. These mix and match possibilities give you independence (while costing you dollars, however).

Check how much you'll do in what time span. Forty cities in forty days is too much—just as a whole list of days "at leisure" may be too much *nothing* for the money. Certainly, you don't have to go everywhere if it's too much and you can go on your own if it's too little, but you're paying double for your whims.

Just so you take the tour and it doesn't "take" you, assume that anything not specified is not free. (This usually includes laundry, cigarettes, postcards, drinks, and other personal items.) You must read the fine print on the boring last page; this is easy to skip since the rest of the brochure is filled with gorgeous photos and glowing adjectives. But read the page that tells specifically what you (and they) are liable for, what the refund policies are, and pretty much what you can expect. You can't complain about second class hotels if that's what the brochure said—albeit in tiny print.

The advantage for the single woman traveler in group (charter) flights is in being thrown in with people of the same interests. Your political organization, public television station, ski club and the like are good candidates for charters. If there isn't already one, organize it yourself by writing for the Charter Flight Handbook, % Travel Information Bureau, Box 105, Kings Park, N.Y. 11754. Since most charters require a six-month club membership, check into this as soon as travel seeds start to sprout in your mind.

A tour that I'll go into in more detail is Bachelor Party's Single-world tours. Only people traveling alone can take these tours. You pay $15 annually as membership dues; and this makes you eligible for their tours and their Singleworld newsletter. Since this newsletter announces weekend trips and special events as well as longer trips, you might want to try out these shorter occasions to see if they're your kind of people. You might find more women than men; in the past men seemed to think it showed some sort of weakness to go on a singles tour—now with sex lines changing, perhaps they'll alter in this area as well. But these or any tours are not for the real swingers: real swingers go alone or with a man. Anyway, some of the Bachelor Party tours and cruises are broken down into age groups (I did not say "broken-down age groups") and especially aimed for the under-35s. On the tours your host gives parties and introduces you around so you'll be sure to meet people. Cruise dining room reservations are guaranteed at the more social second sitting. If you're interested, ask your travel agency or write directly to the Gramercy Travel System, Inc., 444 Madison Avenue, New York, N.Y. 10022.

Gramercy's Singleworld is a rarity; it is a national travel agency exclusively for singles. This New York-based firm promises you a share rate on their cruises (operated out of Miami) whether or not they match you with a roommate. For this, they'll charge you a mere $25—but you can save about $200 on stateroom costs.

TRAVELING WITH NON-HUMAN COMPANIONS

PETS REACT DIFFERENTLY to travel—as do people. If in doubt about your pet's ability to cope, consult your veterinarian before taking your animal anywhere.

Don't feed your pet for several hours before your trip. Take along familiar items—toys, a favorite blanket—to give your pet a feeling of security. Keep owner identification, plus license, fastened to the pet's collar or harness. If driving, keep your pet secured on a leash around open windows since excitable animals may jump out the window!

When going by plane or train, use a travel kennel large enough to let the animal stand, turn around, and lie down. Be certain to arrive early enough to let your pet have time to get used to the new conveyance. Most airlines and trains sell such containers. But if you're using your own, check it out with the transportation company before hand. Some containers are not acceptable because of inadequate ventilation, lack of absorbent floor material, or lack of a water cup. Don't be caught at the last minute at the airport with Fido, an unacceptable container, and the choice of selling Fido to the highest bidder or skipping your flight or train ride!

Some planes require that you ship your animal separately in their cargo department. If this is the case, make doubly certain that your pet's kennel is well marked with the pet's name, your name and address, and your itinerary (in case there's a foul-up). Also clearly state any particular needs your pet might have—as requiring a certain type of food—or any allergies.

Pets are not allowed on all trains or on all parts of some trains. Transatlantic ships sometimes have kennel accommodations. But always check beforehand.

Not all countries welcome pets. Some do, some don't. England, for instance, requires a very long quarantine. The consulate of the country you will be visiting will tell you what the rules are governing pet welcomes, health documents and certificates of ownership.

"Don't be caught at the
last minute at the airport with
Fido, an unacceptable container,
and the choice of selling Fido
to the highest bidder or skipping
your flight."

Getting It Together Before You Go
and
Keeping It Together While You're Away

GETTING YOUR HEAD (AND BODY) TOGETHER

SHAPE UP every part of you *before* shipping out! Local sun permitting, use your bank yard or roof to get a good tan—it'll keep you from burning later and make you look as if you've been traveling for months and not sitting behind a desk! Although it's not nice to fool Mother Nature, you can—by using a sun lamp (carefully!). If you're tanning with the sun, allot five minutes the first day before 10 AM, ten minutes the second day, and so on. Avoid the sun between 11 AM and 2 PM, it's strongest then.

Always use some sort of lotion. A sunscreen lets the tanning rays through while blocking out the harmful ones. Johnson & Johnson's Sundown Sunscreen and Westwood's Pre Sun Gel are good maximum sunscreens. Minimum sunscreens are for those who don't burn easily and can get a great tan: try Bain de Soleil (it gives you a rich orangish tan) or Coppertone (a more yellowish cast). If you want to soak up the sun, but can't take *any* rays on your delicate skin, try either a prescription sun block or an over-the-counter product such as Clinique's Sun Block. They really do block out the sun when reapplied frequently, so don't expect to get much of a tan while using them. A bonus: they also prevent a blossoming-out of freckles!

Strap marks can be tanned to the same color as the rest of the skin by coating the tanned skin with a sunblock while using a light sunscreen on the untanned spots. Use a tinted gel (such as Bonne Bell's Bronze Glo) to help even out the strap marks when you're in an off-shoulder dress away from the beach.

You'll notice I don't hesitate to use brand names—I simply feel it's more useful to share what goodies I've discovered by naming names, than to beat around the bush with Brand X.

Don't go abroad with a broad backside. Start your trip so slim and trim that you'll be able to indulge yourself in a little extra Austrian pasty or New Zealand ice cream! If you don't want to be a pair of walking thighs, start exercising at least six weeks before you leave, and start your diet now. There are usually excellent and inexpensive exercise programs available at the YWCA. Or take a long walk every day; it'll not only shape you up, but will also get you accustomed to sightseeing by foot.

Of course, you should walk a good deal on your trip and thereby continue the slimming process while you absorb the sights. Remember, walk whenever possible. Walk up stairs. Go to the top of the ruins—don't just sit there in the bus and let the guide explain it to you from afar. Take walks around the city to really get the "feel" of a place. Or tour by bicycle—it does great things for the legs, and there seem to be more bikes than cars in many countries, so you won't feel weird. Use your hotel swimming pool to tone up the whole body.

Staying slim abroad also includes watching the munchies! Eat your main meal at noon and you'll have walked off a lot of those calories by evening. When dining, substitute broth for soups and yogurt for lunch. (The latter is readily available, as Europeans like it for dessert and Middle Easterners consider it a staple.) And even in that last bastion of cream sauces, France, there are now some superb restaurants specializing in low-calorie, un-rich foods. Just tell the *maitre d'hôtel* your diet wishes. If the French have come around, you can be sure you can get such food almost *anywhere*! Ask your concierge where to go.

COSMETICS   For packing purposes, a good thing to do is collect beauty samples offered as a bonus by cosmetic companies. ("If you buy $6 worth of Hope, you get $21 worth of cosmetics free.") Or buy the small introductory-size items that you often see in a bin at grocery or drug stores. The beauty samples and introductory-size offerings are almost always in small, unbreakable plastic containers. Perfect!

In packing anything, less is better. I don't know why people assume they'll use more of a product abroad than at home. If it takes two months to use up a tube of blusher at home, it won't be used up in one month abroad! Don't take two bottles of shampoo and three of moisturizer. One of anything will do—you'll be able to replenish your supply with either foreign substitutes, admittedly expensive American imports, or bargains in such duty-free ports as Singapore or Hong Kong. Nothing is irreplaceable, regardless of the claims of cosmetic companies. The only item I would risk over-stocking is deodorant (cream is best for travel since it won't leak) as some countries aren't as odor-conscious as we are and don't always have a good selection.

Cosmetics packaged under pressure, such as hair spray, should be placed in a plastic-lined bag if packed in a case with clothes. But why bother? Buy non-aerosol containers.

If possible, transfer cosmetics to plastic containers. Do squeeze some air from the plastic bottles and recap them snugly. I hope you have allowed enough room in the container for air expansion at jet altitudes. Gather up those goodies in a plastic toilet kit with handles so that you can hang everything on the bathroom door when there isn't adequate sink space.

If you're carrying perfume with you, take it along in a solid form. Remember, every item that is liquid could possibly leak. Besides, many countries are great perfume bargain centers—France, Hong Kong, Singapore—and at the latter two duty-free ports you might find your favorite American scent cheaper than at home. In India, buy sandlewood perfume—it stays on practically forever!

Have your favorite cosmetics with you. You'll probably hear that French ones are the best: it ain't necessarily so. Besides, you don't want to spend that much of your precious time abroad in the cosmetics section. Who ever met a possible evening companion at a mascara counter? At the perfume counter, maybe.

While not encouraging you to spend time on your vacation looking for cosmetics, I must add that there are a few worth ferreting out: Akkar rouge in the Middle East (it stays on until *you* take it off), Talika eyelash cream for longer lashes (France), Belgium's Vallyfix by Adler for a good hair setting lotion, Beten's cosmetics for super-sensitive skin (Hong Kong), and any of the Portugese Thaber products. You'll see gorgeous, black-rimmed eyes in the

Middle East and India—the women use kohl for this effect. But don't you. Kohl can be poisonous if smeared into the eyes. *They* are experts at applying it, but *I* wouldn't chance it.

Do take a moisturizer—you'll need it as much for the sun of Naples as for the winds of Norway. Use it as a night cream as well as for daytime protection against the elements. And speaking of moisturizers, this is a good time to mention the advantage of items which can take the place of many other beauty products in your jammed suitcase. Like that all-purpose moisturizer, baby oil. Use it as a night and day moisturizer, leg shaving lotion, makeup remover, bath oil, chapstick, cuticle cream, body lotion, suntan oil (mix it with vinegar to maintain the skin's balance) and hair conditioner.

If you run out of oil, you can pick up olive oil in grocery stores in most countries. Cleopatra used it for cleansing and moisturizing and she was not exactly history's wallflower!

One small plastic container of Vaseline can be used for a night cream, eyebrow tamer and eyelash conditioner, lip gloss, cuticle cream, and hair conditioner.

Another all-purpose item is Dr. Bonner's Peppermint Soap. It's a liquid, as the title does *not* indicate, comes in a good plastic container, and can be purchased in any health store. It washes the face, hair, teeth, anything. The label is enough to occupy you on a transatlantic flight, as its claims are for almost anything but world peace, but it has been around a very long time and is pure and reputable. And how many of us can say that?

Talcum powder is another all-purpose grooming aid. Put a tiny bit on eyelashes between mascara coats for a fuller look, use it before shaving with an electric razor to prevent friction, dust it through your hair and brush it out if you haven't time to shampoo, put some in your shoes if you don't wear stockings.

If you're into an eye-mask routine at home, you might want to take along Andrea's soothing little eye masks, which come in tiny packets; they're called "Fresh-n-Eyes." Or, to improvise, put wet tea bags over the eyes. (The tannic acid is also good for a facial.)

Non-waterproof mascara is kinder to the lashes than the waterproof variety, and since the former comes off with just soap and water, you don't have to carry eye makeup remover with you. One less thing to schlep.

Makeup colors seem to look different at different latitudes; the shades that look right in a ski resort seem washed out in the tropics and the colors that seem right near the equator look garish in the north. It's because of the light. The pale light of cold places gives blue tones to skin; therefore, you should counteract it with makeup in warm, red-orangy colors such as peach, apricot, or other relatives of red with some yellow in them. Tropical sunlight has a golden cast which neutralizes sun-color make-up. Here is where you should use reds on the blue side such as magenta, burgundy, or, for fair-skinned blondes, mauve and lavender. This lighting factor applies to eye makeup, also: cold light requires warm browns, taupes, and mossy greens while sun country needs blue and mauve.

If allergies are a problem, try a hypo-allergenic line such as Almay. Allergies are a good reason to try your cosmetics at home first so you won't be stuck overseas with a puffy lip or blotchy skin *and* an unusable item which you've just carted thousands of miles!

A HAIRY SUBJECT   It's ideal to wear your hair in such a way that you don't have to waste precious time in beauty parlors. But if you want to go the beauty parlor route, there are some things you should know.

In some countries the whole idea of beauty parlor hygiene is different from ours. I have seen the same hairbrush used on everyone in the shop! So go ahead and bring your own brush if you want. I know one woman who brought her own rollers, but that's a bit much.

If you want to save money, go to the small, unknown beauty shops—not to the salons in the tourist hotels. Ask a stewardess on your flight which beauty salon she goes to. Or relent and go to a safe (but expensive) standby like Elizabeth Arden's (they're sprinkled around the world) or the salon in your hotel. But remember that you will pay much more in any hotel salon or "name" place than at the little shop around the corner. And there are hidden wonders in small towns, long on imagination and short on price. One caution: if your hair is different from the locals (you're a curly-head in Japan), stick to the places that cater to tourists—they'll be used to different hair textures. And while you're at the beauty parlor (especially in the Orient), see if you can have an arm and upper back massage—they're cheap and marvelous.

You should be accustomed to unisex beauty shops by now, so don't be surprised if you venture into one abroad. And always ask what costs extra in a foreign beauty salon; sometimes they charge for things we don't. Also, have instructions translated into the native language by a knowledgeable person (perhaps your own French or Italian hairdresser back home or the concierge of your hotel). And carry with you a picture of yourself with top, side, and back views of your hair set in rollers and after the comb-out; or carry a magazine picture of a style you like. That should avoid most hysterics.

If I had only had such a picture in Rome! I walked into a famous salon, wearing my well-traveled look. (Translation: I looked a little seedy, as I had been traveling for nine months with one small suitcase.) The place was dripping with royalty and the royalty was dripping with furs and jewels. But the glamour of the place faded when the stylist turned my shoulder-length hair into a boyish bob! I started to cry—hair can be a very emotional subject for most women—and told the beautician that while he thought he was a great *artiste*, he really didn't know what he was doing. The management desperately wanted me out of there, as I was causing an embarrassing scene, so they offered to give me a free make-over. I was ushered into a pastel makeup room with scads of jars and bottles. I walked out of there an hour later with the bright light of day hitting my blue/green/yellow eyelids, mauve cheeks, and Fuchsia-outlined lips. I made Cher look like the scrubbed girl back on the farm. An afternoon wasted, money wasted, and six months of hair-growing chopped off! Moral of the story: make sure the salon knows *exactly* what you want.

Cut and style are not the only possible perils. To avoid becoming prematurely green, take a sample of your coloring with you to make certain the salon gives you exactly what you want. Chemicals differ around the world. And if your unnaturally blonde hair quite suddenly turns green or orange, from either an overdose of sun or chlorinated pool water, rinse your hair with a temporary silver color made for gray hair.

If your hair is dark and you want to give it life, consider a henna pack instead of coloring. Since this pure vegetable root is good for the hair, you may not need a conditioner. And it gives the hair body, doesn't need touch-ups, and adds a nice auburn glow.

Bring your own conditioner if your hair has been bleached or dyed or is really damaged. But if your hair is just normal, take a chance on a local product or be lucky enough to find a Pantene rinse and/or conditioner. Pantene products are *everywhere*—actually, they were first available in Europe before invading our markets, and this Swiss product is superior to most of ours.

If you want to take electric rollers, you'll find a small set of just five jumbo ones most packable. But wait until you get abroad to buy them; the appliance you get there will fit *their* voltage and you won't have to fiddle with the fancy American dual-voltage gismos. I once blew out the motor on just such a gismo by asking the hotel clerk in Taiwan what the voltage was: he was inaccurate and that was the end of my drier! If you opt for a curling iron (their advantage is in their really light weight), be sure you know how to use it: put it only on dry hair and don't get it too close to the scalp. Remember, the longer you hold the wand in place, the firmer the curl will be. Don't use an electric wand on bleached or damaged hair. And that goes for electric rollers, too.

Curly-heads should be especially advised to wear their hair short and with the natural curl; this should require no setting or fussing whatsoever. It is impossible to beat the frizzies, whether you are in London or San Francisco, and you'll save yourself a lot of aggravation if you do what comes naturally.

If you insist on fighting Mother Nature, you can straighten your hair nonpermanently. (Sorry, I can't recommend the permanent method as it is horrible for the hair.) Wrap hair around the head as if the head were a giant roller. An hour of this (especially if you've been in the bath or shower in the meantime and let the steam "set" your hair) works nicely. Or, when you're *alone*, sleep with your hair wrapped that way. It isn't uncomfortable, like sleeping on rollers; and you'll awaken with really straight hair.

For you lucky people with straight hair—and I expect to get a lot of letters from straight-haired women saying "lucky?"—either get a non-frizzy body permanent, or wear your hair naturally down and swinging, or pull it back with barettes, colored scarves, ribbons, head bands, etc. And to really save you trouble if you have straight hair, get a short, sharp Sassoon-type geometric cut: it's instant chic and easy care. Being a curly-head myself, I've found Sassoon cuts much less successful on my type of hair. But whatever you decide on, get a good cut *before* you set foot out of town so that you don't have to put your head in a paper bag until you get to that shop you've heard about in London or Hong Kong! After all, you want to look nice *getting* there. I know I always run into someone I want to impress when I look my worst; the best solution is *never* to look your worst.

For any kind of hair, take a light dime-store plastic hairbrush instead of a heavy one.

Do people still really consider hair spray indispensable? If you do, buy a purse-size container. It'll last until you get a replacement, and actually the easily found Pantene—again!—is better than most of ours. Revlon also can be found almost anywhere.

Are you taking a wig? Think twice about it. Then think again. It's far better to have your own hair cut in a manageable way. But if you insist on a wig, the synthetics are definitely easier to travel with than a real hair wig. The former take much more abuse (a friend of mine used to pack hers rolled up in a shoe in her suitcase!) and generally look better. If you completely ignore my advice and take a "set" real hair wig, then you probably won't pay attention to my advice on how to pack it. But I'll try. Stuff the wig with something soft that you have to pack anyway (like stockings) and put it in a plastic bag. Make sure you squeeze air into the bag to soften any blows to your created air cushion. However, do not spoil the wig setting by blowing air into the bag with your moist breath. This

"Dr. Bonner's Peppermint Soap . . . has been around for a very long time and is pure and reputable. And how many of us can say that?"

is very important. Brush your wig after each wearing, rest it at night on an inflated balloon (saves carrying a bulky wig box and stand) and shampoo as directed (saves the wig and your scalp).

If you like manicures, get one before you leave home just to be presentable, but really indulge yourself abroad. Use colorless polish; the chips won't show and you won't have to have a manicure as frequently. Or—since nail polish remover pads dry out and liquid nail polish remover is a disaster to anything it touches if it leaks in the suitcase—you might want to play it safe by just buffing your nails to a high gloss. There are a number of good buffing creams around: get the ones at a beauty supply house instead of the ones in your department store, as the former give more of a shine. Anyway, if you're into manicures and pedicures, you'll really enjoy them in the Middle East, Mexico (probably the best and cheapest in the world), and Europe (Dr. Scholl's pedicures on the Continent are marvelous). If you do the pedicure yourself, remember to cut toenails straight across to prevent ingrown toenails and, again, to wear clear polish or buff your toenails.

SO BE BEAUTIFUL FROM TIP TO TOE AND ENJOY!

WHAT TO WEAR WHERE

WHEN PLANNING your wardrobe, the things to consider are (1) where you are going—and the climate (2) how long you will be staying (3) what you will be doing and with whom, and (4) what mode of transportation you plan to use.

11

What to fly in? Something loose. No girdles or other constricting garments. Dress for your destination. If you're leaving New York in February for Nassau, dress in layers so that you won't arrive sweltering but will also be comfortable on the plane. Pantsuits with lightweight blouses or jacket dresses are good layered combos. If you wear your heaviest (but removable!) clothes on the plane, they won't be weighed. Whatever you choose, remember that it should be in a color that doesn't show soil easily, and of a material that won't wrinkle or bag. And on trains, wear what you would on planes.

Cruises are a whole other story. While shipboard etiquette is not as formal as it was in the past, long evening dress is still *de rigueur* except when in port, Sundays, sailing day and the last night at sea. But that varies, too. Contact the steamship line before leaving; their personnel will tell you in advance what to take. On freighters no one ever has to dress up. Short cruises are usually less formal than long ones. World cruises call for the most glamourous attire. And some liners are dressier than others. First Class is dressiest, with formal clothes (long dresses) worn every night by most of the women, though you'll be admitted in short dresses and evening pantsuits in these more informal days. Formal attire is never required in tourist class, but you can get gussied up if you want to on certain gala evenings. However, more and more ships are classless now. A stole (or any light wrap) for walking on deck and being comfortable in the public rooms is a must on any type of ship. Don't wear a bathing suit in the public rooms on any ship! For days in port, comfortable clothes and shoes are a must, but swimwear or abbreviated shorts should be limited to the beach only. Compare shipboard living with an elegant resort on land and dress accordingly. For any occasion you're not sure about after you're on the ship, ask the purser—he'll tell you what's appropriate.

Remember in selecting your travel wardrobe that a whole new set of clothes isn't necessary since the things you now have will be new to the people you encounter on your trip. If you're not going on a group tour, you'll be in different places with different people, so you won't have to worry about the same people seeing you in the same clothes every day. They'll never know you wore that blue pantsuit yesterday in Paris and the day before in London. And even if you're on a tour and seeing the same people every day, they're all in the same boat, so to speak.

The clothes you know you look best and feel more comfortable in are the ones to travel with—which means you've worn and washed them at least once, so you know how they respond to both wearing and washing. You don't want to find yourself in Paris ready to go out as soon as your dress drip-dries—only to find that when it has drip-dried, it has stretched, bagged or shrunk!

It's important *not* to pick things just because they travel well. A suitcase full of drab easy-care garments is no great shakes. Better they should look good. And great-looking clothes that travel well are good investments since they'll be perfect for home use later.

Always investigate ahead of time to see what they're wearing where you're going. Ask your travel agent, or buy foreign fashion magazines; most big cities have a foreign newsstand. It doesn't matter if you don't understand the language—you can tell by the pictures what people are wearing abroad. Unless you're totally oblivious or exceptionally beautiful, you'll feel more comfortable in clothing similar to that worn by the local residents.

Actually, you can usually get by with the equivalent to what you wear at home. Suburban matrons wear Butte knits or the like everywhere and swinging singles wear lean jeans and T-shirts from New York to Cannes! What is appropriate here is appropriate there —wherever *there* is! Just as you would be out of place wearing blue jeans in a fine hotel lobby in your home town, you'd do better to wear a smart pantsuit or dress in a similar place in Madrid! If you're driving and staying at hotels, dress so that you'll look decent when checking in and out. But if you'll just be traipsing about campsites in a Volkswagen bus, your whole wardrobe can be as grubby as you wish. In general (with the exception of really casual places such as islands or sporty resorts), don't wear jeans or shorts in town (especially in fine shops).

When in doubt, dress conservatively—especially in conservative countries such as Poland, Spain and others where we are regarded as decadence personified.

Once abroad, you can always ask fashion advice of the concierge, or your tour agent if you're on a tour. Or call the restaurant or nightclub and ask what women wear.

Off-season anywhere is less formal, less dressy, less "social" than during the "season." And hotel nightclubs *anywhere* usually require more formal dress than other places—indeed, anything at a "name" hotel is usually the dressiest thing going in town.

Generalities make more sense than specifics when it comes to chic ahoy. It's always more important to know that people dress for dinner than that Gucci is "in" (and maybe "out" by the time this reaches print).

Think climates, not countries. Naples weather can call for bikinis while in Milan you could require a wool sweater on the same day. And consider altitude: sea level resorts may necessitate summer wear while a higher altitude only a few miles away would be cold.

Tweeds, wool knits and ultrasuede are super for colder climates. Synthetics mixed with cotton, crushproof jerseys, and cotton knits are best for hot spots. Remember, in this day of lovely miracles, Qiana can pass for silk, cotton knit for finely woven hand knits.

Pack a *single* color around which to build your travel wardrobe. Basic colors need not be dull. But do choose neutral colors you like that look good on you and that can go with everything. This makes shoes and handbags interchangeable, thus keeping a potentially heavy part of your travel wardrobe to a minimum. You can live without your favorite red or pink purse for a few weeks.

Warning: dark colors aren't flattering for everyone and do collect lint, while white not only shows spots, but also turns telltale gray after repeated sink sudsings. Prints are good travel choices since they effectively disguise spots that might otherwise put a garment out of circulation for the duration of the trip.

Single color wardrobes can be spiced up with smashing belts, jewelry (though nothing so valuable you'll have to guard it constantly), sweaters, and scarves. Scarves are the most magical of the accessories—they can be turned into bikinis, skirts, halters, sashes, purses, turbans—and, of course, neck or head scarves. It would help to have the appropriate sizes, since *small* head scarves turned into skirts might get you arrested for indecent exposure and big scarves that would make dynamite skirts will turn you into a frump if you wear them as babushkas.

Two-, three- or four-piece suits (blazer, pants, short and long skirts) that can be mixed and matched should also be an integral part of your travel wardrobe. Not only can the jackets, skirts and pants be switched, but an entirely new outfit can also be created with the addition of a blouse, sweater, long skirt or dressy blouse. Jacket dresses are also versatile for different occasions and different climates.

Layers are good for sightseeing. You may require a jacket for a heavily air-conditioned modern site, but you'll suffocate in some airless museum galleries unless you have something to remove.

Stoles and sweaters are indispensable for temperature changes between countries as well as between the street and an air-conditioned restaurant. Sweaters are also good under your coat for really cold weather or as a bed jacket in unheated or over-air conditioned hotel rooms.

If you pack one smashingly sexy, no-crush jersey dinner dress, you can get by anywhere. Or a dressy pantsuit—but some places still prefer women in dresses: men do! Long jersey dresses are unwrinklably fashionable, and floor-length T-shirts are considered evening garb in casual resorts and islands. Shoes and purses are not invisible: don't take a gargantuan travel handbag and wear clogs with your sexy little jersey.

If you've met a baron (ah, of such things are dreams made) who wants to take you to a ball, rent a gown. Don't pack anything you'll wear just *once*. Look in a big city Yellow Pages under "Clothes—Hire Services" or "Rental Clothing"—they don't just rent men's tuxes.

Fur coats? Not unless you have someone fetching and carrying.

Such coats are too heavy and too valuable, and you'll just worry about them. But if, dahling, your social schedule is such that you absolutely require one, take it.

More than one word about shoes: every book tells you to buy a sturdy pair of walking shoes. I did that *once*—and left them for the hotel maid at the first place I stayed. Now if you want to go clunking about in heavy sexless oxfords, it's your trip! But you'll never meet your prince in clunky shoes. Better are those lightweight, soft, well-ventilated (perforated) crepe-soled shoes that don't look too bad but will get you through cobble-stone streets and a fair day of sightseeing. I prefer espadrilles. (They were *invented* in Europe, so you can find them everywhere abroad.) They're also canvas and thus "breathe" more than leather. Have rubber tips put on the heels and soles, and they'll last much longer. And no matter what kinds of shoes you choose, take only the ones you've already worn at home. Sightseeing is no time to break in shoes—you'll just break in your feet!

Sandles are especially good for times when your feet have swollen from hot weather or plane rides. Folding slippers are great —use them on planes as well as in the bedroom. If you'll be going to Buddhist temples or Moslem mosques, be sure to wear shoes (or sandles) that slip on and off easily. And tuck some peds in your purse to wear when you must take off your shoes.

Waterproof your shoes before you leave home. And while you're at it, waterproof handbags and scarves. Forget a raincoat— they're like saunas in hot countries and are inadequate in cold ones unless you're well-equipped with layers of clothing underneath.

As for handbags, two should be the limit—one small purse for evening use and a larger one for traveling and sightseeing. They both should be in basic colors to match all of your outfits. The daily handbag should have lots of compartments (some zippered) to hold travel documents and other valuables, and should be a lightweight, durable shoulder bag which frees your hands for other things. Make sure the shoulder bag has wide, flat padded straps so it doesn't cut into your shoulder.

And since your valuables (such as passports) will be in your

"I bought a pair of sturdy walking shoes once— and left them for the maid at the first place I stayed."

purse, it's imperative that you protect it. When you put it down, drape the strap around your leg. Don't carry an open-topped bag: it can spill over and dump out your contents—if the pickpockets don't get to you first. Keep your purse with you; don't think it's safe to put it down for "just a moment." If the purse is one with a long shoulder strap, put the strap over one shoulder so that it hangs diagonally across the body. Then hold the purse between your body and arm. If the strap is short, carry the purse with your arm through the strap, the bag cradled in your arm. It's also advisable to walk with the purse in the hand that is away from the street. If the purse has a clasp, have that side next to you. Another protection tip —this time against your own forgetfulness: slip a piece of paper with your name and address into your purse or a pocket of your overcoat, raincoat or jacket. If you leave those items on the plane or in a restaurant or hotel, your I.D. will help insure return . . . if found by an honest person (admittedly, an endangered species).

If you wear hats, use crushable caps and turbans. Buy inexpensive beach hats at your destination; don't lug a big straw one on the plane.

You don't have to wear gloves these days unless you're going to visit with a head of state or you need them for warmth in a really cold climate. The era has gone when "breeding" meant wearing "little white gloves."

You don't need more than a few pairs of stockings—you can replace them anywhere you would really need them. You may not be able to buy them on a trip down the Amazon—but why would you be wearing them there? Minimum is the keynote: when in doubt, leave it out! If you do forget something you need later, chances are very good that you can buy it where you are. If you can't, it's because no one wears them. Like pantyhose in the Amazon!

You should only need three sets of underwear—one to wear, one to wash and one to spare. Cotton underwear is best for warm climates and disposable paper panties are great for anywhere. And don't forget long underwear for sightseeing or sleeping *alone* in cold, drafty places, and warm socks for bed, ditto when alone.

For hot weather, halter dresses with built-in bras are cooler than separate bra and dress combos. Of course, going braless is coolest of all!

A bathing suit is a good idea for almost any trip—even for not-so-obvious, unresorty or cool weather places. Many hotels have indoor pools and even in non-resorts you might welcome the city municipal pool on a sweltering day. If you have abdominal scars or stomach stretch marks, you might check out bikinis cut fairly high across the stomach but with a very high, cut-out leg. This gives you coverage where you need it, but with the look of bareness. A thin one-piece maillot—high fashion now—will also hide stomach marks. Let your swimming cap double as a shower cap.

Recommended sleepwear: a cotton night gown for warm climates or a nylon one for colder places, and similar fabrics for a robe. And don't forget bath sandles. The robe and sandles should be able to double for beachwear if you are going to a resort area. Indeed, *whenever possible take clothes that are appropriate for several different occasions.* If you're not going to a swimming resort, let your non-wrinkle, waterproof, all-weather coat double as a robe. Remember, the more versatile the outfit the more mileage you can get from it.

Although I'm against weighty gadgets (such as travel irons), there are a few things you'll need in order to take care of the clothes you finally picked out to schlep along on your trip.

Take clothes-pin hangers shaped like this ❓ and a suction cup clothesline, since some hotel bathrooms have no towel racks. And you'll need scotch tape for mending hems and removing lint. Carry large safety pins for pinning skirt tops to the bottoms of hotel hangers. If you take one spool of *transparent* nylon thread, you won't need an assortment of colors—that one spool of thread, a needle, straight pins, and safety pins are all the sewing equipment you'll need. You can use your manicure scissors for sewing scissors.

Another one-color-for-everything tip: you'll only need one container of shoe polish if you use a neutral cream cleaner/polish. And take along a non-flammable spot remover—or use club soda (it really works in a pinch!). Bring little envelopes of laundry flakes (a large container becomes a waste of space when half the flakes have been used up and the other half of the container is empty). If the detergent you bring with you won't suds in the hotel room basin, go out and buy a local brand—it's made for that local water.

If there is anything additional that you need for clothing care, ask the front desk or the chambermaid at your hotel. They'll be able to provide you with an iron, more hangers, or forgotten sewing items. If the hotel can't lend you an iron, it's still better to send out for pressing than to lug a travel iron around.

Do your laundry as soon as you check in, or at least allow the maximum amount of time for things to dry. Get it over with, since I certainly hope it won't be the high spot of your stay! If you wash clothes *before* they're terribly soiled, you'll be able to get them cleaner easier. And if you add a bit of cologne to the rinse water, they'll smell even fresher. Don't wring drip-dries. Let them hang soaking wet (but not on wooden or wire hangers that cause stains) over the tub or basin. The weight of the water "irons" them. If you carry one wooden pants hanger, you can clamp it to the bottom of your hanging wet clothes—its weight will "iron" your clothes even more. But only use this trick on non-stretchables (like cotton); an acrylic sweater could turn into a dress! A steamy bathroom will unwrinkle clothes: just turn on the hot water in the shower and close the door. But don't try this in a drought-stricken area, or you may have more to iron out than just clothes!

Large zip-lock baggies can double as a laundry tub if your sink doesn't have a stopper and can be used later either for clothes that didn't dry or for dirty underwear.

If you do send your clothes out to be laundered, always indicate whether or not you want starch or else Bereny's Law states that you'll get it when you don't want it and won't get it when you do. It's best not to send out delicate fabrics (what are you doing bringing them along, anyway?) because of the harsh soaps laundries use and the even harsher solvents cleaners use. But it beats taking your clothes down to the water and beating them on the rocks.

If you decide to have your laundry done at any hotel, motel, or cruise ship, make certain it can be returned to you before your departure. You can usually get rush service, but it'll cost you more.

Before I go into a country-by-country breakdown of what to wear where, I feel one generalization should be made if you plan to go to rugged country *anywhere*. From the Galapagos Islands to deserted South American ruins, take non-skid shoes, uncuffed (so you won't trip) slacks to protect your legs from vegetation and mosquitoes, sun hats that can be tied to your head, and long-sleeved cotton (porous) blouses. Enough of generalizations—now for specifics. Here's what you'll need:

AFRICA: Summery clothes, but be prepared for cool evenings. In the bush country, you'll do best with khaki-colored (won't show the dust), multipocketed (for purseless jeep travel) outfits. Clothing for safaris is available at stores in large cities throughout Africa, although you can get by without elaborate safari outfits; simple cotton jeans and shirts are perfectly adequate substitutes. Resort clothes are worn for evenings at Tree Tops and other such chic watering holes. Dress up for dinner in Rhodesia and South Africa; remember, anywhere that's British-influenced, the people "dress" for dinner. In Kenya, don't wear very short skirts in the older parts of towns. In Tanzania, the government has banned tight and flared slacks, shorts, and above-the-knee or form-fitting skirts.

AUSTRALIA: Dressy but simple and conservative clothing in Sydney and Melbourne. Styles in those two cities are about three years behind America; Sydney likes to think of itself as another San Francisco, but it ain't. Actually, the styles are similar to Omaha or Des Moines or Peoria—not New York or Chicago. There is one exception, however: the under-25 set has taken to two fads currently popular in America—tiny sundresses and jeans with silk blouses. If you're going into the outback, wear functional clothes, since you'll never find a good dry cleaner out there!

BALI: Rain gear (or a drip-dry hairdo and ensemble) is especially needed during the rainy season from November through January. Very casual, vivid-colored, happy-go-lucky fashions, although not so happy-go-lucky as to tolerate topless per the famed Bali maidens. (Even they don't do it anymore.)

BRAZIL: Rio's beaches are the scanty-clothes capitals of the world. Remember, that's where the "string" and the "thong" got started. I even saw one patriotic bathing suit (?) with stars and stripes—that is, one stripe for the bottom and a tiny star for each half of the top! But no matter how skimpy the bathing suit, hypocrisy demands that you cover it up anywhere off the beach—and that includes the walk from the hotel *to* the beach. It all depends upon your social schedule, but Rio is still less dressy than some of the other big South American cities since life is geared towards the outdoors. If you're going to Carnival in Rio, take something fanciful and gala—anything goes.

CANADA: Dress as you would stateside. Don't forget warm clothing for cool summer evenings.

CARIBBEAN: The only places you'll need to get dressed up are in the bigger islands' big hotel dining rooms. The more British the area, the dressier. Bermuda is the dressiest island I've ever drip-dried through. Government decree prohibits abbreviated outfits in town there, and cocktail dresses are worn in the evening to better restaurants. Outside of Bermuda, islands are not really formal—you can get by with casual dresses or evening pantsuits or party pajamas with pretty sandles. Take light cotton resort wear for day-time and swimsuits with long-sleeved coverups to protect against sunburn as well as impropriety. And if you're a tennis player in the British isles, wear white—they frown on the newish colored togs.

EASTERN EUROPE: Wear simple clothes, nothing flashy; the people are poor—don't rub it in. Dress conservatively, but be especially chic in Hungary (they may be poor, but they have an innate sense of style) and fastidious in Bulgaria (they are the most put-together people I've ever seen).

FRANCE: Trés chic. While *les blue jeans* are still popular, young Parisian women are now wearing below-the-knee unconstructed dresses, and high heels with ankle straps. You can wear your teeniest bikini on the Riviera; anything else will make you look as if you stepped from an eighteenth-century painting.

GREAT BRITAIN: The English still "dress" for dinner. But the young can get away with rather wild attire. Really summer clothes aren't usually needed even in summer—what we call "transitional" frocks would be more apt for those "summer" days when there's no sun! Always have some rain protection unless you're drip-dry from curls to toes.

GREECE: Dress up to go to the nightclubs and tavernas in Athens. Conservative dress is most definitely the order of the day and evening in provincial Greece. But the once-staid islands *close* to Athens now have an anything goes attitude (clotheswise) since their hippy invasion. Less touristy islands require extremely modest knee-length dresses.

HONG KONG: This is one of the less British-influenced places, in terms of clothing, so "dress" or not according to *your* mood. The most popular thing to do is gather up a group of people to share a Chinese dinner—and that requires the simplest attire. Cheong sams are those sexy slit-up-to-here dresses the slender Chinese women wear; unless you have no hips and can walk taking tiny steps, don't wear one. You can come prepared for their rainy season, but forget about the typhoons since there's absolutely nothing you can wear to make you comfortable.

INDIA: Again, take "peds" to wear in temples: if you do it in no other place, do it here, since this is the dirtiest country I've ever been in. (You know where I'll be *persona non grata!*) "Injah" is not as formal as when the British and maharajas were in full power, but it is still not proper to wear scanty, suggestive clothing anywhere! You'll be accosted in a not-too-pleasant fashion. And my personal opinion is that Western women look ridiculous in the saris that they have made for them there—they don't know how to wrap them or walk in them. As for the monsoons, it doesn't matter what you wear—you'll be miserable in anything!

IRELAND: Always be prepared for rain. Be tweedy in the winter. Conservative dress is the order of the day and evening everywhere. Pick up some of their delightfully old-fashioned country-girl fashions and wear them around, but avoid couturier fashions such as Sibil Connolly, which are as dowdy as they are expensive. And Irish linen clothes are impossible to travel in—they wrinkle like a rag. Why pay a lot to look awful?—some people can do it so cheaply!

ISRAEL: A very, very informal country. You don't need nylons ever. Flashy jewelry is frowned upon. You'll need warmer and more conservative clothes in Jerusalem than in Tel Aviv. Don't wear slacks or sleeveless tops into orthodox areas such as Jerusalem's *Mea Shearim*. Israel's fashions copy America's, but new styles take about three years to catch on, so dress accordingly. Also, Israelis still prefer above-the-knee skirts, so if you're uncomfortable being different, shorten your now-fashionable below-the-knee duds.

ITALY: Italian women always look good—they'll skip lunch for a year to buy a great-looking dress—so don't you look schlepy by comparison. This is the place to pull yourself together to look feminine and elegant. Definitely wear a shoulder bag clutched against your body under your arm since Rome's purse snatchers are becoming as famous as its bottom pinchers. And this home of Pucci considers Pucci prints to be the clothing of middle-aged, overweight, rich American women! The bikini coasts allow really scanty bathing suits!

JAPAN: Wear easily removable shoes and bring "peds" to temples, Japanese inns, and restaurants. Also, wear slacks or a full skirt so you'll be able to sit close to the floor (or on the floor) gracefully at Japanese restaurants. Japanese seasons correspond to ours, so wear clothes that would be worn during that season in a comparable latitude stateside. Subdued clothes are the general rule—you'll stand out in bright colors.

MEXICO: Conservative "big city" clothing is fine for Mexico. Pack knits and pantsuits, comfortable shoes for touring, a raincoat and/or folding umbrella for afternoon showers, and a warm coat for winter. Small hotels are not equipped with central heating, so you may also want a warm robe and soft slippers. For Acapulco, pack your brightest, most beautiful resort clothes. If your figure warrants the exposure, a couple of bikinis and a coverup will suffice for the beach; print shifts or wrap dresses with sandles for restaurants and markets; pretty pants ensembles or long skirts for evening. Leave stockings, heavy shoes and heavy jewelry at home.

NETHERLANDS: One of the most permissive countries in the world for everything, including clothes. Lots of cobblestone streets, so have something besides high heels. Always be prepared for rain, mist or fog. Since this country is notorious for putting the pounds on tourists (their breakfasts are as big as our suppers), take some rather stretchable or loose-fitting garments!

NEW ZEALAND: A very conservative country for clothing. Dress is informal, plain, and covered-up.

PAKISTAN: Enter mosques shoeless and with a head covering. Dress modestly or risk being accosted anywhere!

PERU: Lima is one of the more formal South American cities. Women wear rather sedate clothing at night, often black. Wear lighter clothing December-March (their summer) than June-November. For sightseeing at a ruin such as Machu Picchu, wear layers so you'll be warm at night, cooler in the day.

PHILIPPINES: For formal occasions wear long cotton dresses; for nightclubbing wear casual cotton dresses. Dress conservatively in town and be especially careful not to wear anything valuable—hold-ups for jewelry right on the streets are not uncommon. The weather is very warm and humid, so take cotton blends or anything else lightweight, cool, and wrinkle-resistant.

PUERTO RICO: Pack light cotton resort wear, plenty of beachwear, and bright short dresses or pants ensembles for evening. Add sandles without stockings for day and night, a sweater or light wrap to wear in air-conditioning and in the mountains, and a light raincoat for May-December.

PORTUGAL: Dresses and skirts are more acceptable than pants, so dress accordingly. Winters are surprisingly cool for this land of sunshine; be prepared. This is a rather formal country, so don't wear shorts anywhere but on the beach. And don't wear a terribly brief bikini even on the beach except along the cosmopolitan Sun Coast or the Algarve. Don't wear mini-skirts. (Actually they are beginning to look old-fashioned anywhere anyway except Topeka.) Cover up your swimsuit the minute you leave the beach—even if it's just to go to your hotel lobby!

SARDINIA: Skimpy bikinis on the beach—the skimpiest (topless!) in Porto Cervo among the yachting set. Throw on a sheer muslin cover-up and sandals and you have your uniform by day. Maillots (super-thin one-piece suits that fit like a second skin—so your first skin must be in good shape!) have begun to run neck-and-neck with bikinis for popularity here. And jewelry is worn with bathing suits—thin gold waist chains, beaded necklaces, bangle bracelets. You can wear your bathing suit jewelry by day or night. Actually this fad is not confined to Porto Cervo—it's a fad wherever the jet set goes in warm weather: St. Tropez, Portofino, etc. Other *de rigueur* clothes for the jet spots are long jersey clingy dresses with covered arms and bare backs, or midriffs and party pajamas. Don't forget a shawl or cover-up for evening coolness. *Les blue jeans* are worn everywhere—embroidered, sequined, what have you. Cut-off jeans are popular to wear with halter bras.

SCANDINAVIA: Be certain always to have a sweater or coat. (The midnight sun doesn't give off the sun's heat after 9 PM.) Thermal underwear helps in the winter. Stockholm and Copenhagen are the gayest Scandinavian cities with the most permissive dress codes—elsewhere, dress more conservatively. Danish pastries do not seem to go to the Danes' hips, so stay away from their bikini coasts unless you're slim and trim, also. Pick up their comfortable, loose-fitting brightly colored Marimeko designs.

SINGAPORE: Take lightweight, porous cotton or cotton/synthetic mix fabrics. Dress is casual: long skirts or dressy pantsuit ensembles for evenings out. Although many European women residing in Singapore still wear hats and gloves as in Colonial days, you can relax. Rubber sandals have been outlawed (to discourage hippies), so wear regular sandals.

SPAIN: Sedate, conservative clothing (especially in churches). Spaniards are big on black or white dress. Bikinis only when making waves in the Mediterranean, but cover up when walking to your hotel.

TAHITI: Live in bikinis. Wear a brightly-colored *pareau* (a cloth wrapped around your bathing suit bottom which makes you acceptable for meals). Any attire is permissable in town as long as it covers what a bikini would. Women wear *casual* long dresses or skirts in the evening. Wear a brightly-colored cotton Tahitian frock —you'll find them in abundance in Papeete.

THAILAND: Always wear light summer clothes in this sultry climate. A must: sun hats (though you'll see lots of sun umbrellas carried by ladies way under 80!). Women are now allowed to wear slacks in the Grand Palace. Don't be tempted to wear any Thai silks —they wrinkle terribly.

TURKEY: Dress conservatively. Don't wear shorts or bathing suits away from the beach. To enter mosques, wear head scarves, and remove your shoes.

U.S.S.R.: Dress rather conservatively in large cities and public places; dresses and skirts are more acceptable than pants. Save your bikini strictly for the immediate beach area. Since everyone else wears drab clothes, you'll be appreciated if you brighten things up a bit with something colorful (though conservative). Drip-dry clothes are a must since the Russians use a very harsh cleaning solvent. Your heaviest clothes, plus thermal underwear, are in order for the literally freezing Russian winters. Since Russian central heating is as inefficient as their bureaucracy, layer dressing is important; keep that sweater on in an underheated restaurant or take it off in a sweltering one. Do not sell any of your clothes—this is considered profiteering and you'll be sorry—though they'll love your blue jeans so much they'll offer to buy them right off you!

LUGGING YOUR LUGGAGE

ALONG WITH deciding *what* to take, figure out what you're going to take it *in*.

12

Try to make do with your old suitcases. Some of the really old stuff is vinyl. It's heavy, but if you don't want to buy new luggage, coat it with vinyl wax (like that made for vinyl car tops). This will protect it from scuffing en route.

Carry around a prospective suitcase in the store so you can estimate how hard it will be to carry full. If you have to buy new luggage, buy lightweight luggage; some bags are heavy *empty*. And no matter how light the case, make certain the handles are cushioned enough not to give you instant callouses.

I prefer the nylon or canvas bags with double-stitched zippers and good locks that have some "give" for easy closing. Don't buy luggage so rigid that it can't expand to hold little goodies you've picked up along the way.

How much to spend for luggage? I haven't found that the more you pay, the more you get is necessarily so in this case. Lark luggage has taken me from Boston to Burma—it's made of lightweight, durable nylon, and while not the cheapest luggage on the market, it's certainly not as high as the status Gucci or Louis Vuitton bags. Lark makes a hanging bag which has pockets for lingerie and sweaters, and also enables you to put clothes on hangers (thereby allowing you to unpack in a minute by simply lifting them out and hanging them up). And they have a carry-on case which you can divide into three compartments for all your goodies.

It's a good idea to tuck in a light, collapsible suitcase. If someone invites you to spend a weekend at his hunting lodge, you don't want to show up with enough baggage to scare him: he'll think you plan to stay forever. And at the very end of your trip, you can fill your collapsible case with things you've bought along the way.

Since you may have to carry your own luggage at times, it's a good idea to pack as though this will be the case throughout your trip. Porters have become an endangered species and the few left always seem to be helping someone else! Another reason to keep the amount of luggage down: if you rent a foreign car, the trunk will be tiny, and you won't be able to fit a big case in anyway. Traveling light also means you can save money by riding a city bus instead of the airport bus into town and sometimes even walk to your hotel. And luggage wheels to strap on to your suitcase will save your back!

Bereny's Rule: If you cannot carry your case(s) full, lighten your load. If you limit yourself to your main bag plus tote bag you won't have more bags than hands (if your purse is a shoulder bag). I simply cannot stress enough the importance of traveling light. You will be astonished at how heavy your bags are if you have to carry them yourself, even for a few feet. A single lightweight bag, plus a tote, should be sufficient for any two-week vacation; anything over 30″ x 10″ x 20″ will be unwieldly since you should assume you will be doing the wielding!

If you want to eliminate waiting for bags at air terminals, check with the airline *before* you leave for their current size/weight regulations concerning carry-ons. Check with tours as well as with airlines about luggage requirements; they sometimes have certain requirements as to type and amount.

A tote bag is good for two reasons: (1) it's easier to handle two small bags than one large one, and (2) if your other piece is checked through and lost, you still have your essentials in your never-out-of-your-hands tote. Better yet, buy a huge purse that will double as a tote and won't be weighed. Whether you decide on tote and purse or tote/purse combo, it should stay with you at all times and hold anything you simply couldn't be without if your luggage were lost: pills, itinerary, driver's license, passport and traveler's checks, airline ticket, address book, toilet articles, folding slippers, towelettes, and whatever you must have upon landing (i.e., a bathing suit at a hotel resort, or a business-type dress if you are going to a meeting). Your tote bag can later become a beach, shopping, or baby bag if plastic lined.

What can you take on the plane weight-free? A camera, coat (jam the pockets if you must), umbrella, purse, brief case, baby items, reading material. Again, check; requirements change.

So be sure to measure your luggage at home before you leave—and remember that your carry-on tote is counted as luggage if it can't pass as your purse. Give yourself time to weed out any over-the-limit items. Then you won't have any unpleasant surprises in the way of excess baggage charges. Traditionally the limit has been 66 lbs. for first class and 44 lbs. for economy. The new allowance for international economy passengers is two free checked pieces with length, width and depth dimensions totaling up to 106 inches, neither bag to exceed 62 inches. One is also entitled to a carry-on bag with total dimensions up to 45 inches (except where planes have smaller underseats and thus require smaller carry-ons). Using standard bag sizes as a criterion, the 106-inch total will permit both a 24-inch long and a 27-inch pullman case in women's luggage. The first-class international passenger is entitled to two bags not exceeding 62 inches each, plus a carry-on of 45 inches. Excess baggage is charged on a per-piece basis instead of the old weight system; flat dollar amounts are levied according to the destination. While most countries have agreed to the new allowances, not all have—so check. Domestically, you are allowed two checked bags, one with dimensions of up to 62 inches, the other up to 55 inches, and a carry-on of 45 inches, so long as none of the bags exceeds 70 pounds. For a *low* additional charge, you can take some sporting gear such as golf clubs or snow skis. Again, check *before* you pack!

Now if you cannot possibly stay within the lightweight allowances I've prescribed, you can have your excess items sent air cargo. You arrange this through the cargo department of the airport —call them in advance of your trip in case they have special requirements. Air cargo means your baggage will go to your destination via air, but not necessarily on *your* flight. You used to be able to have these extras on your flight with the Unaccompanied Baggage System, but terrorism has made the airlines abandon this practice.

HOW TO PACK There are as many different packing methods as cold cures—and most, to my thinking, are just as ridiculous. But

I'll mention the different methods in case one appeals to you.

Some people prefer to put heavy things (shoes, etc.) on the bottom so they won't crush lighter things—but this loses its advantage in the age of uncrushable travel clothes.

Some people roll everything up and stack as if packing logs. Things don't wrinkle too much and you can fit a lot in, but I think it's a royal pain in the neck and very time-consuming.

Some pack according to when they'll need the items—things needed right away go on top, those that won't be needed for awhile on the bottom. But then you can't really guarantee *when* items will be called for.

Some people pack by categories—all sweaters in one layer, slacks in another. You will know where everything is, but you might have to put it in a space-wasting place. (What if the lower right hand corner is too big for a little cotton top, but that is *the* spot for it?).

Some travelers pack by climates—all summer clothes together, all cold-weather items together. But the best way to travel light in this regard is to avoid many climate changes. If you just go to the Mediterranean in June, you can leave your heavy clothes behind. With one exception. Always take one article of clothing which will get you through unexpected weather. Everywhere I've gone I've heard, "But this weather is most unusual for this time of year." So take a heavy sweater for the warmest spot and a lightweight dress or top for the coldest. Foggy San Francisco's weather is usually in the 60's, but what if you're there one of the four days a year when it's 100°?

Some people pack in complete outfits: a top, pants, scarf, etc. together. While this does allow you to pull out a complete set at once, it doesn't work if you're smart enough to have packed a mix-and-match wardrobe.

Why have I mentioned other packing methods before mentioning my own? So that you will know that I know all about them, but still prefer mine. I've tried them all, but still prefer the following:

I hang items on a foam-covered (so it won't mark your sleeve) hanger and hang pants over the foam covered bar. Then I put each hanger in a dry cleaner's plastic bag and either hang in a hanging case or fold the garments three times into a regular suitcase. Nothing will wrinkle, because of the air cushion from the plastic bags. Hang up everything possible—robes, bathing suits, lingerie, sweaters. If there's a loop at the neck of your blouse or dress, put the hanger handle through it, so that clothes won't slip off en route. Then just grab the hangers at your hotel and unpack in minutes. It's so easy and sure-fire (like the wheel), you'll think it can't work. But it does.

If you insist on *regular* packing, here are some tips:

SHOES: Place them heel to toe in baggies, tuck jewelry or hosiery inside them. Make sure they have decent-looking tips and heels and are sprayed with a waterproofer. (Use the same spray on your leather handbags.)

LINGERIE: Roll complete sets and tuck in suitcase corners. The way to pack padded cups (this goes for swimsuits as well as bras) is to fold the suit or bra in half, turn one cup inside out and place smoothly in other. Then stuff the space with stockings or panties and roll up securely.

SLACKS: Fold slacks lengthwise on natural creases. Place first pair, waistband to the side of the case, back of pants toward hinges and let legs hang outside case. Then place a sweater or blouse, folded in thirds, lengthwise, face down on pants, letting half of it hang at right angles to the slacks. Fold pants over the sweater, then fold the rest of the sweater back on top before folding the last part of the slacks legs back.

SUIT JACKETS: Place these on their skirts, folded in thirds toward the back. Now, with garments facing in opposite directions begin folding them carefully into the case one at a time as you smooth out the wrinkles. This way each garment serves as a cushion for the one around it.

DRESSES AND SKIRTS: Start with the most fragile. Fold it lengthwise, front down, in thirds along natural curves. Sleeves are folded down the back. Put in suitcase, collar touching side and let bottom hang out. Place other dresses folded similarly in direction opposite from the one beneath it. By folding each garment opposite the one beneath it, you'll even the weight and lumps (all bulky hems won't be at one end) and be able to take the desired article out of the case by pulling it gently at the fold while you keep the other things in place with your hand.

GLOVES, SCARVES, HOSIERY, ETC.: The pocket on the side panel of your suitcase is a good place for these items, and it's also a good place to tuck in 2 or 3 plastic bags to use when repacking a damp swimsuit or lingerie.

HANDBAGS: Carry a big one, pack small ones. A flat evening purse can be packed in the pocket with scarves, etc., while a small soft bag can be filled with rolled lingerie to conserve space and shape. Take hard things out of the purse—they'll mark it.

If your suitcase has a divider, one side should be for more crushable clothing, like dresses and suits. The other side should be for less crushable items, like shoes, accessories, underwear and sportswear, evening bag, travel alarm. (A must: hotel clerks often forget to awaken you for planes. I know, I was a hotel clerk in Korolevu, Fiji and there were some people who remained in Paradise longer than expected because I forgot to awaken them.) Remember, what's important to you (i.e., catching a plane), is not necessarily important to anyone else.

Don't pack to the hilt. If you have to sit on your suitcase to close it, it's too full. When you're first packing, everything will be clean and neatly folded and take less space. What happens when you have dirty clothes wadded up and only have time to throw things in? If you've packed to within an eighth of an inch to begin with, you'll end up in rather dire straits.

SOME GENERAL TIPS   Have everything clean and mended. Fasten hooks, button and zip everything before packing it. Empty pockets. Sew loops in anything (sweater, jacket) you'd want to hang up in restaurants or theaters.

Fold crushables like silk over cushioning layers of uncrushables such as knitted sweaters. Tissue paper for this purpose is as outmoded as old steamer trunks. Pack your things in those plastic bags from the dry cleaner—they create a wrinkle-free air cushion and you can see at a glance what you're looking for. And if your suitcase is not completely filled, stuff it with weightless plastic bags—filling your bag tightly keeps things from getting jumbled up. You can always discard the excess plastic as you go along and fill up your case with purchases. And don't waste corner space— stuff film, rolled-up belts and underwear or pack belts flat around the case.

Put liquids—from cosmetics to booze—in plastic bottles and then in sealed plastic bags. Always pack glass in the center of your case. You can also cushion breakables like a travel alarm by placing them among soft items.

Put an extra sweater on top for easy accessibility if you don't have one in your tote bag. Another item that might not occur to you is a windproof lighter (if you're a smoker, of course). You'll need it on breezy boats as well as wind-swept ruins. And you might also consider the tiniest dependable transistor radio you can find. You can often get news in English in other countries or at least get a "feel" for the country through their program ideas.

Allow plenty of time to pack. Here's where I must advise you to do as I say, not as I do, since I once finished packing for a ten-month trip around the world in the back seat of a car while being driven to the airport!

When thinking of what to take, start from your toes and work up; that way you won't forget anything for any part of your body. Toes—what stockings, shoes, to take. Legs—slacks and so on up to your head (sunglasses, hat). As you pack each item, check it off. Then pack the check list. You can use it on the return trip and as the basis for a new checklist for future travel.

Before a final pack, a trial pack is in order. Lay out all your clothes and try everything on. Does the filmy blouse need a bra? Do the khaki slacks need a belt? Does everything fit in the suitcase and is the weight under the limit? Remember, nothing is irreplaceable. They do wear clothes in most places and you will be able to pick up whatever you've forgotten. When in doubt, leave it out, and leave it if you'll just be lugging it!

Now that you've so carefully packed your bags, you should know how to protect them. Use a combination lock set to your birthday. Don't leave your luggage unattended in terminal waiting areas or hotel lobbies. Don't leave your suitcases at baggage delivery areas—always hurry over and pick them up instantly before someone else does. Actually, someone else may pick them up by mistake if you have a common bag; therefore, it's a good idea to individualize yours by a wild decal, bright ribbon on the handle, or colored tape. If you're with a group, take off all old destination tags so your bag will only go to the next one (not the last one). Make sure the agent or porter puts on the right tags to begin with. And be certain you have clear identification both outside and taped to the inside lid, as well as your itinerary also taped to the inside. Of course, you'll worry less if you carry valuables *with* you.

Do keep a copy of any claim you file with the airline, along with the name of any employee you deal with. Also, retain your baggage check and a copy of your airline ticket as proof that you did, indeed, check the luggage involved.

If that rare thing happens and your bag is lost, it'll help you with your claims if you had made a list of contents when you originally packed. Here's what you can expect from the airlines if that bag is irretrievably lost: for most international travel (including domestic portions of international trips), to approximately $9.09 per pound ($20 per kilogram) for checked baggage and $400 per passenger for unchecked baggage; for travel only between U.S. points, $750 per passenger on most carriers. Special rules may apply to valuable articles. Extra valuation may be obtained at 10¢ on trips in the U.S.A. and 15¢ on international trips for each $100 or fraction thereof claimed, up to a value of $25,000. This extra valuation may be obtained through your ticket agent, not through your porter. Private insurance booths at the airport also will give you added valuation, but their prices are sky-high (excuse the pun).

A last word about luggage: on your return to America, you'll have to clear customs, and it's much easier if you've kept your receipts and purchases in a carry-on tote with you: that's not only more convenient, but it also saves you from going back to the airport to go back through customs if the purchases were in a waylaid bag.

MONTEZUMA'S REVENGE
—AND YOURS

CHANCES ARE you'll be as healthy anyway as you were at home. I'm simply going to tell you about possibilities, not probabilities. So read on and ignore what doesn't apply to you, but heed what does!

13

Do go to your doctor several weeks before vacationing. This is a good time for a check-up—plenty of time to fix anything that needs fixing and ample time to leave space between shots if you'll need a series of inoculations. Also, if you do have a shot reaction (often involving fever, chills, etc.), you'll be relaxing in bed at home reading *The Joy of Sex*, not packed into your alloted space on a 747 over the Atlantic! Actually, the Public Health Department can tell you which shots you'll need, but your local doctor will be able to give you an examination at the same time, and he's usually more convenient. Do have whoever gives you the immunizations record them in your "International Certificate of Vaccination" folder which you received with your passport, from a travel agent or the local Department of Health. Each required shot must have an official "Approved" stamp.

Upon your return from the Orient, India, or the Middle East, I strongly recommend that you return to your doctor for a check-up (particularly an intestinal one).

Some medications are better to start quite a bit in advance of a trip: the Pill, for instance. If you're going to take it, start a couple of months ahead of your trip to make certain you don't have adverse reactions to it. You don't need to be wandering around the ruins of Crete *feeling* like the ruins of Crete!

If you will need any medication on a prolonged basis during the trip, either take along an entire supply or carry a prescription with the generic name. It's also a good idea to carry a prescription for extra eyeglass lenses.

Put your medicines into clearly labeled plastic bottles, and tape the caps in place if the medicine is liquid. To allow for expansion, do not fill containers with liquids more than three-quarters full.

Pills or capsules are easier to travel with, so see if you can have your medicine in that form. If you do take pills, don't pack them in an envelope: they'll crush.

If you could possibly be pregnant, check with your physician before taking *any* medications.

Your doctor isn't the only medical person to see—visit your dentist weeks before you leave. Have cavities filled and use this chance to have your teeth cleaned. You'll look good, anyway! (Extraction just happens to be the favored method of treating dental problems in many countries. One of the highlights of your trip shouldn't be seeing your tooth on display in the marketplace in Morocco, where the extractor gets to display it, like a notch on a gunbelt!)

For a mini-medical kit, you might want to include *small* containers of aspirin, anti-diarrheal medicine such as Lomotil, Milk of Magnesia tablets, antihistamine nasal spray, antimicrobial skin ointment, calamine lotion, tweezers, vitamin supplements, band-aids, sterile gauze, a safely encased thermometer, an antibiotic such as tetracycline (but be certain you aren't allergic to it!), a pain killer such as Darvon (or booze!), and Caldesene powder or Desenex ointment for fungus infections of the groin or feet. Speaking of feet, try not to go barefoot anywhere—it's too easy to pick up hookworm or strongyles in hot, moist climates. Sandles are so attractive now, what's the problem?

Be flexible with your mini-medical kit. Adjust these suggestions to your destination(s): less items for big cities (as similar products are usually readily available), more for the boondocks. For example, certain locations preclude calamine lotion because its use is generally intended for mild insect bites and poison ivy. You'll hardly need it in Paris in the winter.

Health-wise, don't bring back more than memories! I met a woman in Belgium who carried a *gross* of condoms as a preventive. She needn't have bothered on *any* count. If you think you have contracted VD, make that part of your return check-up. Don't live in mortal fear that your brain will dissolve during your trip. You can be cured readily when you get back.

For menstrual supplies, take along an adequate supply of tampons as they're much more compact for packing than sanitary napkins. If you insist on packing sanitary napkins, wrap them in small amounts in little baggies and tuck them into your packed shoes. Actually, feminine supplies are usually available anywhere. (The women there do have to use *something!*) Just bring along enough to last until you get to a spot that is likely to sell such items. You don't have to have visions of spending five precious travel days inside a taboo hut for women in Africa! Chances are they buy Kotex down the road.

Because of the different electrical systems, don't take electric pads. If you are dependent upon one to ease monthly cramps, use a hot water bottle instead. Actually, you'll probably notice a lessening of cramps from all the walking you'll be doing.

If you have a problem with water retention as so many women do, give advance notice to your ship or plane and they can provide special food. Also, ask your doctor about taking medications called diuretics which eliminate salt and water from the body. And if water retention is a problem, ignore advice in hot countries to add extra salt to your diet.

Do wear cotton panties. Gynecologists are adamant about this, as synthetic underwear is more likely to foster all sorts of vaginal infections. I can think of more pleasant things than itching one's way around the world.

For many reasons, it's a good thing to carry pre-packaged towelettes such as "Wash 'n Dri." They're good for wiping your face in hot weather (thus preventing or healing skin irritations due to excessive perspiration), freshening underarms, and cleaning off your feet after going barefoot in Buddhist temples or Moslem mosques. They're also good for cleaning off toilet seats . . . though I usually carry a small plastic bottle of Lysol for that purpose. But my nickname is "Germsie," so maybe *you* won't feel so compelled!

Another kind of pre-packaged towelette to buy is a vaginal cleaner called "Tucks." The reason I recommend them over the others on the market is that my gynecologist has them in his office, so they must be pretty good. And while we're discussing *that* area,

I want to pass on a little tip that should make your trip more comfortable. You will quickly discover that America has the softest toilet paper in the world—so to deal with those tough sheets of paper elsewhere, simply crumple them up, thereby making them softer and more absorbent. And when you return home, you will no longer smirk at those commercials claiming that a tissue has "cush" or is "stroft."

GETTING THERE Use nose drops and antibiotics before and during the flight if you have a cold; this equalizes eardrum pressure. If you have an allergy, an upper respiratory infection, or ear trouble, use decongestants and antihistamines like the drippy ones you see advertised on TV and swear you'll never buy. As for that occasional ear pain during flight or descent, chew gum, yawn, or swallow frequently.

When flying (or going by boat or car, for that matter), if you have a tendency to motion sickness, take Dramamine. If it's too late and you start to turn green, don't aggravate your queasiness with liquids, but do take dry food like unbuttered toast or crackers. And stay away from someone else who is sick—he'll make you feel worse.

When flying or cruising, you can have as many as two alcoholic drinks while taking motion sickness pills, without having an adverse reaction. When driving, of course, I hope you will have no alcohol, but also do be wary of the pills themselves as they can make you less alert.

You'll feel more comfortable when traveling by plane if you wear nothing tight that constricts or binds you, like a girdle or long line bra. (Do people really still wear them?)

On a plane, keep your muscles and joints toned by doing isometric exercises in place or walking up and down the aisle every half hour or so. That's another good reason to have an aisle seat! Besides, it's a good chance to scout around for an appealing potential traveling companion. If you're driving a car, stop periodically and get out and walk around if the area looks safe.

Drink either pure tap water or mineral water every hour or so to prevent dehydration. And empty your bladder when the need arises—don't be put off by feeling embarrassed about frequent trips to the rest room. (Remember, you have an aisle seat.) It's not good for the bladder to remain full.

When flying long distances, do allow for jet lag. I say "long distances" but I feel my biological clock is affected when I fly from San Francisco to Los Angeles! Allow enough time to comfortably board your flight—last minute dashes to the airport can exhaust you before you've set foot on board. And don't overpack since you can wear yourself out just by carrying heavy luggage. Also, do take it easy the first day upon arrival so that you can readjust your biological clock. It's a good idea to arrive at your destination toward the end of the day; that way you'll be forced to rest instead of having an entire day ahead of you which you wouldn't want to "waste" by taking it easy. Since your digestive system may also be back in Omaha, eat lightly for a day or two until things settle down. When flying long distances during the day, force yourself to stay awake so you'll sleep at night. Stick to home time for one day after arriving. Don't try to see twenty countries in twenty days. One night stands are as devastating in this part of life as in any other!

If you are going to have a very long flight, break it up with a two- or three-day stopover (usually at no extra air fare if within a straight line). You'll see something extra (but easy does it on the short stopovers) and you won't be so tired when you do arrive. Three time zone changes in one fell swoop are usually the limit your body can tolerate!

A special note about traveling by ship—the major passenger ships have doctors as well as nurses on board. There should also be a well-stocked pharmacy and infirmary. Most emergency surgery can be performed, but the chances of that being needed are infinitesimal. If your illness was pre-existing, you'll be charged a standard fee: if you developed your sickness/accident aboard, there is usually no charge. As to freighters, there won't be a full-fledged doctor or drug store on board, but they do have well-qualified pharmacist mates who perform very adequately. Sea air does stimulate the appetite, so don't over-indulge, especially if you tend toward motion sickness. Try to skip any heavy, greasy, or deep-fried foods, and go easy on the amount of liquids you take in. That goes for liquor, especially. If you do get seasick, get some fresh air and take some seasickness pills. However, the way the new ships are built with improved stabilizers, motion sickness is much less prevalent than it used to be. Since much motion sickness is psychological, try to distract yourself with an interesting companion!

What about sunburn? Remember that the sun's rays are intensified when reflected off water or white-washed buildings—as on the Greek isles, for instance. Wear sunglasses, a long-sleeved blouse of cotton (you can burn through some synthetics), a sun hat that won't blow off in the wind, and sun lotion—and don't forget supersensitive places you usually don't think of, such as ears, ankles and the backs of your knees. Since clouds don't block out the sun, take precautions even on overcast days. If you're not particularly sun-sensitive, use any good lotion. But for those of us who practically burn *indoors*, I recommend Uval. It's a total sun block, so you won't tan either. Reapply after swimming or excessive perspiration. Also, be aware that some pills increase your chances of sunburn—so check with your doctor. If you burn in spite of all my warnings, splash the red-hot sunburn with club soda if you failed to bring along a more traditional remedy.

WHILE YOU'RE THERE   If you are going to a place with a very high altitude (like Mexico City or Bogota), take it easy in the food and drink department, and be absolutely certain to wear sunglasses because of the combination of thin atmospheric conditions and bright sunlight. And how do you know if you have altitude sickness? You'll have headache, palpitations, become short of breath, easily, and feel irritable, depressed and/or euphoric. Sounds like a bad love affair to me.

In any hot climate, tour in the early morning and late afternoon. Remember, there's a good reason that only mad dogs and Englishmen go out in the midday sun! And drink plenty of pure liquids: dehydration is one of the most common tourist health problems in such areas.

Allergies rarely bother people who are traveling, as it takes a while to become sensitized, and thus allergic. If your eyes do start itching or your nose starts running or you begin sneezing, use an antihistamine. Also, reserve air-conditioned rooms at hotels if you have allergies.

If your legs and feet hurt and are swollen from a big day of sightseeing, lie down with legs elevated. Or lie on your back on the floor (on something clean) and "walk" your feet up and down the wall. And to prevent calluses from all of that walking around, put your feet in a damp salt pile, and work them around in it for five minutes. Massage feet all over with salt, rinse in cool water, and dry. Salt is readily available since you can "borrow" it from restaurants.

You've heard the saying "Don't go near the water." Well, don't if it's a tropical river or lake. Parasites love them; you shouldn't. Oceans are fine if they're not close to river and sewer outlets. If a swimming pool is chlorinated, use it freely.

Since I'm sure you don't *like* insects, take heart in knowing that for once something you don't like is bad for you. In the tropics insects are real disease carriers. So use a good repellent such as "Off"—or rub yourself with garlic if that's all you can find. Use a mosquito net if available and avoid perfumes since they attract insects. Between the garlic and lack of perfume, I must warn you that you might be a bit lonely!

Now for that topic which seems to occupy every traveler's conversation: diarrhea or Delhi-belly or Montezuma's Revenge or (E)gypy tummy. Paregoric or Lomotil are highly recommended. I'm sure I owe my life to Ciba's Enterovioform, but it's become controversial lately so check with your doctor.

One used to worry about the water only in out-of-the-way places, but now that water pollution is an international problem, you'd be wise to ask your physician and/or knowledgeable travel agent, before you go, where you can drink safely. If you see a carafe in your room, that's a warning that the tap water isn't safe. And don't fall for the ice trap—remember, ice is made with water. Freezing won't render the germs harmless, and ice can make you just as sick as impure water. And alcohol does not kill the germs in a cocktail, so don't ask for a scotch and water if the water isn't pure. Make up a mysterious and diplomatic malady which precludes your use of ice and/or water to keep your graciousness intact and keep you from offending your host. Stick to bottled water, wine, beer, coca-cola, tea, or coffee. Many modern hotels do have their own filters, but they don't always work, so stay with the above substitutes. Bottled water should be sealed. (Hotels have been known to pour tap water into bottles!) Mineral water with bubbles is pretty much a guarantee of what you are getting. And don't order orange juice for breakfast unless you're positive it's freshly squeezed since frozen concentrate is mixed with water.

Since boiled water kills bacteria, teas and coffee are safe if you're certain boiling, not just hot, water was used. If you're out in the countryside and the water looks slightly yellow, don't be alarmed—actually, that's a good sign that the water was boiled with a tea leaf or so thrown in. If you are going to do the boiling, note that it takes three minutes of a rolling boil to be bacteriologically safe. For you intrepid souls going to really off-beat places where you can't even boil anything, you'll need water purification pills called Halazone. Or for a really simple but slightly iodized-tasting drink, put three drops of regular old tincture of iodine in a quart of water and let it stand for thirty minutes. And don't go through all the trouble of making sure your drinking water is pure and then brushing your teeth with the tap water! Even if you only rinse and spit it out, you are still running a risk.

If you plan to douche, boil the water if it is not pure. So many people go wrong on the water thing—they'll boil it only for drinking, but ingest all those microbes while brushing their teeth, having a cocktail, or douching!

As if it's not enough to fret over water, there's also food to be concerned about. Concerned, not frantic!

In general, remember to be very certain dairy products are pasteurized. Yogurt is the only dairy product that is generally safe. If you must have milk in your coffee, take along the powdered or canned version.

"You don't need to be wandering around the ruins of Crete *feeling* like the ruins of Crete!"

Also, beware of that lovely assortment of cherries or grapes in that bowl full of water in which you are to wash them: if the water isn't good, bypass your fruit dessert. When in doubt, eat only fruit and vegetables you peel yourself. The reason it's not a good idea to eat raw vegetables, fruits or salads in many countries is that they use human waste as fertilizer. (They politely call it "night soil.") There's an old wive's tale that vinegar kills bacteria, thus making it safe to order a marinated salad: I'm not an old wife and I wouldn't count on it. So you say, the natives seem to be walking around and not keeling over left and right. Yes, but remember, they've built up an immunity to it. They also urinate, brush their teeth, and shampoo their hair in the same canals in Bangkok, but I wouldn't suggest that you do it!

Regardless of your personal preferences, avoid rare meat and order it well-done. I met a *mercenary* who gave us all chills when we were eating family-style in Moorea—he asked to have steak cremated! But he was right. Being daring with rare meats or steak tartare invites tapeworm and trichinia infestations. And this is from one who has eaten octopus dipped in peanut sauce on the train through Thailand, raw fish all over Japan, and kebobs in the street stands of Singapore during a cholera epidemic. Why am I telling you this? To assure you that you will survive very well. Do as I say, not as I do!

As if there isn't enough to worry about in Russia (bugged rooms, for a start), the tap water can give you an intestinal parasitic infection called giardiasis. It's a delayed-reaction sickness which produces cramps and nausea to weaken capitalist tourists!

The use of so much oil in the food in Spain, Italy, and Greece gives some people an upset stomach. If this should happen to you, ask for poached fish and devour rice—it's a good stabilizer. Actually, if you do get mildly sick *anywhere*, recover with weak tea or bouillon (from boiled water), poached eggs, and unbuttered toast.

In Japan and certain South American countries, indulge in the national speciality of raw fish if the fish is salt-water, but avoid raw sweet-water fish because of the possibilities of parasites. Shellfish should always be well-cooked because of the chance of hepatitis and intestinal diseases. Fresh fish is fine if well-cooked. Actually, a good general rule is that cooked foods are safer than uncooked ones, since germs lose their potency when heated.

While spices can be a preservative, they can also disguise slightly spoiled ingredients. And be suspicious if mayonnaise, pastries, and desserts with cream fillings are served warm: they spoil easily unless properly refrigerated.

Restaurants aren't the only culprits, nor are hotels. Many a touristy tummy has started with the foods catered to planes, so unless your plane has been catered in the U.S. or Northern Europe, be wary of the same things I've already warned you about. Most cruise ships have adequate water filters, though, so this is one thing I'm actually declaring safe!

If you're going to rent a place abroad that has its own kitchen, avoid frozen foods, since you have no idea how many times they've been frozen and refrozen en route if you're off the beaten path.

Also, sometimes stomach upsets may seem to be related to food, when they're really due to excitement, long hours on your feet, general tiredness, jet lag. I've had more Delhi-belly in California than in Europe! Most places are safe and most travelers come back intact. My cast iron stomach rusted only in Russia.

On that really small chance that you do get seriously ill, it's best to have with you a list of physicians recommended by your own doctor. Failing that, consider the International Association for Medical Assistance to Travelers (IAMAT), 350 Fifth Avenue, New York, N.Y. 10001. Or join INTERMEDIC, 777 Third Avenue, New York, N.Y. 10017. They both issue a directory of their centers in major cities of the world. Each recommended doctor speaks English, will respond promptly to calls from members, and promises to abide by set fees: no high prices because you're an American! Both organizations also give you a chart for your personal medical history, which could be invaluable to a physician treating you overseas. The cost for a one-year membership in INTERMEDIC is $5. There's no charge for IAMAT, but they do appreciate donations.

The Medic Alert Foundation, Turlock, California 95380 provides a bracelet or necklace that identifies your health problem—a heart condition, say, or an allergy to penicillin. There's even one for those who wear contact lenses. In the event that you should faint or be knocked unconscious in an accident, such information could be vital to the doctor summoned. Actually, you should wear one at home!

One may obtain (again, in advance) a good list of approved hospitals from the American Hospital Association. If you are caught in an emergency without any recommendations, contact the American Consulate. One other alternative is to go to the closest university hospital: these usually have the most up-to-date methods and equipment, as well as a superior staff.

Sometimes, if you're staying at a really good hotel, the management can recommend a physician. Many hotels have house doctors. But first read on about my experience in Italy. I doubt that it would have happened in a medical school hospital with full diagnostic tests. I found myself doubled up with abdominal pains one day in an Italian hotel. The concierge called a doctor who practically pronounced me dead on the spot and had me taken to an immaculate clinic, where the diagnosis (sans proper tests) was to remove an ovarian cyst and my appendix. I was in such pain and so frightened that I acquiesced. Back in this country almost every doctor I saw questioned the operation—and you know how reluctant doctors are to question each other's practices! But my Italian doctor was handsome and charming and gave me a rather gay, if not too lengthy, convalescence! Anyway, there is a moral to this story: if you must have surgery, go to two or three different places for confirmation of the diagnosis and treatment. I'd certainly do the same thing here!

Sometimes politics enters medicine. Once I had gotten coral in my foot in Tahiti (note: to prevent that, remember to wear thongs while swimming in the South Pacific) and by the time I got to New Zealand I could barely walk. New Zealand medical care is cheap and good, but not apolitical. As I lay on the emergency room table moaning while the coral was being taken out of my inflamed foot, the doctor asked me what in the hell we Americans were doing in Vietnam!

But relax: around the world there is excellent medical care. Israel has the highest doctor-patient ratio in the world and the Hadasah Hospital in Jerusalem is outstanding. Korea's Seoul Medical Center has good English-speaking doctors and dentists. There are good English-speaking gynecologists at the Tokyo Women's College Hospital and the Shibuya Central Clinic and Hospital for Women. The Hospital Center in Helsinki, Finland, can help you in an emergency or you can just call 008 for a doctor in a hurry. In Rome there are English-speaking attendants and many American products at Lepetit and Evans pharmacies. The Parisian police can tell you the closest open pharmacy, and you can obtain difficult-to-get medicines from home through the Ministry of Social Affairs in Paris. You're even safe in Africa's bush country—the East Africa's Flying Doctor's Society can help you out! This is just a sample, to show you that they aren't going to leave you to die if you get sick over there.

If you do become ill, there are no cheaper places than Russia, Scandinavia, or England—their socialized medicine will pick up the tab! I want to clarify that. Always ask if you will be covered by the program, since sometimes there are catches. For instance, in England your bill will be tiny *unless* you go to a famous specialist. Women may be happy to note that in Russia you stand a better chance of getting a female physician than a male one. I don't particularly see that as better, but you might.

Since you can't pick the country (if any) you get sick in, pay a small extra premium on your medical insurance to cover you for travel. You might check into an accident insurance floater that'll take care of you on everything from a camel to a Concorde. If you carry Blue Cross, make sure your payments are kept current and won't expire while you're abroad. Pay in advance if need be. Your Blue Cross policy should take care of you abroad, but you won't get reimbursed until later, so pay your own bills and keep the hospital and physician's receipts.

People do differ, so if any of this medical advice conflicts with either your doctor's recommendations or your own experience with your particular medical history, I will be modest and say disregard what I've written and follow the counsel of someone who knows *you!*

Above all, remember that millions of Americans travel every year and stay perfectly healthy. And there's no reason you shouldn't be one of them!

PASSPORTS AND VISAS

TO DO ALL of this traveling, you will need a passport, unless you will be staying within the U.S. or its territories. The usual passport is valid for five years from the issue date. Apply for a passport as early as possible, and at least two weeks before departure.

14

For your initial passport, you must complete a passport application (Form DSP-11) at one of these Passport Agencies:

Boston, Massachusetts 02203: Room E 123, John F. Kennedy Bldg., Government Center. 617-223-3831

Chicago, Illinois 60604: Room 331, Federal Office Bldg., 230 South Dearborn Street. 312-353-7155

Honolulu, Hawaii 96813: Federal Bldg., 335 Merchant Street. 808-546-2130

Los Angeles, California 90261: Hawthorne Federal Bldg. Room 2W16, 1500 Aviation Blvd., Lawndale. 213-536-6503

Miami, Florida 33130: Room 804, Federal Office Bldg., 51 Southwest First Avenue. 305-350-4681

New Orleans, Louisiana 70130: Room 400, International Trade Mart, 2 Canal Street. 504-589-6161

New York, New York 10020: Room 270, Rockefeller Center, 630 Fifth Avenue. 212-541-7710

Philadelphia, Pennsylvania 19106: Room 4426, Federal Bldg., 600 Arch Street. 215-597-7480

San Francisco, California 94102: Room 1405, Federal Bldg., 450 Golden Gate Avenue. 415-556-2630

Seattle, Washington 98174: Room 906, Federal Bldg., 915 Second Avenue. 206-442-7945

Washington, D.C. 20524: Passport Office, 1425 K Street, N.W. 202-783-8170

If you don't live near any of these agencies, get an application from any federal or state court of record accepting applications or at a post office designated by the Postmaster General.

WHAT YOU NEED TO GET A PASSPORT

1. *A properly completed passport application.*
2. *Proof of U.S. citizenship: a previously issued passport, a certified U.S. birth certificate or a notice from the registrar stating that no birth record exists, in which case send instead the best combination of secondary evidence you can get, such as a baptismal certificate, early census, newspaper files, etc. Such secondary evidence should be created as close to the time of birth as possible. All such proof must be in the form of original or certified documents. A Certificate of Naturalization should be submitted if you claim citizenship by naturalization. A Certificate of Citizenship issued by the Immigration and Naturalization Service must be submitted if you became a citizen through the naturalization of a parent. If you can't obtain such a document, your parent's certificate of naturalization and your foreign birth certificate and evidence of admission to the U.S. must be submitted.*
3. *Two identical photographs. These can be either color or black/white and must be close-up front views not more than 3" x 3", nor less than 2½" × 2½". There are photographers who specialize in passport photos, usually at a low cost.*
4. *A fee of $10 in the form of a bank draft or cashier's check, personal check or money order. Submit cash only if you are applying in person.*
5. *Proof of identification: previous U.S. passport, driver's license, a Certificate of Naturalization or Citizenship, a governmental i.d. card or pass, personal knowledge of the passport official, or an identifying witness who has known you for two years.*

Children may have separate passports; and a parent can make application for an under-12 child. You may include your children in your own passport; your child must accompany you when you apply if he/she is 16 years of age or older.

Your passport may be changed at your request for such things as showing a married name or legal change of name (to exclude a former husband, for example). Use the Passport Office Form DSP-19 "Application for Amendment of Passport."

You may apply for a new passport by mail if (1) you have been the bearer of a passport issued within eight years prior to the date of a new application, and (3) your previous passport was not issued before your eighteenth birthday, and (4) you aren't applying for an Official, Diplomatic or no-fee passport, and (5) you do not wish to include a member of your family, and (6) you can carry out this whole procedure in the United States.

If you are eligible to apply by mail, get Passport Office Form DSP-82 ("Application for Passport by Mail") from an office accepting applications. Fill in *all* requested information. Sign and date the application in the space provided for certification of the truth of the statements made therein. Attach the required passport, two duplicate photographs signed on the front left-hand side taken within six months of the date of the application, and the passport fee. You'll save the $3 execution fee when applying by mail. Then mail the *completely* filled out application and attachments to the nearest passport agency for processing.

What do you do if your passport is stolen or lost? Report it immediately to the nearest American consulate if you're abroad. If you're in America, report it (also immediately) to the Passport Office, Department of State, Washington, D.C. 20524. If stolen, the theft should also be reported to local police; insist on a written statement from them stating that you have reported the loss. There may be quite a delay before you're issued a new passport since the circumstances of loss will be reviewed as well as your file in the Department. A replaced passport is limited in validity. Remember, while you're without your passport you're also without appropriate evidence of identity and citizenship. So make certain your passport is safe. According to the U.S. Passport Office, the main cause for losing a passport or having it stolen is carelessness. Protect your passport by always carrying it in a safe place in your handbag or putting it in the hotel safe. Do not put it in a suitcase either in transit or in your hotel room. Believe me, losing your passport is worse than losing your Pills!

VISAS A visa is usually a stamped notation placed in the traveler's passport; and is permission granted by the government of a foreign country for an alien to enter and stay in that country for a certain period of time. You get a visa by submitting your passport (along with completed visa application forms) to the consular official in the U.S. of the foreign country requiring the visa. That official should approve the visit and enter it into your passport. Carry extra passport photos with you overseas for spur-of-the-moment visits when you may need to get an extra visa on the spot.

While some countries don't require a visa, they may insist upon a tourist card or entry permit (obtainable from travel agencies or airlines serving the country).

Don't Listen to Your Mother: Talk to Strangers

MEETING YOUR KNIGHT IN SHINING GUCCI'S

JUST BECAUSE you start out alone, doesn't mean you have to remain alone. Indeed, the fewer people you're traveling with (solo is the very best), the better your chances of meeting people.

15

☛ Look and *be* friendly and inviting. Don't listen to your mother —talk to strangers. Your chances of meeting people will increase in direct proportion to your adventurousness. Be approachable. Even in travel situations, many people are hesitant about approaching a complete stranger. Melting the ice may be up to you. Do it! And anytime you meet people whose company you enjoy, ask them to be *your* guests for cocktails or tea. Don't hesitate; you don't have much time.

☛ Go to places that interest you—you'll find others there with a similar bent. You dig archaeology (excuse the pun)?—go to the ruins in India or Greece. Water baby? Go to the bikini coasts. Culture vulture? Make a grand tour of European music festivals. For a single who's not too outgoing, the best trip is one where she gets involved in an activity, so that meeting someone is just an offshoot of the trip and not the sole aim. But you must do something you genuinely enjoy so that if you don't meet the love of your life, you'll still have a good time. Hate hiking but want to meet a rugged outdoor type? Forget it—if you don't meet anyone, all you'll have to show for it are blistered feet. Love tennis? Take a tennis tour and you'll have fun regardless of the love prospects après-game.

☛ Be a sport. If you can't afford a day of sailing, water skiing or whatever, buy an hour's worth. An hour of three different activities exposes you to three times as many people as one three-hour session anyway! Or go to a tennis camp.

☛ Golf courses usually have a great male-female ratio. If you belong to a private club at home, have the club manager write on letterhead stationery to the foreign club requesting that they extend privileges to you. And carry a letter of introduction and/ or your home club membership card to get admitted to private clubs. If you don't belong to a private club at home or do but forgot to plan ahead, once you arrive somewhere look up sporting clubs of your choice in the English directory. Or ask the local Department of Tourism to set you up with a sports club that welcomes visitors.

☞ Take lessons—even just one. French cooking in Paris, scuba diving in the Caribbean, tennis and horse back riding at resorts, dancing and languages on cruise ships.

☞ Go off the beaten track. The more remote the area, the more the foreign travelers band together for companionship. Tourists will be rarer, so they'll be more noticeable. Also, I've always found more interesting people the farther I've gone from "civilization." You'll meet more well-traveled, "with-it" people in an African bush oasis than at the London Hilton!

☞ Solo females don't have to avoid couples. Many couples enjoy a new face and also know a single man—but pay your own way when with couples. Or invite them to your room for cheap, duty-free liquor which you have wisely stocked up on at the airport.

☞ Chat with anyone interesting in large crowds—no one is going to rape you with 80,000 bullfight fans around or guards aplenty at the Louvre.

☞ Pretend you're a reporter—ask everybody lots of questions. If it'll help you carry off this little deception, carry a note pad or tiny tape recorder.

☞ If you fly to a city frequently, try to get on the mailing list of your favorite museum, art gallery, etc., so you'll be invited to any openings or premieres.

☞ Pick a lounge chair near an attractive man at your hotel pool. If you're a bathing beauty, walk around a lot: you'll be noticed. Sun on the porch. Run out of sun tan lotion—borrow his and ask him to apply it to your hard-to-reach back.

☞ Lounge in a well-trafficked hotel lobby.

☛ Stay at a business hotel. You'll meet the businessmen who stay there.

☛ Resorts thirty minutes or so from a big city are like suburbia—very couple- and family-oriented. Avoid such places: being a one among twos is like being alone in the Ark. And singles resorts are out—they get a rather desperate crowd.

☛ If you plan to visit a resort and big city in the same country, visit the resort first. Friends you make there will provide companionship in the city. It's easier to get acquainted in resorts than in big cities.

☛ If you're not going far, call up a resort to check out their guests. Ask if they're mostly singles, or families, or older couples. Or drive over for a look before settling in for two weeks.

☛ On a pauper's budget but want to meet a prince? Have cocktails or spend the day sunbathing at a super deluxe place you can't afford to *stay* at. No one will throw you out if you act as if you belonged. Or stay at first class hotels—but get the cheapest room. Your prince won't know the tariff.

☛ Avoid room service unless you have an eye on the waiter, since he's the only one you'll meet.

☛ If you're an older woman, go to those wonderful countries where such females are adored—like Denmark and France. Youth-oriented cultures (like our own) can be a downer!

☛ Go to a city's marketplace—it's an informal way to meet another tourist. Ask him how to haggle, or whether this pottery looks like a good buy, or what this strange-looking fruit is.

☛ Take half- and full-day city tours. Be among the last to board so you can choose a seat by an interesting-looking traveler. It's a great way to meet someone for later-in-the-day activities.

☛ Go to folk dances—the klutzy audience is often asked to join. You'll meet *someone*.

☛ Plan your trip around a festive celebration like Papeete's Bastille Day or Rio's Carnival. There's literally dancing in the streets. Europe's cultural festivals are also great places to meet people since *everyone* gets caught up in the ebullient mood.

☞ Get lost in a safe area during the day—it's a good way to find things and meet people since you'll *have* to ask directions.

☞ Chat with the people you do business with. The ticket agent or shop clerk or druggist are also *people*. But beware of guides— they usually have a woman in every bus.

☞ In southern Europe, sit in the piazza or stroll the quay for your quarry or eat family-style at long wooden tables in outdoor harbor restaurants; everyone talks to everyone else.

☞ Go to big city amusement parks (like Copenhagen's Tivoli). They're not tacky like ours, and they are a friendly, fun meeting ground.

☞ Be active, not passive. Get your own tickets for concerts and theaters; you never know who you'll meet in line but you must know you won't meet anyone alone in your room.

☞ Check to see if there is a U.S.—Foreign Country friendship society. Attend a function.

☞ Whenever there's a "Meet the Danes" (or Swiss or Italians or whatever)—go. Someone there may have an attractive relative or friend hovering about, or they may fix you up with one later. Anyway, it will be nice company for an evening. Arrange as far in advance as possible and indicate the type of people you're interested in. Take a little gift.

☞ Get to know people before you go, through the "Globetrotters Club." Travelers the world over share experiences via the printed word. Write Globetrotters Club, BCM/Roving, London WC1 V6X England.

☞ Try to arrange contacts through organizations or friends. Someone's third cousin twice removed in Naples just may be better than arriving totally friendless. Take names and ad- dresses with you if you will be looking up a friend's friend or relative. I know that sounds obvious, but many people forget. And do bring a little gift.

☞ Meet people through a function of an international organiza- tion to which you belong—like the Red Cross, the Jewish Wel- fare Federation, the Catholic Relief Charities. Your professional or political organization may have a branch overseas. Write ahead of time introducing yourself and suggest that you'd like to attend a social function.

☛ Take a special-interest cruise (theater, bridge, etc.) to meet simpatico people. For the same reason, participate in the ship's many activities. And talk to the cruise ship's hostess—tell her if there is someone in particular you'd like to meet and ask her who might need a partner for chess or a foursome for bridge. But don't come on too strong with men at sea—neither one of you will have any place to escape to if either one of you cools. Jumping overboard is a bit extreme.

☛ Optimize your social life on board by choosing the second dinner seating; the ship's social activities revolve around it. Reserve a table as soon as you go aboard. Tell the Chief Steward you wish to be seated at a large congenial table; otherwise you may end up at a table for three—you and another couple! If you're traveling with a man, reserve a table for two immediately—they're scarce and go quickly. (I'm talking here about tables, but this could also apply to attractive men!) If you don't like your table, let the maitre d' know immediately so he can have you moved—the longer you wait, the more embarrassing it'll be.

☛ Book cruises at optimum times: the best time for singles to meet other singles on cruises is in the summer and during holiday periods, on transatlantic voyages for those in their 20s, and on short-term Caribbean cruises for older singles. The cruises that draw the most singles tend to be activity ones on the Norwegian Caribbean Cruise Lines' Southward, which go to Grand Cayman and Cozumel and are big on skindiving.

☛ Mix business with pleasure. Set up your next convention or seminar aboard a ship or at a sociable resort. Your company might just bite because of the tax break. As the planner, you'll meet people before and during. Actually, you can plan *any* trip around a convention or seminar—and you'll be thrown in with your colleagues constantly.

☛ Get as many business letters of introduction as you can. Even business acquaintanceships have been known to blossom beyond the briefcase stage. Bring your business card—it's an excuse to give someone your name.

☞ Look up professional colleagues. If you're a nurse or doctor, visit a hospital. If you're a teacher, visit your department at a university. If you're a reporter, visit a newspaper. Go to a spot that appeals to a profession whose members you like. You'll probably find a psychiatrist reverently touring Sigmund Freud's old stomping grounds in Vienna; chances are you'll meet a writer or two at Hemingway's old haunt in Key West. If you want a *starting* chance to meet someone in a particular profession, see if you can latch on to an affinity-group tour that interests you . . . a tour of bankers, physicians, psychiatrists, stockbrokers.

☞ On a plane, train, or bus, exchange pleasantries with your neighbor if you have a common language. Nothing earthshaking, but comfortable things like "Where are you going?" If you happen to be going to the same city, you might end up with a date for your first night in town. If he isn't going to your stop, perhaps you can get together later on in the journey if your itineraries coincide.

☞ Don't be the first to board your plane—look over the other passengers first. Tell the check-in clerk at the air terminal to put you next to that great-looking man. And inquire whether it's cheaper to take a taxi to or from the airport; it may be if you can share. And what better way to strike up an acquaintanceship with a man than "Going my way?"

☞ Bring small versions of popular games (Scrabble, backgammon, cards) and ask others to play on planes, trains, and at poolside.

☞ A good place to meet English-speaking men is in bars, lounges, and lobbies of the *best* hotels around 5:30 PM when they've just finished their business for the day.

☞ Meet the *locals* by going to the cafes and bars off the beaten track, away from the fancy hotels. You and your friends don't go to the Hilton bar for a night out at home, do you? But, just as you would at home, be wary of leaving with just anyone. Remember Mr. Goodbar.

☛ You'll meet more locals than tourists on public transportation and at free facilities such as parks and public beaches. Picnics in the park are a super way to meet people.

☛ Stop at a coffeehouse or gathering spot whose clientele attract you. Say you're doing research for something and must locate all the fun places in town. It is an instant conversation opener, and one place will lead to another.

☛ Buy the local underground or student newspaper and go to advertised spots if you want to meet hip young people or older people trying to be hip and young.

☛ See if there are communal saunas, steam baths or whirlpools. Nothing breaks down the barriers faster. Or break down inhibitions immediately and go nude *en masse*. Vacations in the Buff (244 E. 46th Street, New York, NY 10017) arranges group trips for those who want the Caribbean in the nude.

☛ Go to a Club Mediterranee anywhere, though the best Club Med spot for a single to commingle is Buccaneer's Creek in Martinique. These resorts have built-in congeniality with shared dining tables, scads of activities, and an atmosphere which guarantees meeting people. If you go alone, you'll be assigned a female roommate.

☛ Go on a Lindblad Tour. These are for comfort-seeking adventurers who want to go to such off-beat places as the Amazon and the South Pole. You'll meet a relatively small group of well-traveled people.

☛ Go where you're "trapped" together in small groups—a long schooner trip, for instance. One suggestion: Windjammer Cruises, P.O. Box 120, Miami Beach, FL 33139. They have a smaller (70-130 people) and younger group than the big ships. Or take a barge trip and float with a friendly group down the rivers of France or the Netherlands.

☛ Remember, the more you get locked into plans ahead of time, the harder it'll be to tear yourself away if you should meet someone with whom you wish to travel. Sure, you're free to cancel everything and take off with the man of your dreams, but since you've already paid for everything, you might hesitate. I'd certainly find it harder to go off with a man in the Austrian countryside if I had to think of my money dripping away daily on unused hotels and other junkets.

☛ Take along your own address labels (mail order firms can print them up supercheap); you can give these to a new man to make sure you'll hear from him when you get home. And bring a blank address book for new names and addresses.

☛ Swear to yourself that you will not meet Mr. Right (or Mr. Wrong if you're a practicing masochist) and you most assuredly will.

OTHER FACTS OF NIGHT LIFE

1. *Don't ask taxi drivers for night spots—they'll tell you about either some dump their brother owns or a well-known place you already know about.*

2. *No matter where you go at night, always make arrangements in advance to get back to your hotel: some towns don't have 24-hour taxi service. And never go anywhere without a card from your hotel in your hot little hand so that you can get back!*

3. *Countries start swinging at different times (e.g.: Caracas, Venezuela just begins to come alive at 11 PM). Check with the concierge.*

4. *Check the English language newspaper for daily (and nightly) activities. And read the local "Where" or "What to Do in. . . ." You can also get free booklets of local events put out by the city tourist bureau.*

5. *Ask your plane's stewardess for her suggestions on where to go. Later, at your hotel, ask your concierge what places you'd like —he can size you up quickly.*

6. *Don't go the regular bar route alone if expenses are a concern. Beer gardens are popular and cheap abroad. Other cheapie fun places are coffeehouses. These are not to be confused with American coffee shops; they're intimate, atmospheric places with some kind of music (from classical to hard rock). Coffeehouses and cafes are such a European institution that you can spend hours over a cup of coffee and no one will hassle you to order more. And they're so respectable, you can talk to anyone there—and you will.*

7. *Go to a big hotel entertainment complex, especially if you're staying at the hotel, since it eliminates traipsing about dark streets at night. Many large hotels have revolving restaurants, cocktail bars and outdoor patios.*
8. *Remember, with all your good intentions to save money and with the above tips notwithstanding, you may not be back again—so think twice before economizing to the point that you'll miss an unrepeatable event.*

THIS IS YOUR MOTHER SPEAKING Now I haven't told you to go out and meet people just to turn around now and tell you not to. But I feel it my duty to give you some warnings about finding fun. Don't worry yourself silly—I feel much safer wandering the streets of Athens or Lisbon at night than I would feel in most American cities.

Want to gad about at night? Do it and enjoy. But think. Use common sense—don't go off just anywhere with just anyone! If you've met a charming man that afternoon who wants to see you in the evening, go! But have him meet you in your lobby, and take a taxi (not his car) to a public place such as a restaurant or theater or disco. Ditto a taxi coming home.

Remember that if you do go to a bar, the general rule is that the nicer the man, the shyer he is. And the *way* you dress will generally determine the *type* of person you'll end up talking with!

If that man you've just met is more rogue than Redford, there are some things you can do to get rid of him. Forget your English. Pretend you're married and your husband is expecting you back at the hotel *now*. Stay in crowds and lose him. Tell him "Good-bye, I've just seen some dear friends" and go over and talk to a couple (*any* couple). If all else fails, call the police.

Want to go nightclubbing, but you haven't found the man? Go on a nightclub tour. It'll be safer, cheaper and more comfortable than going alone.

Since most tourist joints are watched over by everyone from the local police to the Chamber of Commerce, the worst that can happen to you in a "name" place if you do go alone is a too-diluted drink!

There's usually safety in numbers, so feel free to walk alone at night if there are lots of people out. And stay away from dives and seedy neighborhoods—this usually means the waterfront area.

Carry a little whistle in your pocket (not in your purse because you'd never find it quickly).

Have a good time!

WHEN IN ROME. . . .   In Europe, unescorted women are welcome at brasseries, trattorias, and other eating places except for some really chi-chi spots. I'm not telling you to fold into the wallpaper, but do modulate your voice; you wouldn't believe the number of complaints I've heard from European restaurant owners on this subject—they feel that unescorted women seem driven to prove (loudly!) that they can have fun without a man.

Be especially wary of accepting invitations from local males in Middle Eastern and Latin countries; to them, women's place is still more or less in the home (especially in the Middle East), and a solo woman is often assumed to be plying her trade!

One more thing that's peculiarly Middle Eastern, before we leave that area. Bars there are strictly male provinces. Even some restaurants are male only, not by official policy, but rather by custom.

In Latin countries, you should expect to be ardently pursued— ogled and pinched right on the street. Don't be alarmed; if you're in a safe part of town, it won't go beyond pinching and ogling. Be flattered and smile. This is not the place to launch into a tirade about being a sex object.

Some Latin countries won't admit unescorted women to bars, discos, and dance places. (By the way, an escort can mean one man and ten women!) But in general Europeans and Latins expect to see unescorted women just about anywhere in street bars and night-clubs—that's why those night tours, folklore spots and student hang-outs have become so popular.

In certain countries, like the Virgin Islands and parts of Africa, you shoud not go into a bar or nightclub with or without a date; the racial tension is such that unless you're black, you'll feel unwelcome because you'll *be* unwelcome.

Asia is different even again. Asians always marry and assume everyone else does. So you may be looked at as a bit of an oddity, but you will be politely treated. Asian women usually remain at home, and when they are in public they remain in the background, wear subdued clothes, and defer to the men. Don't try to liberate the women—you're on their turf!

Whatever continent you're wandering about, you'll usually feel more comfortable going into a casino unescorted than into a bar— you can always wander around pretending you just wanted to play and watch the games! There's something less obvious about it.

And wherever you are, observe the formalities of bringing candy or flowers to your hostess and calling people by their surnames. In informal countries like Australia, they'll immediately say "Call me Mike, Mate," but in England you'll be saying Mr. and Mrs. and Miss for ages. By the way, they won't know who you're talking to if you address someone as "Ms." Err on the side of formality. One other behaviorial note: easy on the booze in different climates and altitudes; in hot or high places you may have one too many with only one. A lush does not look pretty even in a Valentino original.

COUNTRY-BY-COUNTRY CAROUSING Here are some tidbits I've gleaned about different countries. I'm being brave mentioning places by name—you know how fast they change.

AUSTRALIA: In Sydney, meet your Australian artist at Paddy's or go to the market in the Haymarket on Friday. The King's Cross area is Sydney's night life center. Something you must see: Sydney's all-*male* revue at Les Girls. Don't just wander into bars—many don't allow women.

AUSTRIA: Vienna's Raimund or Kammerspiele coffeehouses attract theater people, while football fans go to the Hummel and Zögernitz. Take a streetcar to Guinzing (a suburb) and go for a sing-along at an open-air wine house. And go to park bandstands to be surrounded by friendly people and good music in the summer. If you already have a date, dance outdoors at the Cobenzel Bar in the Vienna Woods—utterly romantic. The Atrium is the best of Vienna's lively discos.

BELGIUM: Americans hang out at the Main Street in Rue des Dominicains. Elegant bar/meeting places are in the name hotels—the Hilton's Le Bar, the Westbury's Penthouse. If you've already met a man, have him take you to such popular discos as The Great American Disaster, Watergate, Au Broadway.

BOLIVIA: Don't go into bars unescorted. Confiterias are popular all over La Paz; the best are the Club de La Paz (Avenida Camacho, Esquina Ayacucho) and the Confiteria Toko (Avenida 16 de Julio 1832): these are leisurely drinking places to go *with* a man or another woman.

BRAZIL: In Rio de Janeiro the Copacabana Beach is where everybody shows up. In the early morning you can literally run into handsome joggers . . . later in the day the place will be alive with soccer and volleyball teams. If you want free-wheeling, uninhibited fun (and huge crowds), go to Rio's February Carnival. There are continuous parties and balls with people always Sambaing (learn before you go or at Rio's top-rated dance studios: Portela's, Mangueira's, the Imperior Serrano). Singles go to the Crazy Rabbit (Avenida Princesa Isabel 185) and you can mix with the locals at Canecao (Rua Lauro Muller, Botafogo).

CANADA: Beer parlors seem to be male preserves, so stay away. British Columbia is filled with Americans in the late 20—early 30 age bracket; they fled our draft some time ago and have stayed on, favoring the area around the university. The summer brings Ontario's Shakespeare Festival, a wonderful experience both artistically and socially. For wild (by Canadian standards) socializing, go to Quebec's Laurentian Mountains during Winter Carnival. Go to Quebec's best disco—La Traite du Roy. (It has a good French restaurant upstairs.) In general, the pubs are rather tame and the main sources of entertainment for you to really enjoy are the special festivals in various provinces—such as the stampede in Calgary, Vancouver's Oktoberfest, Montreal during the International Film Festival or St. Jean Baptiste Day.

CARIBBEAN: In the Bahamas, Harbour Island attracts yachtsmen and fishermen. The Bahamas' social life centers around Nassau, where the Pilot House Club collects sportsmen and fishermen. Everyone goes to Charley's La Fin or Dirty Dick's (both bistros). El

Casino is the main social center for Nassau, where you can gamble, dance, and mix with *everyone*. You'll feel comfortable with or without a date. Nassau's discos (as well as casinos) attract a young single crowd. Go to local limbo shows with a date but decline low limbos for your back's sake. The little Bahamian isles like St. Kitts, Nevis, and Montserrat do not have much planned activity: you'll have to make your own.

In Barbados you might want to stay at the Paradise Beach Club or the Rockley Beach Hotel if you're looking for the under-30 set. Both the small Island Inn and Bagshot House have a clubbish atmosphere where you'll feel an instant camaraderie.

Bequia has the Friendship Bay hotel, whose clients are mostly New England doctors, so if M.D.'s are your thing, take heed.

In Bermuda the Hamilton Princess hotel attracts a swinging crowd at the Princess Room and Regency Terrace. Front Street's Rumrunners is a young-people's favorite for disco and dining. The Holiday Inn has a social hostess and lots of entertainment, as does the Hotel Inverurie. The Newstead in Paget Parish appeals to re-fined types while the Castle Harbour (at Tucker's Town) attracts a rather boisterous crowd intent on having fun. The Belmont Hotel Golf and Beach Club (in Warwick Parish) makes sure you meet people at their swizzle parties and outdoor barbecues.

The British Leeward Isles have the Callaloo Beach Hotel where the professional men go. Businessmen go to the Cortsland. Lord Nelson's Club is usually filled with British and American expa-triates. The Admiral's Inn and Cobblestone Inn dining rooms at-tract yachtsmen. American and Canadians go to the Coconut Beach and the Habberock Beach Club hotels. Both yachtsmen and water sports enthusiasts go to the Mariners Inn. Meet Antiguans and a young American crowd at the Halcyon Cove.

In Haiti the Grand Hotel Oloffson attracts celebrities, especially writers and other such eccentric creatures. The Habitation Leclerc is for rich but hip travelers.

The Netherlands Antilles sports the Avila Beach resort, which has a convivial outdoor bar where everybody talks to everybody. Meet cruise passengers at the Avila's shared swimming facilities. The Manchebo Beach resort attracts tennis buffs and honeymooners (so if you've met some attractive man, get their honeymoon package). Go on weekends (only women and children go on weekdays) to the Shell Clubs—the Yacht Club, Golf Club, and Country Club; do call ahead first.

The Virgin Isles have an arty crowd staying at Sebastians-on-Tortola and The Sort. Businessmen stay at the Windward Hotel and Treasure Isle. Meet the locals at the Holger Danske. The Club Comanche has an "in" group of repeaters—so at least pretend you've been there before. The really rich stay at Little Dix Bay. Yachtsmen go to Drake's Anchorage. The Bali Ha'i Hotel's bar and Sunday brunch are easy places to meet both guests and locals.

Don't go near the water in Aruba and Curaçao—the local women outnumber the local men 3-1. So stick to the non-local spots like the Curaçao Hilton; you will meet some male locals at the Hilton's "In Touch With the Dutch" weekly parties. Also, meet male (as well as female) locals through the Gezzelligheid and Societeit Curaçao clubs.

CHILE: There has been a general curfew from 1:00-5:30 AM in most of the country, so if it's still in effect, time your evening festivities accordingly. Linger with the others at the Haiti Coffee House (Bandera St.) and the Do Brasil (Ahumada). You can go there unaccompanied, but not to nightclubs and street bars. If you latch on to a date, have him take you to the best disco in town, the Portada Colonial.

COLOMBIA: Meet South American millionaires at the Jockey Club, Los Lagartos and the Executives Club (all in Bogotà). The San Diego Hotel attracts non-millionaire Colombian businessmen. Americans gather at the Capri. For a fun night spot go to the Tequendama's Monserrate Room. The Unicorn (Calle 94, 7-75) is a private club where singles feel welcome; even though it's a private club, you can easily get in—ask your concierge for the how-to's. Have a date take you to the popular discos Tizca (Calle 28) and Cafe Europa Billares (Calle 22). Don't go into bars or cafes alone except in a big name hotel. And don't go about the streets alone at night *anywhere*.

DENMARK: You're bound to meet a great Dane at the grandmother of all amusement parks, Tivoli (open May-Sept.). Wander about freely—it's refined, safe, and very friendly. Women can comfortably go into bars and cafes except in the Nyhavn district. Copenhagen's locals mix with tourists at such hotel bars as the Palace, Royal, Europa, Kong Frederik. Want to meet artists and journalists? Then eat at Copenhagen's Bronnum on Kongens Nytorv. Copenhagen's lively bohemian district is filled with music and dance spots—it's an area called "The Minefield" on Nikolaj Kirke. Young people in Copenhagen love the sandwiches at Cheval Blanc while society and artists (theater) gather at the d'Angleterre Hotel dining room. Meet tourists at the Plaza. Vacation on a farm in Denmark— you'll be instant family with those gorgeous Danish men! If you are invited to a Danish home any evening, nibble a bit first since you may be invited only for entertainment, not dinner.

FINLAND: Be prompt for any invitation; the Finns are a punctual people. Shake hands with everyone you meet. Wait until your host has toasted you before you drink. Helsinki's Toolonranta Cafe with its open-air grill is a popular spot, as is the Vanhan Kellari cellar bar. Go to the twice-weekly folk dancing exhibitions (dial 058 for information in English on upcoming events). Spend some time on a Finnish farm or chalet. Sign up for an English-speaking seminar on a subject of interest (the Finnish Travel Association will arrange it): remember, small groups are good for meeting people.

FRANCE: In Paris, you must go to a sidewalk cafe; the most elegant are the Cafe de la Paix and the Grammont. Go with a date to such "in" (now, anyway) discos as New Jimmy's on Blvd. Montparnasse or Castel's in the Rue Princesse. Young people flock to the less chic (and alcohol-free) Bus Palladium in Pigalle. Parisian nightclubs and theaters are heavily (no pun intended) into nudity—so if you're straight-laced or have a date with a new man, be forewarned. In Paris businessmen go to the Ambassador and the Scribe hotels to stay. The Hôtel de Paris has a very wealthy clientele. In Cannes, Americans fill the Hôtel Carlton. In St. Tropez, go to the cafes and quay to meet the jet set. Back in Paris, the Chez Ginette (101, rue Caulaincourt) is a place for great inexpensive food and dancing so informal that strangers will ask you to dance; you needn't be shy about going there with another woman. Long Hiep is a Vietnamese restaurant on 3, rue Pot de Fer, in Paris and the good, nonfattening food makes it a meeting place for architects, artists, models, photographers and other such arty types.

GREAT BRITAIN: Meet a fellow pervert at the sex shops in Piccadilly Circus. Go to one of London's legitimate theaters (a money and taste bargain), but do check curtain times—they're different from ours. Mingle in the lobby. Night life centers around the Mayfair area—go with a date to the nice hotel nightclub/dancing spots such as the Dorchester, Grosvenor House and the Mayfair. Visit the coffee bars on King's Road on Saturday afternoons—lots of friendly, hip young people. Do drop in at a pub; the ones off the tourist track welcome women. Where to *stay* to meet people? The theatrical crowd goes to the Savoy. A rather conservative group goes to the Hyde Park or the Park Lane. Businessmen stay at the Tower Hotel. The Connaught attracts VIP's and royalty. Join a gaming club. (Allow at least 48 hours: write to Secretary, Curzon House Group, 20/23 Curzon Street, London W1.) If you're invited to a private party, don't expect to be introduced around—the host or hostess will smilingly mutter something and leave you to your own devices. London is a safe place to walk about at night: you've always heard "The English are so civilized"—it's true.

GREECE: Search for Greek millionaires in Athens at the Neraides nightclub, the bar at the Grande Bretagne or the casino at Mount Parnes. Go to the Plaka section of Athens and eat at a little outdoor taverna—the wine and music loosen everyone up. You needn't be afraid to pick up strangers—there are practically no rapes or crimes of violence in Greece. Women should not, however, go into ordinary street bars or they will be assumed to be practicing the world's oldest profession. This is especially true in small towns. Go to the islands, especially Hydra and Corfu—they're jumping with social activity which always revolves around dockside cafes.

HONG KONG: Take the cheapest and most exciting ferry ride in the world—between Victoria Island and Kowloon Peninsula—and talk to the other tourists while you see one of the most spectacular skylines in the world. If you take the ferry after 5 PM, you'll meet the businessmen returning home. The Mandarin Hotel attracts businessmen while the Peninsula attracts old money. If you can't afford to stay at the Peninsula, at least hang around the lobby! Most of the "respectable" entertainment is at the hotels. For a romantic but sedate spot (if you've already found a date), go wining, dining, and dancing at the Mandarin Hotel's Harbour Room . . . and see a floor show (not yours!) as well. You can go unescorted to the Chinese theater restaurants with stage shows while you eat a Chinese banquet. Rent a *male* escort for the evening at the reputable Alliance Escort firm. Go people-watching in the coffee shop of the Hong Kong Hilton. The Hilton's Dragon Boat Bar is rife with people ready to meet people. Go to a gaudy Chinese-style supper club such as Kowloon's Highball or Oceania, or Hong Kong's Blue Heaven or Gloucester. 'Kowloon's The Scene (in the Peninsula Hotel) is the scotch and watering hole for young jet-setters. You can stroll safety at night through the poor man's nightclub—the open-air park of stalls, vendors, entertainers, and fortune-tellers. Stay away from bars and ballrooms in the Wanchai area: they're girlie bars with their own girlies. See what's happening culturally year-round at City Hall by checking with the very active Tourist Organization.

HUNGARY: Sit on the sidewalk cafes along the river. Romantically schmaltzy gypsy music will fill your soul if you dine at the restaurants in the Hotel Budapest and the Intercontinental Hotel. There's not much night life, though you might try the rooftop nightclub at the Duna Hotel. In the summer, go to an evening goulash party with Hungarian food and folklore; check with Ibusz, the state travel agency. If you latch on to a hand-kissing Hungarian or a lonely tourist, have him take you dancing at the Moulin Rouge (VI, Nagymezó Út 17) and the Casanove Night Club (1, Batthányi Ter 4).

INDIA: Don't go anywhere alone except to big name hotel bars. The respectable places to meet someone in Delhi are the Peacock Room at the Ashoka Hotel and the Sensation at the Oberoi Maidens. Though prohibition is no longer generally enforced, the night life is still subdued. Bombay's social center is in the public rooms of the Taj Mahal Inter-Continental Hilton, really! Calcutta has a few spots that try (and fail) to capture Parisian gaiety, but the town itself is so dreadful I can't imagine anyone being there in the first place. Fripo's (18/2 Chowringhee) and the Blue Fox (15 Park Street) are the *très gayest* of the dull. The Mocambo (25-B, Park Street) has a lunch concert where it's easier to meet a male in not so aggressive circumstances. I had more difficulties with unwanted super-aggressive male strangers in India than anywhere else. They seem to think any single American woman is "available." Anyway, you are forewarned—let your only sexual experiences in India be seeing the pornographic carvings on the ancient caves of Kharjuraho!

INDONESIA: Make a play at the Copacabana Casino. Dance and watch the best floor shows in Djakarta at the Hotel Indonesia's Nirwana nightclub. The most "in" discos currently are the Mini Disco and the Tanamur. Don't go near the waterfront area at night even though some of the bars like the Yacht Club may be recommended.

IRAN: During the day you may be the only unescorted female in a restaurant, so you can imagine how awkward you'll feel alone in a bar! Hotel bars in Tehran such as the Tavern in the Intercontinental and The Hunt Bar at the Hilton are okay, though. Have a date take you to the best discos in Tehran—La Boheme (Avenue Shemiran) and the Casbah Stereo (Avenue Pahlavi).

IRELAND: Dublin's pubs now welcome women, but do go in the evening—they're more fun then. Irish women stay in the lounge bar of the pub since they still acknowledge a male-only atmosphere for the public bars. The Palace Bar and the Silver Swan attract literati and journalists. The Bailey (Duke Street) is where literati, students from the university, and businessmen meet. Bowe's attracts newsmen. Many ballrooms welcome unescorted women—it's considered proper—but check which ones with your porter. In the country, stay away from pubs. They're totally male bastions away from the city. Bad taste in any social situation here: profanity, religious jokes, and giving your opinion of the Protestant/Catholic troubles.

ISRAEL: Women are welcome everywhere men are, so go ahead into bars such as the Alara (Ben Yehuda Street) and Navah (Jaffa Street), both in Jerusalem. For fun discos in Tel Aviv, try the Omar Khayam or Tavern. Go to a sidewalk cafe in Tel Aviv. Jerusalem is to the spirit what Tel Aviv is to the libido. Dizengoff Square is *the* place in Tel Aviv to chat with people or to promenade. Meet the people on a kibbutz; you'll eat and work (only if you want to) with the kibbutzniks—what better way to get to know them? Find immigrants from your country at the Newcomer's Club in Jerusalem (tel. 33718) or Tel Aviv (tel. 244768). For organized group hikes contact Hachevra Lehaganat Hateva (tel. 35066). Saturday in Israel is like Sunday in America so check to see what's open on the Sabbath.

ITALY: A boost to the morale: Italian men ogle and pinch anything female. I was practically mauled even at my scrawniest worst while recovering from surgery! A fun Roman restaurant where you'll meet other tourists is Da Meo Patacca. Diplomats favor the Giggi Fazi on Via Lucullo. Unescorted women can feel free to sit in the outdoor cafes on the Via Veneto, but you'll get more "action" in the cafes below the Cafe de Paris. The discos and slick bars of the jet set are on the back streets off Via Veneto, but don't go alone. Rome's Excelsior Hotel is a popular spot for theatrical personalities and affluent tourists. Businessmen go to the Berini-Bristol on the Piazza Barberini. Have a date take you to the Hilton's rooftop bar/dance floor on a nice summer night. Meet some interesting people by gallery-hopping in the Piazza di Spagna area. Go to a summer-time outdoor opera in the ruins of the Baths of Caracalla. The Italian cinema shows much more explicit scenes than American censors allow—so make a beeline to the movies or avoid them like the proverbial plague, depending upon your sensitivities and/or escort. The Italian Riviera is très gay around Portofino but not as social as the French Riviera.

JAMAICA: The Half Moon Hotel has "Get Acquainted" parties so you can't help but meet people. If you stay at the Casa Montego you'll be entitled to guest privileges at the Montego Bay Country Club and the Doctor's Cave Beach Club. Meet high-class tennis partners at the Montego Bay Racquet Club. (Charleton Heston is a member, which should give you some idea of the caliber of guests.) Friendly Canadians stay at the Upper Deck Hotel. The Sheraton Kingston (a commercial hotel) is a real meeting place in Jamaica—their supperclub is especially popular. The disco in the Casa Monte Hotel is where the action is. Kingston hotels usually are filled with businessmen, not tourists, since Kingston is not resort-oriented.

However, the Hotel Terra Nova is a popular place for government business, and social affairs. The mod set goes to the Club Caribbean and Chela Bay hotels. The Richmond Hill Inn's bar attracts locals and visitors. College age and under-30's go to the Summit Hotel. The Verney House makes you feel as if you're living with a family —it's up to you whether that's pro or con. You must go to Doctor's Cave Beach to socialize (though I can't guarantee you'll meet a doctor). Don't wander around Kingston after dark without a male escort who knows the area. And take a taxi. The Montego Bay area is where the action is. See the real back country Jamaica with a ''Night on the Great River'' (Tuesday-Friday evenings); you'll be canoed away to a country picnic with music and dancing. You can't be anti-social there, nor can anyone else!

JAPAN: Japanese night spots can be very expensive, so unless you or your date is loaded (with money, not booze), go on a Grey Line Night Tour. Tokyo's Byblos in the Akasaka district is filled with young people. Theatre types go to Charlie Mano's bar in Akasaka. There's a lively disco called the J & R (5th and 6th floors, 4-9 5-chome, Ginza); or try Mugen (8 3-chome, Akasaka, Minato-ku). The Shinjuku area is where the young people gather. In general, the Ginza's bars are second class compared to those in Akasaka. Club Night in Akasaka has *hosts* to attend women guests. Don't worry— it's respectable and safe, and you won't be hassled. Do you want to try a dance hall? Go to the one in Yurakucho—there are thirty male professional dance partners and it's also respectable! For folk danc-ing try Shichi-go-san on Tawaramachi. Tokyo's first-class hotels have their own deluxe clubs and bars, but your hotel can also recommend night clubs and cabarets in the city. You may, even with a date, face a rejection at a small Japanese bar—some want to keep them for their Japanese regulars and also feel you'll be more trouble than you're worth since no one there speaks English. Bars close (or are supposed to) at midnight—at which time the last subway train leaves the Ginza, leaving you looking for very scarce cabs. You can go to a cabaret-cum-hostess place with a date if you don't mind being ignored while your date has a fuss made over him. On weekend afternoons the city's young flock to the pop concerts in Tokyo's Hibiya Park—it's a great place to meet people: they're all anxious to try to practice their English on you. Or you can loll away hours in Tokyo's coffee shops for just the price of a cup of coffee. These coffee shops have non-stop stereo music (classical, rock, jazz) and are a place to meet the under-35 Japanese. Beer gardens are often found atop the roofs of downtown buildings and hotels in summertime; the food and drinks are very cheap and there is some sort of entertainment, from rock bands to sing-along with Kenzo music. Everyone is very friendly. There are also "Mammoth Bars" or "Compa Bars" which are huge, folksy bars where groups of singles congregate and enjoy moderately priced snacks and drinks. If you do go to someone's home or to a Japanese-style restaurant, do remove your shoes.

KENYA: Jet setters mix with the rest of us at the Aberdare National Park's renowned Treetops and Noah's Ark hotels as well at the Mt. Kenya Safari Club in the Mount Kenya National Park. Out in the bush, they sort of force togetherness with the midnight calls of the (non-human) wild game. As you roam about in your mini-bus with the trap door in the roof (so you can poke your head out and take pictures), you might not find a Humphrey Bogart type or even a fascimile of the African Queen, but those great white hunters leading you lucky travelers can be pretty exciting. Let those helmeted and husky hunters lead you through the most exciting parks: Tsavo, noted for great herds of elephants and hippos; Masai Amboseli, known for both Masai tribesmen and the rhinos who share their grazing space; Lake Nakuru, the bird sanctuary where thousands of flamingos cover the water like a pink carpet. Back in "civilization," meet some other interesting people at the Thorn Tree Cafe in Nairobi's New Stanley Hotel. Do not walk about unescorted *anywhere* at night.

LEBANON: Women should not go to cabarets or nightclubs unescorted in Beirut. This once-swinging fun capital of the Mideast is now unsafe and will take many years to get back its old reputation for gaiety. Right now women are pretty fair game for impassioned terrorists—so stay away.

MEXICO: Women should never enter men's drinking establishments, known as cantinas or salones de cerveza. There is mixed drinking in bars, but women should not be unescorted. In Mexico City have a date take you disco dancing at the Barbella at the Hotel Fiesta Palace or the Hotel Aristos (Camino Real, Alameda). Acapulco is much more jet-setty and flamboyant than Mexico City.

MOROCCO: (Marakech) If you want to splurge somewhere, do it at the Mamounia hotel—dress up, wander around the grand public rooms, go to the restaurants (one's French, the other's Moroccan) and meet a sheik or such. No pikers here. Stop by a sidewalk cafe (always an unobtrusive way to meet people and pleasant even if you don't); I recommend La Renaissance in the new section of town on Ave. Mohammed V. If you like folk-dancing and the ambience that conjures up, stop in at Dar es Salam, 95 Derb Djedid. For an evening of absolutely fascinating sights, wander through the largest *souk* in Morocco—Marakech's Djemaa El Fna.

NETHERLANDS: In Amsterdam there are two restaurants where you'll find fellow Americans—the Port van Cleve and the Gaslight. Good for dancing *with* a date are the King's Club (Korte Leidsedwarsstraat 85) or the Voom Voom (Raamstraat 14-16). Nightlife centers around the Rembrandtplein and Leidseplein: that's where you'll find bars, *boîtes* and discos. The Zeedyk is the liveliest area, but it's a tough sailors' quarters so go only with a burly escort or your own black belt in judo. Amsterdam is one of the most permissive cities on earth: don't be shocked by this anything-goes town. There are almost no taboos. If you don't let it all hang out, you'll miss everything! Main spots such as Amsterdam, Rotterdam and The Hague have women's groups who'll organize contacts and tours for you.

NEW ZEALAND: Nice people but dull social life. Their idea of a good time is a country fair, not a night on the town. Even dinner dancing is so rare that you must always check ahead to be certain that the hotel is having music that night! They're big on sports, so check with the National Tourist Board for clubs which will admit you; it's a nice way to meet the people.

PANAMA: Go to the Executive's Club at the El Continental Hotel. Socialize at the Panama Golf Club and the Riding Club when you stay at the El Panama. The smart set dines at the Portobelo Room at the Hotel El Panama. Panamanian socialites go to the Unicornio Disco. Casinos are an easy place to meet men since you'll be wandering about—go to the casinos at hotels La Siesta, Continental and El Panama. Two very popular and friendly cafes are the Café Rizzo and Café Boulevard Balboa (both on Avenida Balboa).

PERU: Women should not go into street bars, but they can go into hotel bars and cocktail lounges. The Sky Room in Lima is an expensive society gathering spot. The Unicorn (Paseo de la Republica 3030) is considered the best disco in Lima, but many of the younger set gravitate to the crowded but romantic Sunset Club in San Isidro. Combine good food with good dance music at the Country Club Acquarium.

PHILIPPINES: Manila newsmen hang out at the Taza De Oro restaurant on Roxas Blvd. and the Front Page on Plaza Ferguson. Go to the Sky Room (Jai-Alai Building, Taft Avenue) where you can watch or bet on games if you don't want to dance. Good night spots to go with a date are the Where Else (Hotel Intercontinental Manila) or the Bayside Club on Roxas Boulevard, Pasay City.

PORTUGAL: You'll be the only unescorted woman in a bar: women tourists should go to nightclubs in groups or twos if not with a male. Go to a Fado cafe (I recommend the Taverna do Embucado where the songs are sadder soap operas than "The Guiding Light.") Fado singers are highly respected, so don't talk when they're singing. You'll have fun at the unsleazy Lisbon version of Coney Island —Feira Popular. Tourists go to the Archote Club bar in Lisbon as well as the rooftop of the Embaixador Hotel. Gambrinus is a restaurant that attracts the society set—so go there if that's your thing. The international jet set goes to Lisbon's Ritz Hotel. (But don't *stay* there unless you're really flush.) You must go to that scotch and watering hole for royalty—Estoril. You'll see a lot of kings and princesses, mostly in exile, alas, but with titles and Swiss bank accounts intact, again if that's your thing. Meet your prince in shining Pierre Cardin suit at the super deluxe Estorial Palace—it's a hotel, not a palace. The casino in Estoril attracts the royal set for entertainment.

PUERTO RICO: A super cosmopolitan clientele flock to Lutece on the Beach. Businessmen go the Melia and the Pierre. Singles stay at

El San Juan and take advantage of all the action there. There's a string of raunchy but colorful bars on the waterfront, but only go with an escort. The more sedate shows are at the big-name hotels along the San Juan strip. The Helio Isla and Hyatt hotels have very social casinos. The El Guajataco Hotel lets you mix with the locals at their basketball games, meals, and town square festivities. Tennis love-matches are made at Puerto Rico's Cerromas and Dorado Beach Hotels—all the outdoor sports in Puerto Rico attract a young single crowd. Like non-absentminded professors? Go to the Sea Beach Colony Hotel. Surfers go to the Villa Cofresi. In Old San Juan, go to Mago's for lunch—businessmen fill the place. And on Saturday and Sunday afternoons, the sailing set gathers at Mike's Bar. In June, the Casals Festival is a must for music lovers who want to meet other music lovers. Culebra Island has become a gathering hole for writers, readers, and scuba buffs.

SARDINIA: A small but "in" place. Rent a boat with others from Marinasarda at the Costa Smeralda. Go social at the Cervo Tennis Club. Ask the pro to set you up in a doubles game in the late afternoon (when more people are there). If you prefer drinks to doubles, go to the Tennis Club Bar from 5-7 PM. Plop down in the piazza or wander the quay to meet attractive men. The yachting set yachts over to La Pizzeria for lunch—while the jet setters go there for dinner.

SINGAPORE: Unescorted women can go into *hotel* bars. Most of the discos have been closed by the government because of the drug/crime problem among the young, so it's not the swinging town it used to be.

SOUTH AFRICA: Women are not permitted in bars except for the special women's bars in certain hotels. Forget any entertainment on Sundays since just about everything is closed. Other times try nightclubs such as Ciro's (45 Kruis Street, Johannesburg) or the Sable Room (Savlan Bldg., Cape Town). If you're in Cape Town during January or February, go to the Maynardville Open Air Theater. It's a good respectable way to meet men—and even if you don't, you'll enjoy the show!

SPAIN: Try to bump into a Spanish prince during the Gran Teatro del Liceo's opera intermission. While in Madrid, go to Botin's for meals—it attracts fellow Americans and literary types. Las Lanzas attracts the local society. Meet the Spanish social set if you stay at the Luz Palacio. American women are *tolerated* unescorted in night clubs; the Spanish women aren't, but they think we're decadent beyond redemption. Don't go unescorted into "dives"—even the Spanish "hostesses" object, and will tell you so!

SWEDEN: Above all, remember that Swedes go to Copenhagen for fun—that should tell you a lot about their own nightlife. In Stockholm, if you've met a man who is on an expense account, have him take you to such affluent nightclubs as Berns (Näckströmsgatan 8) and Bacchi (Järntorgsgatan 5). The young set favors such clubs as Bobbadilla (Svartmangatan 27) and The Racing Club (Birger Jarlsgatan 95). Most night life is found on Stora Nygatan Street in the Gamla Stan area. In Stockholm the Riche and Teatergrillen (Birger Jarlsgatan 4) is a worthwhile restaurant; the Teatergrillen is the gathering place for actors, actresses, and the theater crowd. For *cultuh,* see what's going on at the Royal Opera House and the Stockholm Concert House. Always check ahead of time if you plan to go hotel dinner-dancing since they don't always have it every night. Public ballrooms are perfectly respectable and are not at all seedy. You can wander about unescorted through the Giöna Lund amusement park . . . you might even find someone to take you dancing outdoors there. There's more marvelous outdoor entertainment at Skansen, where you might find yourself sitting next to a smashing Swede! The Swedish Lifeseeing Tour shows you social conditions in progressive Sweden: since they visit such places as schools, old age homes, and factories, you'll probably meet interested professionals who have come along on your tour. With all the talk about swinging Swedish ways, you'll also notice a reserve and formality. Men take off their hats in places American males would not, they'll rush to light your cigarettes and pull out your chair. Don't be startled; go along with it and love it! Entertainment (including dinner) starts and ends early. Be punctual. When invited to a Swedish home, don't assume it means dinner.

SWITZERLAND: In Zurich, go to de wine keller in the Old Time.

There's tea dancing at 3:30 PM at Le Grillon, 5 Pl. de la Fusterie. Go to the Hit Club disco at 3 Rue de Marché in Geneva. Also in Geneva, attend the August outdoor festival Fête de Genève. There's all sorts of good entertainment, plus dancing in the streets —a sure way to meet people. The casino is usually the center of social activity in resorts—but even that can be dull here. Swiss night life just ain't got it! Zurich perks up a bit at Queen Anne or Churchill's (discos). Dinner and drinks in a fun atmosphere can be had at La Ferme disco, also in Zurich. Recommended Zurich nightclubs: the Hazyland and the Terrasse.

TAHITI: In this truly uninhibited paradise, women can go anywhere unescorted. Women (and men, too) can even advertise their availability; both sexes wear a flower behind the right ear if "looking." Don't be discouraged by the gorgeous looking Tahitian women in those travel posters—in reality they're usually toothless (if you'll notice, they're usually smiling through closed lips!) and fat. You'll look great by comparison—I should hope!! Try Vaima's Cafe for fun. Since the Hotel Tahiti has the most activity and is quite big (for Tahiti), you'll have a good chance of meeting other people, especially on Saturday nights when *everyone* goes there. Dance outdoors with tourists and Tahitians at the Puooro Plage on weekends. The Hotel Bali-Hai on Moorea is a continuous party. If you want action, stay *away* from the Moana Nui Hotel near Papeete since they discourage noise and frivolity (a most unusual attitude in Tahiti).

THAILAND: Although many of the Bangkok night spots revolve around "hostesses," you'll feel more welcome at the night spots without them, at such places as the Erawan Hotel's Ambassador, the Oriental Hotel's Bamboo Bar, the Honey (on Suriyong Rd.) and the Dusit Thani Hotel's Tiara. The Napoléon on Patpong Road offers lively jazz sessions on Sunday afternoons. The verandah of the Sorn Daeng restaurant is popular for drinking, people-watching (it overlooks Bangkok's main street), and people-meeting. The Bamboo Bar and the Pool Bar are also popular scotch and watering holes. The respectable discos and cocktail lounges are the President Hotel's Cat's Eye Bar and the Sheraton's Cavern. Non-respectable places are after-hours bars and go-go spots which may be whispered to you by a hotel clerk. If you're lucky enough to be invited to a Thai home, take off your shoes before entering (just as you must do in a Thai temple), don't pat children on the head, and do eat without a knife.

U.S.S.R.: Not much night life—bad music and worse food usually combine with atrocious service! Also, most workers start work early in the morning and don't have the energy (or the rubles) to play late! Try to meet people through the professional clubs for writers, artists, etc. If you can claim ties with any international or national governmental, labor, academic, or cultural organization, contact these organizations or the Office of Soviet and Eastern European Exchanges, Dept. of State, Washington, D.C. 20520. Don't try to have a grand affair with a Russian—you could be charged with being a sexual provocateur!

VENEZUELA: The Caracas Hilton has a rooftop supper club and attracts businessmen because of its in-town convenience. Caraqueños gather at the Holiday Inn (of all places). The Macuto-Sheraton is a good compromise if you're in Caracas on business but also want resort life . . . the nightclub really swings on weekends. El Emperador attracts businessmen for lunch. For folk music and its attendant crowds, go to the Underground (Centro Comercial del Este). A lively crowded disco is the Blow Up (Avenida Avila Su Altamira). Most discos and dance places will only admit women who are escorted by a man. The supperclubs at the Tamanaco and Hilton are popular. Enjoy good Venezulan entertainment (such as flamenco dancers) at the Café Las Chinitas Nelos (in the La Castellana area); it's a good mixing place since patrons sing and dance with the music. Chic sidewalk cafes abound in the eastern part of the city. Don't stay at the Avila Hotel in Caracas—you'll be out of the action.

Getting Down to Basics: Food and Shelter

LODGING LOGIC

PICK A HOTEL by location, price, plan preference (American or European), and reputation. A good hotel in the **16** center of town usually attracts a lot of businessmen. The charming little hotels tucked away attrach the more romantic, younger (thirtyish) souls.

Do not ever stay at a youth hostel if you're over 21 or you might be the oldest living relic there. *Pensions* are at the opposite end of the age scale.

Don't go to a place with only American Plan meals—it ties you down and is only good if it's a really remote place. (At Isashima, Japan or Moorea, Tahiti there's nowhere else to go!) Also, one tends to eat much more when on the American Plan because of the attitude: "I've already paid for it . . ." and those added dishes add pounds.

You can take more chances in countries with higher standards of cleanliness: Switzerland and Sweden have clean *anythings*, India and Southeast Asia seem to have dirty *everythings*. Sorry, but I'm going to tell it like it is. Even if going to the "safe" countries, I would still recommend a reservation for the first night.

MAKING RESERVATIONS Before you get all involved in the wonderful world of reservations, you should be able to decipher hotelese:

CHECK OUT TIME: Time posted at hotel, beyond which you are obligated to pay for an additional day. For late-departing flights, special arrangements can sometimes be made with the hotel management.

ON AND OFF SEASON: "On" or "high" season is the period when the hotel or resort is busiest and most expensive. "Off" or "low" season is the slack period, when rooms are usually less expensive. A few resorts have interim fall and spring rates.

EUROPEAN PLAN (EP): Prices quoted are for accommodations only, excluding meals.

MODIFIED AMERICAN PLAN (MAP): Prices quoted include room and two meals per day, generally breakfast and dinner.

AMERICAN PLAN (AP): Prices quoted are for room and all three meals per day.

CONTINENTAL PLAN (CP): Prices quoted include room and breakfast, either a complete American-style breakfast or a European-style repast of rolls with butter, and coffee or tea.

SINGLE: One person in a private room.

DOUBLE: Two persons sharing a double-bedded room; prices may be quoted either for the room or per person, but should always specify which way the price is applied.

TWIN: Two persons sharing a room with twin beds. Priced as a double room.

SUITE: Parlor and one or more bedrooms, in some cases including kitchen facilities.

THIRD ADULT IN ROOM: Unless prices for triples are quoted, availability and price must be checked with the individual hotel or resort.

CHILD'S RATES: Some hotels add a cot or crib to parents' room at no charge; some permit one child of *any* age to occupy parents' room without charge; some permit one child free but charge for additional children. Price should be stated by the hotel or resort, or checked in advance.

Always make reservations as far in advance as possible. And do make them, unless you're flexible and going somewhere off season (and at a time when there's no convention, festival, or fair). It's just not as easy to gad about without a place waiting for you as it used to be. I know. I took one ten-month trip around the world without a single reservation—but that was several years ago; just a few months ago a friend and I drove to Florida's Sanibel Island without reservations and ended up sleeping in our car in the Ramada Inn parking lot (without the knowledge of the Ramada Inn!).

If you're booking into a large hotel or chain in America, use their toll-free number in the U.S. Call 800-555-1212 to find out the number for a big chain, 800-323-1776 for independents. And check the Yellow Pages under "Hotels and Motels—Reservations" for local numbers of reservations bureaus and offices of out-of-town lodgings. Get immediate and free international reservations by using the computerized services of the big chains like Hilton, Sheraton and Hyatt. Or make reservations through airlines, tourist offices, and travel agencies. You can make your own hotel/motel arrangements by writing to the reservations department. If you write abroad, enclose an International Reply Coupon (available at U.S. Post Offices) for confirmation by airmail. Use English unless you're totally fluent in the other language!

Mention (1) the number of people in your party (if more than one, do you want a double bed or two singles?); (2) whether or not you want a private bath (they're not automatically included); (3) if you'll need air-conditioning; (4) how long you'll be staying; (5) time of arrival; and (6) how much you want to pay. You might also request a particular room (ocean view, off the street, etc.) but hotels won't usually guarantee it, though they'll try to please you.

Should you send a deposit? Only if required, but if so get the cancellation and refund policies in writing. Be sure any amount you may have paid as a reservation deposit is credited to your final bill.

Be certain to get confirming letters and carry them with you. Just as that is your guarantee, a confirmation is the hotel's—you may be charged if you're a no-show.

But sometimes you will be told there's no room at the inn, even when you've reserved in advance and are standing there clutching a confirmation slip. A reputable hotel will try to get you a comparable room somewhere else (and taxi fare there). If not, raise hell. They'll do anything to stop you from spoiling their image.

TRAVELING WITHOUT RESERVATIONS If you arrive in town without a reservation, ask a stewardess for recommendations before you even get off the plane. Most tourist offices, hotel reservation services, airport and railroad stations, and highway border crossings have up-to-the-minute information on what rooms are available. If you go to a hotel sans reservations and they don't have room, don't just leave. Ask them to give you leads or to call other hotels for you. And once you do get into a hotel, ask for help in getting reservations in the next town. If you're ad-libbing while driving, start looking for a place to stay around 4 PM—the later you're on the road, the fewer the choices left—they've all been taken by those who did get off the road earlier! If you're ad-lib traveling, do not budge from your room during a holiday such as Christmas—you'll never find another one. Sure, the hotel won't be happy, but they won't carry you bodily out!

O.K., you've found a vacancy. Leave your bags in the lobby under the watchful eye of the desk clerk and check out the room. If your bags are still downstairs, you'll be more willing and able to turn the room down and ask to see another.

Pick a hotel by perusing guide books you trust. How can you tell? By checking, if possible, the author's comments about places —such as a hotel you've already stayed at *anywhere*; if you agree with the author on that one, you'll probably agree with his/her choice on other places. Taste is taste, whether it's in Peoria or Pago Pago. Or get a list from tourist offices—they're objective, if not so descriptive. Or ask friends who have the same taste and budget as you. Ask a travel agent. Don't, don't, don't go by brochures—they make dumps look like Versailles.

I do not automatically turn up my nose at "plastic palaces" like the much-maligned Hiltons and Holiday Inns. After two months of staying at quaint little places down side streets, I greeted the Istanbul Hilton's unlimited hot water and orthopedic mattresses as if they were paradise on earth!

$$$ LODGING LUCRE $$$

$ Travel off-season and book into more expensive hotels at mid-week instead of during the more expensive weekends (though sometimes that's reversed and weekdays are more expensive: check, as always).

$ Steer around big events and festivals. While they inspire fun, they also inspire innkeepers to raise their prices.

$ If you're traveling with a man, ask for honeymoon rates at the hotel. It doesn't have to be your honeymoon.

$ Check into the possibilities of getting special rates for families if you're traveling with children.

$ Rates are generally based on double occupancy of a double room. So if you can share a room, it'll cost you less (but, if with another woman, might not be worth it!). On tours you'll pay a single supplement. (This is usually in the miniscule print hidden away at the back.)

$ If you insist on going alone (I wouldn't go any other way), you can still scavenge out some bargains. Check with the tourist bureau in the country. Their personnel know the inns and outs of the country; they're well-acquainted with every type of accommodation and can often dredge up a budget place at the last minute. And, of course, their services are free . . . as are all government tourist offices.

$ Upon arrival at a hotel sans reservations, look disappointed with the quoted price and ask in a firm but pleasant voice, "Haven't you anything for less? I'd really love to stay here."

$ Take advantage of any specials—such as packaged holidays programmed for a particular interest such as golf or tennis packages.

$ Sometimes you can get a bargain at the last minute. If you have a firm reservation at an expensive hotel, when you arrive in the city go in person to a couple of cheap places you've heard about (but don't spend too much money on cab fares doing this or you'll wipe out your savings). You might get in on a last-minute cancellation, and if not, you always have your other reservation. No, guilt pangs are not overtaking me about that hotel left holding your reserved empty room. They generally overbook to cover such contingencies.

$ When you do stay at cheap little places off the beaten path, you must be forewarned that maybe no one will speak your language, and you may be taken for some extra francs. So you'll have to weigh the advantages of that atmospheric little hotel vs. a cheap room in a grand hotel.

$ Consider location. A hotel far away from everything you want to see and do, even if it's a good deal, means mounting taxi fares.

$ You don't have to have the same kind of accommodations every night. You can switch to a simple hotel every few days, particularly if you are in a city like Paris or Rome that has scores of interesting little hotels.

$ At hotels go without a bath, a chambermaid, a balcony, a view. Going without a private bath is where you can really save a bundle. But I would rather cut my trip in half. It's up to you how much of a problem a bathroom down the hall is—and it might be more of a problem at some times of the month than others!

$ Ask what meal plan your hotel offers so you can take advantage of *all* the meals you are paying for.

$ Have meals in the hotel restaurant instead of your room. Breakfast in bed may be romantic if you're not alone, and may give you a great feeling of luxury, but room service prices are usually much higher and carry a big service charge. However, when breakfast is included, sometimes breakfast in bed does not carry an additional charge. Ask.

$ Find out whether the hotel automatically adds a service charge (usually 10 to 15%, but it can be even higher) to your rooms and meals. If so, adjust your tips accordingly.

$ Inquire about weekly or monthly hotel rates—they're usually discounted.

$ Be willing to experiment with new hotels or lesser-known "established" ones.

$ Be open to new *types* of hotels. For example, in Japan there is a new category of western style hotel. Locally, they're known as "business" (not what you think) hotels, on the theory that they are run in a business-like fashion. Nothing fancy, but high marks for efficiency and low on costs. They cut down on frills and pass on the savings to guests in the form of simple, comfortable rooms. And because they cater to the traveling Japanese businessman, a good many of the rooms are singles. In Spain and Portugal you can stay at converted castles which are now country inns. Since they are run by the government, the costs are kept down. In Ireland and England there are inexpensive bed-and-breakfast guest houses, farmhouse accommodations and thatched cottage rentals. And you'll get a warmer reception than at the bigger city establishments! In parts of Southeast Asia you'll find government Rest Houses to be simple but clean, comfortable, and reasonably priced.

And so on around the world, if you'll keep an open mind.

$ Pensions (boarding houses) are cheaper than hotels, but also crowded and less private. Vienna has the best pensions in Western Europe. They are homey and you won't be lonely—you won't be left alone even if that's what you want.

$ When you've made your hotel choice, do your own thing (laundry, theater ticket brokerage, etc.)—don't pay extra for extra services.

$ Take advantage of any free services your hotel offers: transfers to and from the airport, bus service to beach or town, parking, welcome drinks, etc.

$ Be sure to return any beach towels, chairs or equipment you sign for. Even if you don't take them with you (but leave them on the beach when you leave), the hotel can charge you for them.

$ Make telephone calls from a public telephone, if possible. Calls made from your room can cost two to five times as much.

$ There are day hotels where you can rent rooms inexpensively for a few hours. They'll save you the price of a regular hotel room if you have a brief layover between planes.

$ Stay in a suburb if you have a rented car or if the local transportation is cheap and reliable.

$ Rent a cottage or apartment/condominium. A condo can be rented in *advance* through Condomart, 655 Madison Avenue, New York 10022. Or rent a home through At Home Abroad, Inc., 136 E. 57 Street, New York 10022. These are great for, say, two divorcees with children. (Pooled resources will always save you $$$.) Or swap your home through Loan-A-Home, 18 Darwood Place, Mount Vernon, New York 10533.

$ The crème de la crème of ultimate bargains—stay with friends or relatives. Or camp out!

ONCE YOU'RE ENSCONCED You're settled in to the bargain or non-bargain place of your choice. What to expect? (1) Hot and cold water faucets indicated by dots (red for hot, blue for cold). (2) A bidet (a low sink which you use as a bottom-washer-offer by straddling it while you face the wall: close the drain and open up the faucets). (3) Shoes cleaned for you if you leave them outside your door in a hotel where you see *other* shoes outside other doors. (4) Such fast room service that you may be caught in your skivvies after you order. (5) Illustrateed buttons to indicate service—one to call the floor porter, the waiter, chambermaid, etc. (The chambermaid can literally put you back together. She'll sew what needs to be sewn, get you extra hangers, draw your bath, clean your room, remove clothing spots, zip you up—you'll wish you could find a lover like that!)

Anything you can't buzz for, the concierge will tackle. He'll mail your letters; get tickets for events; make plane or train reservations; tell you where to park your car overnight; obtain and explain street maps; hire a car and driver; tell you what's going on in town; recommend restaurants and shops; arrange for a doctor; hand out currency advice; give a weather report; tell you what to wear where; order flowers and have them delivered; arrange for packages to be wrapped and mailed; arrange for escort services when available, and find a baby sitter. The top concierge has the day shift (big deluxe hotels have a concierge on duty at all times), so give *him* your *major* problems.

Protect yourself in hotels by using your "Do Not Disturb" sign even when you're out. Burglars are looking for an empty room and they'll assume someone is in a room with such a sign. Use your chain lock and keep it on while you're checking to see if that knock is really the guest or service you were expecting. If "Laundry," "Room Service," or "Security" should arrive unordered, don't open the door. This saved my life in Shiraz, Iran. A powerful Iranian official had his eye on me and had intimidated the front desk clerk into telling him my room and the time I was in. He then went to my door and proclaimed himself "Room Service." I'm sure it would have been! Was I glad I had chained the door!!

If there is someone you're avoiding, instruct the hotel not to give out your room number. When asking for mail, just give your name, not your room number.

Another thing to keep in mind for your personal safety: some hotels do not stay open all night. If you plan a night on the town, ask when your hotel closes.

Guard your valuables by using the hotel safe. If you are protecting something small, put it in an envelope and write your name **GAIL** across the flap closure. If the envelope has been steamed open, the signature will be disturbed.

Your stay has ended. Now what? If you have an early morning flight to catch, tell the operator or front desk clerk to awaken you with a call at whatever time you request. If you are leaving early in the morning, see if you can take care of your bill the night before. Other pre-departure things to take care of: transportation arrangements to the airport or railway station, rental car return, tips for hotel personnel, packing and then checking *everywhere* to see if you've left anything in the closet, bathroom or mixed in with the bedspread. Put all your bags in one spot so that *nothing* is left behind, but leave a forwarding address so your hotel can send your things in case you've slipped up. Leave a note by the door reminding you of anything important—you won't be able to leave without spotting it. Always allow plenty of time for pre-departure items so you won't miss a plane or train if there is a snafu. If your plane is leaving, say, four hours after checkout time, see if you can leave your bags in a safe place in the hotel and use their lobbies, restroom, and lounges.

THE MICHELIN GUIDE
OF THE LADIES ROOM SET

DON'T LEAVE your hotel room without using the john. **17**
"Never pass up a good john" should be emblazoned
across your pantyhose.

How do you find a good restroom once you've left your hotel?
You know where to look. Facilities at government-maintained
places such as parks, monuments, or forts can be pretty raunchy.
Deluxe hotel lobbies and restaurants are usually the best places.
I've used many a restaurant and hotel restroom without being a
paying customer, so don't you be embarrassed. You may want to
tip the attendant, so have some small coins handy. Large department stores usually have good facilities, and you never have to tip.

Be prepared: other peoples' concept of privacy is often different
from our own. There may be just the tiniest bit of wood for a "door"
or no door at all or even co-ed facilities. You have to decide if
modesty is more important than walking cross-legged through
town.

Toilets will also *look* different than what you are used to. Those
with foot prints are used by placing feet there and squatting; there's
often no flushing device. When there is a flushing device (be it
urinal or turkish toilet), it may be a button, chain, or foot pedal.
Look around—you'll discover it.

Since some restrooms don't have the facilities we're used to at
home, you might want to carry soap leaves. They come in a packet
about the size of a match book. With the passing of slips, we've lost
an emergency towel for those towel-less restrooms.

You can spot ladies' rooms by the skeletonized figure of a
woman in a skirt. Others have names so coy you could have an
accident figuring it out. The names below are the words for ladies'
rooms in different countries, and should help you when the doors
are not clearly distinguished.

Argentina	baño de damas
Austria	damen

Belgium	damen or dames
Bolivia	damas
Brazil	señhoras or damas
Canary Islands	señoras
Costa Rica	damas or señoras
Czechoslovakia	dámy or zeny
Denmark	damer
Egypt	hajmam sayyedat
Finland	naiset
France	dames
Germany	damen
Guatemala	dama or señoras
Hungary	nök
Indonesia	perempuan
Iran	tuualet or khandomhah
Ireland	mná
Israel	sh erutim lenashim
Italy	signore
Japan	o-te-asai
Jordan	toilette or WC
Kenya	wanawake
Lebanon	beit-el-ma lilsyidat
Malaysia	peremouan
Mexico	damas
Morocco	dames
Netherlands	dames toilet
Nicaragua	damas
Norway	kvinner
Panama	damas
Philippines	babae
Poland	dla pán, dla kobiet, or damska
Portugal	lavabos de senhoras
Romania	wc femei
Samoa	tama'ita'i
South Africa	dames
South Korea	buin yong
Sweden	damer
Switzerland	damen, dames, or signore
Tahiti	wahines
Thailand	sukha ying
Tunisia	dames
Turkey	bayanlar-kadin
USSR	twalet (toilette)
Vietnam	quy ba

"WHAT DO YOU MEAN, YOU'VE NEVER HAD SEAWEED FOR BREAKFAST?"

I LIKE TO eat anything at all that flies, crawls or swims, and if *you* do, you'll enhance your trip tremendously. Try anything. Don't turn up your nose at raw octopus or broiled seaweed—it's less peculiar to *them* than frogs' legs or Kool-Aid!

18

There is no right and wrong—eating is simply habit. You may have to fight for this liberated attitude since many head waiters will guide you to the Americanized versions of everything: chicken chow mein instead of lotus root in sesame oil.

Eat in the foreign sections of your city before you go, to get used to different foods. So when you're in Japan, you'll have a Japanese breakfast (soybean soup, seaweed, pickles, broiled salmon). Or you'll gorge yourself in Holland on a hearty Dutch breakfast of assorted meats and cheeses. Why have the two poached eggs on toast that you could get in Topeka? And for another change in routine, try foods not only foreign to you, but also foreign to the country you've traveled to (e.g., Polish food in London).

I haven't talked you into experimenting with your food? Then rest assured you can find familiar foods. Hamburgers and pizzas have conquered the world more surely than any army. You can eat your heart out at McDonald's (from London to Tokyo), Wimpy's, or Kentucky Fried Chicken; and you can get kosher hot dogs in London, pizza in Switzerland, and cherry pie in Australia! Actually, fast food places are the only places where you'll have a quick meal—the rest of the world believes in *enjoying* long repasts, so relax and expect to spend at least an hour over a meal.

And don't just eat their food—eat it in the same *way* they do. Use your hands (mid-East), chop-sticks (Orient), or keep your fork in your hand even while not eating (the rest of the world). And eat *when* the locals do—many Europeans eat a gargantuan lunch and a miniscule dinner!

If no one speaka da language, go into the kitchen and point out which foods you want. Don't be embarrassed; I've done it many times. Or point to an appealing dish someone else ordered: it's a great conversation starter, anyway. Or use sign language.

Don't add salt, pepper, and ketchup to everything before even trying it. Americans are known for this peculiar trait. Don't worry about a completely well-balanced diet. In some places it won't be possible. Just take your vitamins and forget about Gaylord Hausner! It takes more than a three-week vacation to develop rickets!

If you have gained a lot of weight from the rich sauces and desserts in other countries, try eating a few meals without the entré—just soup, peelable fruit, and cheeses. Or eat your main meal at noon and walk off the calories by evening.

Make reservations. If you feel funny about eating alone, bring a book. Pick it up if there's no one interesting around, put it down if there is. Go with a group and have everyone order something different—sample each other's dishes. Or go to a small family-style place where everyone eats together at long wooden tables.

Don't shy away from foreign railroad station restaurants just because ours are so terrible. Foreign train station eateries are often outstanding—especially in Europe. As a class, they have better food than airports do.

There are two terms you'll constantly encounter. One is *table d'hôte*. It means a full meal for a set price, usually with no substitutions permitted and usually a good buy for hearty eaters. *À la carte* means a meal in which each item of food is ordered and priced separately, or the entré includes only specified vegetables (other items are additional).

And now for the liquid part of your moveable feast. Consider an electric immersion heating coil for making your own coffee, though it's fun to try coffees around the world since they vary as much as the foods. If you must have decaffeinated coffee, bring little packets of your own.

You won't get water unless you ask for it. And you must ask for ice—it's not automatic. Foreigners are not the ice water drinkers we are. Indeed, there's a marvelous (and supposedly true) story of a young German man who was about to immigrate to this country. Instead of dire warnings about being mugged in the streets or having the IRS after him, he was told simply "not to drink the ice water that Americans ruin their stomachs with." Actually, you'll be better off with bottled water—it's available everywhere.

Since wine seems to be an intimidating subject to American women, a few words on the subject are in order. You'll be poured a small bit of the wine if you ordered a full, unopened bottle. It's for you to taste a sip or two and then indicate by saying "Very good" (or something on that order) or "I don't care for it." The house wine comes in an open carafe (a quarter-liter yields two wine glasses) and is good if you're not a real wine buff. It's also cheap!

CHEAP EATS!

$ Don't be shy. If you're not sure what is included and what is extra—ask.

$ Since the workers and students of any country are usually on limited budgets, eat where they do! You'll be able to spot them. Stay away from places with fancy cars, etc.

$ Go to the self-service cafeterias that the locals patronize. Remember, you eliminate tipping in cafeterias.

$ There are always cheap (if uninspired) eats at McDonald's or Kentucky Fried Chicken or other recognizable fast-food slurp-ups.

$ Use the dining rooms of department stores, or other reasonably priced restaurants which are found on the streets, in downtown arcades, and in large office buildings.

$ The non-touristy part of any city has non-touristy prices. The farther you get from tourists' habitats, the cheaper the prices anywhere. The very same drink that costs $2 at a deluxe hotel will cost you 75¢ in a local non-seedy bar.

$ Browse through the older sections of different cities and pop in on the trattorias (in Italy), taveranas (in Greece), etc. for lower priced food and the real local flavor.

$ A rule of thumb: the higher the bar or restaurant, the higher the prices. Sky restaurants and lounges of hotels and office buildings are usually very expensive. So even if they do offer a fabulous view of the city, don't plan on eating or drinking much there.

$ Wine or beer are usually taken with meals. Experiment with local brands; they're much cheaper and often better than the American imports. If you're used to cocktails beforehand, either again order the local brand or have a drink in your room with the duty-free liquor you so wisely purchased at the airport.

$ Don't insist on imported food. Eat the specialities of the countries—they're as low-budget as they are an exciting adventure. After all, the reason they're the national dish is that their ingredients are cheap and plentiful!

$ Have your main meal at lunch—the same thing would cost you more at dinner.

$ Sometimes soups are so filling they can be a whole meal—this is especially true in Eastern Europe and the Orient.

$ Whenever you order the prix-fixe dinner, you'll get a complete meal at a fixed price, but you won't be allowed a substitution. Tax and service charges are included. The cost can be one-third lower than the other dinners on the menu, and there's ample food.

$ Don't run up a multi-itemed bill. In certain restaurants, especially those which serve mainly drinks, the tax and service charges can accumulate rapidly. So ask for an itemized bill each time you are served and before you order again.

$ If you are on a packaged tour, you'll probably be given one banquet of the local foods. These are the kinds of dishes that can cost dearly if you try them on your own. So find out what you get "free" and try other foods in the restaurants.

$ Have a picnic in your room, on the roadside, or at a city park (safer than ours) by going to a local grocery store for bottled water and/or wine, cheese, bread, and fruit. Besides that, picnics in the park are a super way to meet people.

Money Matters: Getting It and Spending It

DIAMONDS AREN'T
A GIRL'S BEST FRIEND:
MONEY IS!

THE FIRST question usually is, "How much can I spend?" To figure this out, calculate your annual expenses—food, clothing, medical bills, rent and incidentals. When you have all the essential expenses out of the way, that's what you have left for travel. Figure what you plan to spend per day on hotels, meals, sightseeing, transportation, gifts, sundries and multiply by the number of days you plan to be away. Then add 10% as a safety factor. Allowing this extra amount is especially important if you don't have an international credit card to bail you out.

The only thing that is certain about the money situation is that nothing is certain. A lot has changed recently with the American dollar. Where it used to be sought after, it is now sometimes refused or given unfavorable rates of exchange. Another uncertainty is the unpredictability of devaluations—theirs or ours. Devaluations can work *for* you if it's the other country that has it: you'll get more for your money there. But if the *American* dollar is devalued, your money is worth less.

Money fluctuates everywhere. Check for the current rates or exchange right before you leave and during the trip itself to be sure that you have a regularly updated idea of general values for each country. In this day and age of constant and often dramatic changes, it would be foolhardy to include a currency conversion chart here (a standard chapter in travel books of old). But such charts are available, constantly updated and free of charge, at hotels, banks, and tourist information offices.

Purchase foreign currency packets from your bank before you go. Given time, even the smallest bank can send away for the coin and paper packages sold by foreign exchange brokers. This allows you to enter a country with small bills and change for cabs and tips.

And keep a handful of this small change in your coat pocket so you won't have to open your purse in public places.

Another thing about local currency: it is always to the tourist's financial advantage to use it when traveling. Whenever possible, change your U.S. money in banks or licensed money exchangers' offices. Many hotels, restaurants, and shops not only offer a bad rate of exchange, but also sometimes refuse to exchange, especially on weekends.

Carry such international cards as American Express, Diners Club, and Carte Blanche. Their directories will tell you who takes what where. Do travel with a *major* credit card—the local one from your friendly Peoria bank won't help very much in Majorca. And make sure your credit card(s) won't expire while you're away. A major advantage of such cards is that they often allow you to cash personal checks (otherwise impossible!) or get travelers' checks. Before you go, find out the company policy on where to go for what. For carriers of lots of cards, you can protect yourself against theft or loss through the International Charge Card Registry, Federal Way, Washington 98003 (tel. 800-426-8112). This entitles you to one toll-free call from anywhere in the world, and you are fully taken care of, with literally instant notification of your card issuers, $300 in emergency cash, an airplane ticket home, plus other benefits.

There's also an international "cash card" called Visacard, good in thirty-one countries for accommodations, meals, pearls, antiques, and custom tailoring, allowing you a 10% discount on these items. For further information write to Visacard/Asia International Club, Ltd./American Representative: Bernard Kessler and Associates, Ltd., 11891 Martha Ann Drive, Los Alamitos, Ca. 90720, USA. The card is $10.

I strongly urge you to carry travelers' checks. They're sold by banks and agencies for major currencies—American, Japanese, British, Canadian, German, French, Swiss. You can get foreign travelers' checks at the Bank of Tokyo, Perea, Thomas Cook, American Express and Barclays. It's only advantageous to buy foreign checks if you aren't going to many different countries and will spend awhile within one border. Why? (1) Your American checks will get you the fastest refunds if lost; (2) with dollar checks you'll be better able to keep track of what you have left than if you had to convert those yen mentally into the rest of your budget; and (3) if you're going to many different countries, you always have to change to the next currency or back into dollars before moving on, and you're apt to lose on the transaction. Better to have dollars in case. Also, when you come back home, you can always use them.

The important questions to ask when deciding which travelers' checks to purchase are: Where are they sold? Are they available in foreign currency? What, if any, is the refund policy? Is there a charge for the checks and if so what is it? Some travelers' checks can be purchased on sale. Bank of America runs its sale in May, but if you aren't going until December, you might do better to put your interest in the bank; it's that low! And sometimes your bank will give you free travelers' checks if you badger them a little.

Checks range in denomination from $5 to $5,000 and up, but experienced travelers stick to five's, ten's, and twenty's. The smaller range is particularly important in foreign countries, where you get checks cashed into local money. If you need the equivalent of a few dollars to pay a dinner tab or buy a small gift, you don't want to cash a $500 check and get $490 worth of it back in foreign currency; you'd be crazy to carry around that much money. Another reason not to carry large sums of foreign currency: what if the exchange shops are closed at the airport and border crossing spots? But do cash enough so that you won't keep paying a transaction surcharge and you won't be stuck over a weekend or holiday or in some remote place without being able to cash a check.

You will render your precious travelers' checks void by countersigning them before cashing, gambling with them, or using them in illegal transactions or an attempt to defraud. There's a big black market for travelers' checks, so don't be tempted if someone offers you money for your checks if you'll "lose" them to him. Travelers' checks representatives are familiar with just about every scheme imaginable, so don't think you're outsmarting them.

Protect your travelers' checks by keeping a duplicate list of the numbers; and have your purchase agreement with you—both of these will help immeasurably to speed up your refund should something happen to your checks. Leave one list at home with a contactable friend and carry the other with you—apart from your checks, of course. If you lose your checks in America, call the toll-free 800 number that's on your purchase agreement. They'll tell you where to go for a refund. Abroad, ask at your hotel or consulate to determine the nearest bank or travelers' check representative where you can get an immediate refund.

If you do lose your money, or simply run out of it, all is not lost. Call someone back home to contact a local bank for a foreign remittance. Or have your contact send money through the local American Express office. Your contact should take either cash or a certified check to the bank or office. If the money is cabled to you, it will take one or two days; if a foreign check is mailed, it'll take seven to ten days. You will need your passport as identification to claim the money. Use an international credit card in the meantime to charge purchases and to get cash.

TIPPING   I must confess that women the world over are known as bad tippers and given service accordingly. Remember the women who will come after you.

That old standard, the 10% tip, has gone the way of the five-cent newspaper. The general rule now is 15-20%. The easiest way to figure out a 20% tip is to figure 10% of the pre-tax total, drop the last decimal place and double that amount. If I can do it, you can, since my math is so bad I've been known to take out a pen and paper and make long calculations to divide in half a lunch check of, say, $12.57. Let me give you an example of this mathematical tipping marvel: If a dinner costs $8.00 before tax, 10% would be 80¢—double that to $1.60 and you have a 20% tip for an $8.00 meal. Voila! But wait. Just when you think it's standardized and foolproof, there's a catch. In some restaurants and hotels, a service charge has been included in your total bill. The information below should help you out of that mess. If in doubt anywhere, ask your hotel clerk, tour operator, other tourists or the maitre d'hotel.

RESTAURANTS: In addition to a service charge of 10-20%

Waiter:	1-5% extra (with service charge), 15% without
Wine steward:	75¢-$2

HOTELS: In addition to service charge of 10-20%

Porter, station to hotel	
room:	50¢-$1 per bag
lobby to room:	50¢ per bag
Chambermaid:	30¢ per service
Floor porter:	30¢ per service
Concierge: For each	
day's stay	small service: 40¢
	several services: 80¢
	many services: $1.25
Room waiter, per	
service:	30¢-70¢
Table waiter, per 3	
lunches and	
dinners:	30¢-70¢
Bartender, bar	
waiter:	small change

NIGHTCLUBS: In addition to service charge of 10-20%

Maitre d', for table	
of your choice:	$3
Waiter:	50¢-$2

MISCELLANEOUS:

Sightseeing tour	
escort, per two	
weeks, per person:	$12-$15
Half-day bus tour:	50¢-75¢
Washroom	
attendant	20¢-50¢
Usher:	20¢-50¢
Railroad porter,	
per bag:	40¢
Taxi-driver:	15%
Beauty shop,	stylist: 15% shampooer: 5%

CRUISE SHIP:

Cabin steward:	$1.50 to $2 per person/ per day
Dining room steward:	same as above
Deck steward:	$3 per person per trip
Head dining room steward (maitre d'hotel):	$10, half on departure
Table captain (if any):	$5 per trip
Wine steward:	15% of the wine bill
Night steward:	50¢-$1 per service
Bartender:	15-20% of the bar each time

On a cruise it is proper to give most tips the last evening of the trip. Two exceptions are the maitre d' and bartender. Also, if the trip is more than two weeks, give half of your tips mid-way through the trip. The crew will not only be able to use the money in port, but they'll also be even more inclined to give you better service for the rest of the trip.

When traveling abroad, don't judge tipping amounts by U.S. currency standards. Fifty cents would be extravagant bad taste for a porter in India, but not really enough in Sweden. Again abroad, look around you for clues as to people to tip. In some countries, it's the theater ushers. And conversely, don't tip where you don't have to: in countries with no tipping, like Tahiti, don't do it!

FOREIGN MONEY/REGULATIONS

COUNTRY	MONETARY UNIT	AMOUNT ALLOWED IN	AMOUNT ALLOWED OUT
Argentina	Peso	No limit	No limit
Australia	Australian Dollar	No limit	Same amount taken in
Austria	Schilling	No limit	15,000
Belgium	Belgium franc	No limit	No limit
Brazil	Cruzeiro	No limit	No limit
Bulgaria	Leva	No limit	No limit
Burma	Kyat	No limit	No limit
Cambodia— Khmer Republic	Riel	No limit	No limit
China (Peoples Republic)	Renminbi	No limit	No limit
China (Taiwan)	New Taiwan Dollar	1000	1000
Czechoslovakia	Koruna	No limit	No limit
Denmark	Krone	No limit	2000
Egypt	Egyptian Pound	No limit	No limit
Fiji Islands	Fiji dollar	No limit	No limit
Finland	Finmark	1000	1000
France	New Franc	No limit	500
Germany (East)	Ostmark	No limit	No limit
Germany (West)	Deutche Mark	No limit	No limit
Great Britain	Pound Sterling	No limit	25
Greece	Drachma	750	750
Hong Kong	H.K. Dollar	No limit	No limit
Hungary	Forint	200	200
India	Rupee	No limit	No limit
Indonesia	Rupiah	No limit	No limit
Ireland	Pound	No limit	25
Israel	Israeli Pound	100	100
Italy	Lira	No limit	50,000
Japan	Yen	No limit	20,000
Kenya	Kenya Shilling	No limit	Not more than brought in
Lebanon	L. Pound	No limit	No limit
Liberia	L. Dollar	No limit	No limit
Lichtenstein	Swiss Franc	No limit	No limit
Luxembourg	L. Franc	No limit	No limit
Malaysia	Mal. Dollar	500	500

Monaco	Mon. Franc	No limit	No limit
Morocco	Dsrham	No limit	No limit
Netherlands	Guilder	No limit	No limit
New Zealand	N.Z. Dollar	10	10
Nigeria	Naira	No limit	No nairas
Norway	Krone	1000	350
Papua New Guinea	Kina	100	100
Philippines	Peso	100	100
Poland	Zloty	No limit	No limit
Portugal	Escudo	No limit	No limit
Romania	Leu	No limit	No limit
Russia	Rouble	No limit	No limit
Samoa, American	U.S. Dollar	No limit	No limit
Samoa	N.Z. Dollar	No limit	No limit
Singapore	Singapore Dollar	1000	1000
South Africa	Rand	50	50
South Korea	Won	No limit	Same as taken in
Spain	Peseta	50,000	10,000
Sweden	Krona	6000	6000
Switzerland	S. Franc	No limit	No limit
Tahiti	Cen. Pac. Franc	No limit	$100 U.S. unless more declared
Tanzania	Tanzanian Shilling	No limit	No Tanzanian currency
Thailand	Baht	500	500
Tonga	Patanga	No limit	No limit
Turkey	T. Lira	100	100
Yugoslavia	New Dinar	100	50

TIME DIFFERENCE/BANK HOURS
Mexico, Central America & South America

Country	Time Difference to: EDST.	PDST.	Banking Hours
Mexico	−2	+1	9 AM-1:30 (M-F)
Caribbean:			
Antigua	0	+3	8 AM-noon (M-F); also 8-11 (Sat.)
Aruba, Bonair, Curaçao	0	+3	8:30-noon; 1:30-4:30 (M-F)
Bahamas	0	+3	9-3 (M-Th); 9-5 (Sat.)
Barbados	0	+3	8-noon (M-F); also 3-6 PM (Fri.)
Bermuda	+1	+4	9:30-3 (M-F); also 4:30-6 (Fri.)
Cayman Islands	−1	+2	8:30-1 (M-F); also 4:30-6 (Fri.)
Dominica	0	+3	8-noon (M-F); also 3-5 PM (Fri.)
Dominican Rep.	−1	+2	7:30-1:30 (M-F)
Grenada & Grenadines	0	+3	8-noon (M-F); also 3-6 PM (Fri.)
Guadeloupe	0	+3	8-noon & 2-6 PM (M-F); 8-noon (Sat.)
Haiti	−1	+2	9-1 (M-F)
Jamaica	0	+3	9-2 (M-Th); 9-noon & 2:30-5 (Fri.)
Martinique	0	+3	8-noon; 2:30-4 (M-F)
Montserrat	0	+3	8-noon (M-Th); 8-noon & 3-5 (Fri.)
Puerto Rico	0	+3	9-2:30 (M-F)
St. Kitts & Nevis	0	+3	8-noon (M-F); also 8-11 (Sat.)
St. Lucia	0	+3	8-noon (M-F); also 3-6 PM (Fri.)
St. Martin	0	+3	8-1 (M-F)
St. Maarten, Saba & St. Eustatius	0	+3	8-1 (M-F)
St. Vincent	0	+3	8-noon (M-F); also 8-11 (Sat.)
Trinidad & Tobago	0	+3	8-noon (M-F); also 8-11 (Sat.)
Br. Virgin Island (Tortola, V. Gorda, Anegada)	0	+3	9-2 (M-F)
U.S. Virgin Islands (St. Thomas, St. Croix, St. John)	0	+3	9-2:30 (M-F); also 4-6 (Fri.)
Central America			
Belise (Br. Honduras)	−2	+1	8:30-noon & 2-4 (M-F); 8:30-noon (Sat.)
Costa Rica	−2	+1	8-11 & 1:30-3 (M-F); 8-11 (Sat.)
El Salvador	−2	+1	8-4 (M-F); 8-12 (Sat.)
Guatemala	−2	+1	8:30-12:30 & 2-4 (M-F)

Honduras	−2	+1	8-12 & 2-4 (M-F); 8:30-12 (Sat.)
Nicaragua	−1	+2	8:30-noon & 2-4 (M-F); 8:30-11:30 (Sat.)
Panama	−1	+2	8:30-12:30 & 2:30-3:30 (M-F)

South America

Argentina	+1	+4	12 noon-4 PM (M-F)
Bolivia	0	+3	9-12 & 2-4:30 (M-F)
Brazil	+1	+4	10-4 (M-F)
Chile	0	+3	9-2 (M-F)
Colombia	+1	+2	9-3 (M-F)
Ecuador	−1	+2	9-noon & 2:30-4 (M-F)
French Guiana	0	+3	7:30-1 (M-F)
Guyana	+¼	+3¼	8-noon (M-F); 8-11 (Sat.)
Paraguay	0	3	7:30-10:30 AM (M-F)
Peru	−1	+2	9:30-12:30 & 4-7 (M-F)
Surinam	+½	+3½	7:30-1 (M-F); 7:30-11 AM (Sat.)
Uruguay	+1	+4	1:30-5 (M-F)
Venezuela	0	+3	8:30-11:30 & 2:30-5:30 (M-F)

TIME DIFFERENCE/BANK HOURS
Europe, Africa & Middle East

Country	Ahead of U.S. (EDST)	Banking Hours
Austria	5	8-3 (M-F) to 5:30 PM (Th)
Belgium	5	9-4 (M-F)
Bulgaria	6	8-noon (M-F)
Czechoslovakia	5	8-2 (M-F)
Denmark	5	9:30-3 (M-F) & 4-6 (Tues. & Fri.)
Egypt	6	8:30-12:30 (Sat. & Th.) & 10-noon (Sun.)
Finland	6	9-4:15 (M-F)
France	5	9-4:30 (M-F)
Germany	5	9-1 & 3-4 (M-F) to 5:30 PM (Th)
Great Britain	4	9:30-3:30 (M-F) to 6 PM (Th. or Fri.)
Greece	6	8-1 (M-Sat.)
Hungary	5	9-1 (M-F)
Ireland	4	10-3 (M-F) to 5 PM (Th)
Israel	6	8:30-12:30 (Sun.-Fri.) (some) 4-5 PM
Italy	5	8:30-1:30 (M-F)
Kenya	7	9-1 (M-F); 9-11 (Sat.)
Lebanon	6	8:30-12:30 (M-F); 8:30-noon (Sat.)
Liberia	4	8-noon (M-F); 8-2 (Sat.); closed Fri.
Lichtenstein	5	8-noon, 1:30-4:30 (M-F)
Luxembourg	5	8:30-noon, 2-5 (M-F)
Majorca	5	8:30-2 (M-F)
Monaco	5	8-noon, 2-4 (M-F); 9-noon (Sat.)
Morocco	5	8:15-11:30, 2:15-4:30 (M-F)
Netherlands	5	9-4 (M-F)
Nigeria	5	8-3 (M-F)
Norway	5	8:15-3:45 (M-F)
Poland	5	9-12:30 (M-F), 9-11 (Sat.)
Portugal	5	9-12:30 (M-F), 9-11 (Sat.)
Romania	6	8-noon (M-F), 8-11:30 AM (Sat.)
Russia (Moscow)	7	9-1 (M-F)
South Africa	6	9-3 (Mon., Tues., Th., Fri.) 9-1 (Wed.) 9-11 AM (Sat.)
Spain	5	9-2 (M-F)
Sweden	5	9:30-3 (M-F)
Switzerland	5	8-4:30 (Tues.-Fri.), to 6 PM (Mon.)
Tanzania	5	8:30-noon (M-F); 8:30-11 (Sat.)
Turkey	6	9-noon, 1:30-5 (M-F), 9-noon (Sat.)
Yugoslavia	5	7-3 (M-F)

TIME DIFFERENCE/BANKING HOURS
Pacific, Orient, and Southeast Asia

Country	Time Difference From U.S.A.		Banking Hours
	PDT.	EDT.	
Australia	+17	+14	10-3 (M-Th), 10-5 (Fri.), closed (Sat.)
Burma	+13½	+10½	9-4 (M-F); 9-12:30 (Sat.)
Cambodia-Khmer Republic	+14	+11	8:30-3:30 (M-F); 8:30-noon (Sat.) Closed on religious holidays
Ceylon-Sri Lanka	+12½	+9½	9-1 (M-F); 9-11 AM (Sat.) Closed on religious holidays
China, Peoples Republic	+15	+12	Hours vary drastically Open Sat., closed Sun.
Fiji Islands	+19	+16	10-3 (M-Th); 10-4 (Fri.) Closed Sat.
Guam	+17	+14	10-3 (M-Th); 10-6 (Fri.) Closed Sat.
Hawaii	−3	−6	8:30-3 (M-Th); 8:30-6 (Fri.)
Hong Kong	+15	+12	10-3 (M-F); 9-noon (Sat.)
India	+12½	+9½	10:30-2:30 (M-F); 10:30-12:30 (Sat.)
Indonesia	+15	+12	10-3 (M-F); 9-noon (Sat.)
Japan	+16	+13	9-3 (M-F); 9-noon (Sat.)
Macao	+15	+12	8-4 (M-F); 9-1 (Sat.)
Malaysia	+14½	+11½	10-3 (M-F); 9:30-11:30 AM (Sat.) Closed Friday in some states.
Micronesia	+17	+14	9:30-2:30 (M-F)
Nepal	+12½	+9½	10-3 (Sat.-Th.); 10-noon (Fri.) Closed Saturday
New Caledonia	+18	+15	7-10:30; 1:30-3:30 (M-F); 7:30-11 AM (Sat.)
New Hebrides	+18	+15	
New Zealand	+19	+16	10-4 (M-F)
Papua New Guinea	+17	+14	9-2 (M-F); 8:30-10 AM (Sat.)
Philippines	+15	+12	9-6 (M-F); 9-12:30 PM (Sat.)
Samoa, American	−4	−7	9-2 (M-Th); 9-5 (Fri.)
Samoa, Western	−4	−7	9:30-3 PM (M-F); 9:30-11:30 AM (Sat.)
Singapore	+14½	+11½	10-3 (M-F); 9:30-11:30 AM (Sat.)
South Korea	+16	+13	9:30-4 (M-F); 9:30-1 PM (Sat.)
South Vietnam	+15	+12	8-11:30; 2-4 (M-F); 8-11 AM (Sat.)
Tahiti	−3	−6	7:45-3:30 (M-F)
Taiwan	+15	+12	9-3:30 (M-F); 9-noon (Sat.)
Thailand	+14	+11	8:30-3:30 (M-F). Closed Sat.
Tonga	+19	+16	No banks. Change money at Treasury Building or hotels.

PUT *THAT* IN YOUR STRING BAG!

BEFORE YOU set foot out of town, there are some things **20** you can do to enhance your buying abroad. One is to comparison-shop at home for items you might purchase overseas; many things are cheaper at home than in foreign countries. This is also the place for a sneaky suggestion: if you have a large import store in your town, like Pier 1 or Cost Plus, you can pick up gifts for friends there (but make sure they are stamped "Made in Japan" or whatever country you'll be in) and save yourself the time and trouble of looking elsewhere and lugging friends' treasures home. I know: I hand-carried a clay drum all the way from the Middle East for a friend only to have that gift break upon my arrival home! And then I found better, cheaper ones at San Francisco's Cost Plus.

If you have a specific large purchase in mind, you can inform your banker to take care of the currency registration ahead of your purchase by specifying the type of item. The seller, when you're abroad, forwards a package description and a bill of lading to the bank. This protects you because the seller isn't paid until he sends the bank a stamped receipt showing that your purchase is really on the way.

And if you don't go through a bank (say it's a small purchase), always make certain any item is properly insured before it's sent home. Give the purchase three months to reach its destination. If it hasn't been received by then, send a letter plus photocopies of your receipts to the store and the local tourist office. One other hint to insure that your packages will arrive at the same place you do: take along typewritten or clearly printed labels with your name and address on them. (Sometimes they simply can't decipher your chicken-scratchings.)

The most reliable way of transporting the packages you bought is to hand-carry them—but that means pre-planning your packing to allow room—or send them by parcel post. You can also send them via a commercial airline, as air cargo. The minimum charge for an air cargo shipment is $32.00, though. (The approximate rates are: $2.04 per pound up to 100 lbs., $1.46 per pound from 100 to 220 lbs., and $1.10 per pound from 220 to 660 lbs.) Or have your gifts accompany you as unaccompanied baggage on the plane. If you don't want to try these approaches, get an all-inclusive transport quotation before buying. Any way you do it, make certain purchases are well-protected from the rigors of transport. And only have things sent from established shops with lots of experience in sending things overseas for fussy Americans. Seek out the shops the big tour operators use. Ask the concierge and the local tourist organization. Never trust it to a tiny souvenir shop or other such place.

Before you go, you should also have friends' clothing sizes if you're going to pick up something along that line for them. And since clothing sizes vary, refer to this list of comparative sizes.

JUNIOR MISS

AMERICAN	9	11	13	15	17
EUROPEAN	34	36	38	40	42

WOMEN'S CLOTHING

AMERICAN	10-30	12-32	14-34	16-36	18-38	20-40
EUROPEAN	40	42	44	46	48	50

WOMEN'S GLOVES

Same as U.S.

WOMEN'S STOCKINGS

AMERICAN	8	8	9	9½	10	10⅜	11
EUROPEAN	0	1	2	3	4	5	6

WOMEN'S SHOES

AMERICAN	4	5	6	7	8	9
EUROPEAN	34	35	36	37	38	39

CHILDREN'S DRESSES AND SUITS

AMERICAN	2	4	6	8	10	12
EUROPEAN	40-45	50-55	60-65	70-75	80-85	90-95

MEN'S SUITS, OVERCOATS, SWEATERS AND PAJAMAS

AMERICAN	34	36	38	40	42	44	46	48
EUROPEAN	44	46	48	50	52	54	56	58

MEN'S SHIRTS

AMERICAN	14	14½	15	15½	16	16½	17
EUROPEAN	36	37	38	39	41	42	43

Women's sizes in foreign countries are determined by bust and hip measurements. Buy children's sizes by ages (one year is size 2, etc.). In countries where people are smaller (like Japan), buy a size larger. I know, I wear the average American shoe size (7B) for women. But when I went into a Tokyo department store for a pair of shoes, the clerk looked at me and said, "But we don't have anything that big!" I felt like Gulliver. Because of this difference in the way we're built, always try on ready-made clothing. And since most of the world measures things by the metric system, it behooves us to know something about it. One inch equals 2.5 centimeters—that should get you started. For further specifics, consult the chart below. A really useful gadget (if you leave this book back in your room) is a double tape measure with centimeters on one side, inches on the other.

If you're going to have something custom-made, there are some special things you ought to know. For instance, you'll be sorry unless you go to a place with a fine reputation for tailoring, allow enough time for at least three fittings, have a photograph or detailed drawing of the item you want made, and are willing to pay a little more for a really good job. Make certain the tailor understands your needs, and be very specific about details (linings, seam widths, length, buttons, etc.). I personally think having clothes custom-made wastes a great deal of precious sightseeing time. After all, the inside of a dressmaker's shop is not too different in Paris, France or Paris, Illinois. But if you're going to do it, at least do it right. The one woman who will truly find it worthwhile is the woman who wears an irregular size.

Pearls and jade range from the ordinary to the out-of-sight, with prices to match. And unless you have a trained eye, you probably won't know the difference. So go to a really venerable old place—more expensive, perhaps, than the smaller shops, but at least you'll be sure of what you're getting. Jade is judged by evenness of color, shade, and size, and by absence of flaws. The best type of jade is jadeite since it's the hardest; it is commonly called Imperial Jade. Good jade does not scratch easily. Pearls are rated by size, luster, color, and shape. The finest quality pearls are silvery white, then light pink, darker pink, yellow and plain white in that order. The pearl should be round and without imperfections or minute bubbles.

Jewelry is such a popular gift for women to give themselves that I must speak out on it specifically. Buy expensive jewelry only at name places. Actually, buy expensive *anythings* only at such establishments. And have your new gems appraised at home by a member of the Gemological Society of America. Second best, but also reputable and knowledgeable (and more easily found), are the members of the American Gem Society.

The good watches, with prices ranging from moderate to astronomical, are: Audemars-Piguet, Patek Philippe, Vacheron et Constantin, Borel, Clarenzia, Jaeger-Le Coultre, Longine, Movado, Piaget, Rolex, Vulcain, Zenith, Omega and Tissot. Jewels are placed at points of stress in the instrument; seventeen jewels are considered perfectly adequate for any hand-wound watch, twenty-six for an automatic. You'll pay a higher price for more jewels, but won't necessarily get a better watch. Check with the seller to establish that your watch (if non-electronic) has a "jeweled escapement." Buy a watch with shockproofing built in if you're at all active. If you're very sedentary, stay away from self-winding instruments since they are wound by the movement of the wearer's wrist. If you do buy a self-winding watch, make sure it uses the newer "rotor" principle rather than the old-fashioned controlled swing. Waterproof watches are better shields against moisture (of course), dust, and air than non-waterproof ones, but don't make a practice of swimming with even a waterproof one; it won't last long. And don't order a leather strap for a waterproof watch. If you're going to buy an ultra-thin watch, make sure you have an excellent repairman back home who can fix it. (Not everybody can!) If you buy one of those digital read-out watches, be certain the figures are luminous—otherwise you'll be in the dark *in* the dark. Allow enough time when purchasing for your dealer to give an accuracy check so that your watch will be adjusted to your particular wrist movements. It's also good to allow time leeway in case you change your mind about such changeable things as the watch strap or dial design. Many brightly-colored dials fade quickly, so beware.

When shopping for a camera here are some guidelines for you to follow: (1) Buy the camera as soon as possible, so if there is a problem with the equipment or your understanding of how to work it, you can have the shop straighten things out. (2) Read the instruction booklet in the store and try to operate the camera then and there. (3) Let the seller know the type of pictures you like to take and how knowledgeable and experienced you are as a photographer; that'll allow him to make an intelligent choice of cameras for you. (4) Make certain that all auxiliary equipment is fresh—such as batteries, light meters, and flashguns. (5) Go only to well-established, reputable shops and buy only known, guaranteed products.

Now for the question of bargaining. Do you or don't you? In some places you do and in some places you don't. You don't in department stores, government-operated stores or important smaller shops. But haggle your head off at little souvenir shops, flea markets and outdoor bazaars. How to do it? Don't knock the merchandise. Start out by offering one-quarter of the seller's asking price. He'll throw up his hands in despair and say that's much too little and are you trying to drive him out of business? Then he'll come back with a counter-offer. As will you. And so on until you come to about 60% of the original price. The whole process takes a bit of getting used to, but actually merchants where this is a common practice *miss* it if you don't give them a chance to carry on like this. And they won't respect you as much. When you think about it, it's at least a way of carrying on a conversation instead of our dehumanizing practice of mumbling "I'll take it. Charge it" and off!

Other ways of saving money: ask for a cash discount if you don't use your credit card; request a discount if buying a substantial amount; check into special buying incentives of some countries, like having your purchase tax refunded when you take the product out of the country; don't go shopping with professional guides (they usually get a commission on your purchase from the store—and guess who unknowingly pays the commission!). And shop at duty-free airports. (The best are in Shannon, Paris, Amsterdam and Frankfurt.) There are also good tax-free shops at some highway border-crossing points, not to mention whole areas which are free ports—this means you are free of the local duty, but you still must pay American duty when you bring the purchase home. When free-port shops have items "in bond," they must be delivered to your plane or ship—so be sure to purchase early enough for them to get there! The best buys in such places are high-duty things like cameras, perfumes, tape recorders, liquor and tobacco. Just make sure the item is not restricted or trademarked (see the "Customs" chapter) or it will be kept out! Don't buy *anything* without keeping a running record (with receipt) for customs.

If you don't shop at the duty-free places mentioned above, where should you shop? Places you can trust are department stores, government-operated shops and large hardware/houseware stores. Have fun at little souvenir shops, flea markets and gift stores in smaller towns, but be very alert as to what you are getting and for how much. Many people believe that the further off the beaten track you get, the lower the prices. It ain't necessarily so. Bigger stores can often buy in such huge volume that they can offer lower prices. And you're not getting tourist junk—you're shopping where the locals do.

Some don'ts: Don't buy tacky little momentos such as ashtrays which have a picture of the Eiffel Tower and say "Greetings from Paris." If they don't look tacky at the time (simply because the atmosphere is overwhelmingly exotic), they will by the time they are back home! Avoid items which are so fragile they could break easily in transit. Don't buy things without figuring out if you have room to pack them—or buy a tote bag for them. Don't count on storekeepers to provide you with shopping bags; that's a unique American extravagance, so carry your own—a nylon string bag is strong and collapsible. And if you don't want to be collapsible, don't shop in the heat of the midday sun if you're in a hot climate. Anyway, the locals are smarter than you and usually close up the shops for an hour or two at lunchtime. Don't wait until the last minute and then grab *anything*—desperation purchases are never optimum buys. But also don't buy the first thing you run across. Compare before, not after your purchase. (The latter is pure masochism, because you'll really get depressed when you find something better and cheaper). Don't offer to bring back specific items for friends—you can waste a whole day looking for an item which you probably won't be able to find and which is probably available back home. Don't put off buying something with the thought that you'll get back there again on your trip; you probably won't, or if you do the shop may be closed or your tour will bypass it or the item may be gone! Don't buy something just because it's cheaper than you could get it at home. (That's an increasingly rare phenomenon anyway.) Don't expect spectacular bargains everywhere. You will find some, but they're getting rarer and rarer. Don't buy lots of inexpensive doodads—buy one good thing you'll cherish. Concentrate on finding things truly representative of a particular region. But don't buy those women's outfits that only look good on the locals—American women don't know how to wrap the Indian sari and are too busty and hippy for the Chinese cheongsams and Japanese kimonos. Along these lines, don't buy anything you won't be able to wear comfortably at home. I've known women to come back with gold Indian saris or elaborate Hong Kong brocades or exotic-looking Guatemalan peasant blouses which would never fit into their life style back home. They aren't exactly *de rigueur* for the office, a date for the movies, or the PTA. Don't expect to get into a French couture showing unless you can convince your concierge to wangle an invitation for you, or you've lined it up before leaving home with your local department store's couture section. (They'll only do it if you're a big buyer.) Otherwise, stick to the couturiers' boutiques—they're much cheaper, anyway. Don't buy brands of watches, cameras, and other serviceable items that can't be serviced back home . . . or that don't have a guarantee valid in America. Don't buy electrical equipment which works on different voltages and cycles than you have at home. Don't buy just the amount you need of anything fragile—buy several extra. Don't buy an exotic-looking souvenir without checking the origin or you'll get home and find "Made in U.S.A." stamped underneath. Don't buy anything unless it's suitable, useful, packable, or shippable.

Think small in terms of (1) price—you can send gifts that cost $10 or less back to the States duty-free; and (2) size—to save room in your suitcase or to save mailing charges.

One last tidbit that doesn't really "fit" anywhere, but has added so much to my trip memories that I must pass it on. Buy records with music representative of the country you're visiting. You'll be able to recapture the drums of Bora-Bora, the sitar of India, the koto of Japan, and folksongs the world over! There has been many a night when I've really re-lived my South Pacific experiences by playing "The Drums of Bora-Bora."

WHAT TO BUY WHERE?

AUSTRALIA: (SYDNEY) Stores are open 9-5:30, later on Thursdays. Good buys are aboriginal artifacts at the Australian Board of Missions (417 B Kent Street) and black opals at the Opal Skymine (6th level, Australia Square). Proud's and Percy Marks are good stores for *anything*. Woolens are of excellent quality and about half of what they'd cost at home (but don't forget to figure in the shipping or overweight costs).Sydney's Centrepoint contains 200 speciality shops in one building. Touristy koala bears are good buys for the young or young at heart.

AUSTRIA: (VIENNA) Store hours are 8 AM-noon, closed for lunch, open 2-6 PM, closed Saturdays at 12:30 PM. Good buys are colored stone jewelry, painted enamel boxes, petit point, cut-glass bowls, leather goods, antiques, china. For kids buy dolls, dirndl dresses, and Tyrolean hats. Dirndles and regional wear are best at Loden/Plankl (Michaelerplatz 6), but check the fabric in the aprons since some don't iron well after washing. Great Viennese handicrafts can be found at Elfi Müller & Co. (Kärntnerstrasse 53). For leather goods go to Mädler Gmbh at Graben 17. Buy exquisite petit point at the J. Jolles Studios (Andreasgasse 6) where the really fine work is sold at a 10% discount to boot. The leading department stores are Boecher and Steffl. For a real bargain, go to the Dorotheum Auction. There's a flea market at Am Hof place on Saturdays from 9-5.

BAHAMAS: (NASSAU) Store hours are 9-5 with a Friday noon closing. Shop Bay Street in Nassau and Freeport's International Bazaar. For jewelry go to Alpina. Ernest Borel Swiss watches, Wedgewood and Spode are best at The China Shop in Nassau. John Bull (that's really the name!) has the best selection of cameras and equipment. Buy native craftwork at the Rawson Square outdoor market. Get children's fashions and Hummel figurines at Vanite off Bay Street. If you're looking for a gift for a man, go to the Pipe of Peace for a great selection of pipes and tobacco.

BELGIUM: (BRUSSELS) Department stores are open from 9:30 AM-6 PM except Sundays and holidays. Smaller shops often close for a couple of hours at lunch, but remain open until 7. Almost all stores stay open until 9 PM on Fridays. All shops must close one day a week and since it doesn't have to be Sunday, Belgium's individualistic shopkeepers close at various times (though they usually ignore the one-day closing in summer). Buy lovely Belgium lace at Maria Loix at rue d'Arenberg 52-54. Purchase beautiful jewelry and silverware at Wolfers Frères at 82-84 avenue Louise. You'll find a great selection of antiques at Delplace (rue de la Regence 11), the country's largest and most respected antique dealer. The best department stores are L'Innovation and Bon Marché. The nicest cluster of couture shops are the Garden Stores Louise at 45 boulevard Louise. From the chic to the cheap—the Flea Market is in the square of the Place du Grand Sablon, Saturday (9-6) or Sunday (9-noon). The duty-free shop at the Brussels airport is the only one in all of Europe to carry precious gems. Stockings and nylon underwear are poor quality here and their shoes will never fit you (wrong "last").

BERMUDA: The best shops are on Front Street and the best buys are woolens, crystal, watches, perfume, silver and china. Shetland and cashmere sweaters are cheaper here than in London! Also, the caliber of the goods and reputation of the merchants is often higher here than elsewhere in the Caribbean. Trimingham's (in the better hotels) has the most wonderful selection of woolens, children's clothes, and leathers. Archie Brown's (on Front Street) has the best Pringle cashmeres. For china and antiques go to William Bluck & Co. (on Front Street West). Bermuda Crafts on Front St. has great-looking copper enamelled jewelry and Bermuda perfumes. If you have a male friend who smokes a pipe, buy a good English one for him at Outerbridge's Salmagundi.

BRAZIL: (RIO) Store hours are from 9-6. You may get a 10% discount in shops if you ask for it. Good buys are gems (especially topaz, aquamarine, and amethyst), antique silver, alligator bags, wood carvings. Buy fabrics rather than ready-made clothing as the workmanship is often inferior in the latter. But shoes are well-made. The main department stores are Sloper (Rue do Ouvidor), Mesbla (off Praca Mahatma Gandhi), Sears (Praia de Botafogo). There is a "hippie" fair at Ipanema on Sunday from 9 AM to sunset where you can pick up handmade items. For the children on your list, pick up Bahiana dolls and kites.

CANADA: Hours are the same as ours. Best buys are furs, deerskin leather, British woolens, Nova Scotia weavings, British Columbian jade, and cigars. Children on your list will like totem poles, Indian moccasins, and dolls. The good reputable department stores which operate throughout the country are Eaton's, Simpsons-Sears, and The Bay Company.

CHILE: (SANTIAGO) Best buys are copperware, Chilean woolens, lapis lazuli jewelry, Chilean wine, leather goods. The main department stores in Santiago are Los Govelinos and Flano and Rosenblith. Buy your clothes at Cador (Merced 732) or pick up a gift of clothes for that man back home at Juven's (Huérfanos 1034).

COLOMBIA: (BOGOTÁ) Buy emeralds—they're cheaper here than anywhere else in the world. Fine jewelry shops in Bogotá are Willis F. Bronkie y Cia (in the Bavaria Building) and H. Stern (in the Hotel Bogotá Hilton). Another good buy, though certainly less expensive, are ponchos made from Colombian wool; these have an added asset in that they're practically waterproof, being made with a natural oil *in* the wool which is water-resistant. Buy one for $12-$15 at Almacen Tropicana in the Hotel Tequendama. For native handicrafts go to Artesanias de Colombia. The main shopping area of Bogotá is on Cannera 7.

CURAÇAO: Widest selection of duty-free goods are at Willemstad: sound and movie equipment, Dutch tiles, Delftware, Swiss watches, French perfumes, china, silver, liquor, Oriental silks, Spanish shawls. The Punda area of Willemstad is the chief tourist shopping haunt and rightly so. The main shopping streets are Heerenstraat, Breedestraat, and Madourostraat. For anything good (from jewelry to china), go to Spritzer & Fuhrmann, Ltd. (They have 5 stores in town.)

DENMARK: (COPENHAGEN) Store hours are from 9-5:30, Saturdays 9-2 PM, Friday night until 7 PM. Shop in the pedestrian precinct known as Strøget. Check out Georg Jensen for modern silver jewelry. Margit Brandt is the best-known Danish designer. Den Permanente offers new Danish designs in crystal, stainless steel, modern furniture (which is still a good buy—about 40% less than you'd paid here—even when you consider transportation costs). Magasin du Nord is a superb department store, and Illums Bolighus will make you drool over their marvelous home designs: they have everything for the hostess. For Bing & Grøndahl porcelain go to Amagertorv 5. For furs 30% below U.S. prices, go to the reputable Birger Christensen (Østergade 38). A great fabric shop is Per Reumert (Hyskenstraede 1). A chic, youthful sportswear boutique is Bee Cee (Østergade 24). The equivalent of the Danish Brooks Brothers is Brodrene Andersen (Østergade 7-9)—keep that in mind for the men on your list. For finished or to-be-finished-by-you needlework go to Clara Weaver (Østergade 42). For the little ones at home, bring back toys from Thorngreen (Vimmelskaftet 34). Savings tip: don't take anything of value *with* you: if you have it sent directly to your home, you'll get a 15% discount.

DOMINICAN REPUBLIC: Their free port shopping area is La Zona Franca. Calle el Conde is the main shopping street in Santo

Domingo. Go to Mimosa Boutique for locally made women's clothes. Or to Noa-Noa for gifts of men's clothing. The Mercado Modelo is *the* place for island artifacts. The Dominican Republic has the lowest-priced amber in the world.

EGYPT: (CAIRO) Haggle at the Khan El Khalili Bazaar in the middle of the Old City and the larger bazaar on Mousky Road. Best department stores are Hanneau, Circural and Chemla, all on 26 July Street. Smart shoppers buy lengths of printed cottons, leathergoods and gold and silver jewelry. And Egyptian primitive paintings are truly lovely and colorful.

EQUADOR: (QUITO) Shops are open 9 AM-1 PM and 2:30 PM-6:30 PM. The best shopping in Quito is to be found in the Avenida Colon and in the arcades under the Government Palace on Avenida Guayaquil, around the Plaza de Independencia. La Ronda Street in the old section of town has nice tourist shops. There is an Indian Market on Calle 24 de Mayo, every Tuesday. Good buys are woolen ponchos, rugs in brilliant colors (bring along a color sample of the room you're going to decorate), embroidered blouses, raffia place mats and other handicrafts. Children will enjoy embroidered shirts, native reed flutes, and ski caps.

FINLAND (HELSINKI) Shops are open 8:30-5 PM, with 8 PM closings on either Fridays or Mondays. Saturday closings are 4 PM in winter, 3 PM in summer. First go to the Finnish Design Center (Kasarmikatu 19) for displays of the best Finnish weaving, furniture, silver, whatever. While you can't buy anything in this nonprofit center, the people can direct you to places where you can purchase any item that has caught your fancy. I would not advise shipping home that great-looking Finnish glassware, since packaging, shipping and insurance will negate the savings. The main shopping areas are around the Palace Hotel, the Hotel Helsinki, and Senate Square. For less "polished" native wares, go to the Market Square any day (except Sunday) from 7 AM to 1 PM. Opposite the Central Railway Station there is an underground shopping center with stores open till 10 PM, including Sundays. Stockmann's (Aleksanterinkatu 52) is a justly world-famous department store. Best buys in Finland: jewelry, porcelain, handwoven rya rugs (they make great wall hangings as well as floor coverings), ceramics, decorative wood, furs, and textiles.

FRANCE: (PARIS) The hours for shops are as individualistic as the people operating them. Fancy stores are open Monday and closed Saturday while department stores close Mondays except for the summer months, but they are open Saturdays. Small shops close for a couple of hours at lunch, while the big guys stay open. Best buys are perfumes, gloves, lingerie, sacheted scarves and lingerie cases, and gourmet foods. The top shops are on the Faubourg St. Honoré, Arcades de Rivoli. The department stores are Aux Trois Quartiers, Bon Marché, Au Printemps, Galeries Lafayette, Samaritaine de Luxe, and the boutiques of the Grand Couturiers. Since you'll probably be unable to go to the courturier houses of Dior, Chanel, Givenchy, and St. Laurent, stop in at their chic boutiques, which are less expensive than their courtier parents. Dior does have dreamy lingerie . . . as does Cadalle (14 rue Cambon) and Cordelia (21 rue Cambon). French lingerie is beautiful and seductively exquisite, but the top half does not seem to fit American women as well as the bottom part. If you're really loaded, buy a fabulously expensive Hérmes handbag (Princess Grace does). Or pick up gorgeous alligator bags. (Do it without a heavy heart. Alligators are proliferating so in Florida, they're going to remove them from the endangered species list.) And beaded handbags cost half what they would back home. Buy a hat to wear in Paris, even if you don't wear one anywhere else; they somehow feel right there! A good spot for such a top is Willoughby, 7 rue de Castiglione. For gloves and scarves go to Denise Francelle at 244 rue de Rivoli. Buy great-looking costume jewelry at Line Vautrin (3 rue de l'Université). For what must be the sexiest bath essence you've ever indulged in, go to Charles Blair at 374 rue St. Honoré. You can pick up *haute couture* sample dresses at Anna Lowe's shop on the Avenue Matignon; they're about the best bargain in Paris except for finding something really good amid the overpriced junk at the Flea Market at Porte de Clignancourt (Sat., Sun., Mon.). Trousselier on boulevard Haussmann has bouquets of handcrafted silk. Buy inexpensive (relatively) French art at the tiny galleries on the atmospheric

"You'll probably find
a psychiatrist reverently
touring Sigmund Freud's
old stomping grounds in Vienna;
chances are you'll meet
a writer or two at Hemingway's
old haunt in Key West."

streets of Montparnasse and St.-Germain-des-Prés. Sevrés and Limoges porcelain is expensive, but still half what you would pay at home. Ditto beautiful Baccarat crystal. If you're a gourmet cook, you'll go wild over the gallic cooking items at de Hillerin (18 rue Coquillière). And to further please your taste buds, you'll find the world-famous Fauchon edibles at 24-26-28 place de la Madeleine. And while at Fauchon, buy your perfume (it's certainly reputable). For the children on your list, go to Au Nain Bleu on Rue St.-Honoré for wonderful toys, or buy lovely children's items at Chez Perrette (15 bis, rue de Marignon); at the latter you'll be helping the mentally handicapped who have crafted these gorgeous items. Sommer (15 Passage des Princes) is the Dunhill of Paris, so pick up a pipe for a friend there—or for yourself if you're *that* liberated. Name stores make their sale merchandise available to you at self-service places such as Prisunic or Monoprix. More ways to save money (and you'll need them in this expensive country): always ask if you're eligible for the 17-20% discount available, and carry your passport since you must produce it for such a savings; and stay clear of the airport shops in the International Zone at Orly since virtually none of their products are tax free. More warnings: Neither furs nor shoes are a good buy; the former are too expensive and the latter don't fit American feet. Don't buy perfumes anyplace except established shops . . . or you'll end up with "Essence of Dimestore." Don't plan to surprise your male friends with French ties (they're better in England and Italy) or shirts (they're also better in London). Nylons are poor quality. And don't buy mechanical anythings—they're just not reliable, even in reliable stores.

GERMANY: Shops are open from 8-6:30 weekdays; Saturdays, 9 AM when they stay open until 4 PM. Best buys: cameras (Rollei, Zeis, Leica), cutlery, Rosenthal and Meissen porcelain, crystal, fine china figurines, leather goods, and eyeglasses. Children will love you if you bring them back cuckoo clocks, electric trains, and leather shorts. And a really good thing to stock up on for the rest of your European travels are German nylon stockings (called perlon and very long-wearing). Get the 11 percent tax reduction by having goods sent directly out of the country.

GREECE: (ATHENS) Shops are open 8 AM-2 PM and 5 PM-8 PM. From 2 to 5 PM they're closed for lunch. Buy handwoven fabrics, clothing, wall tapestries, long-haired rugs (called flocates), decorative plates, handworked jewelry. When buying icons (particularly when they appear ancient), be aware that special export permits are required. And remember that hand-embroidered peasant blouses look more apropos in Greece than in Chicago! Do try clothing on since Greek women are shorter and broader than we are. Frankly, much Greek clothing is pretty dowdy, but one zingy exception is Tseklenis's clothing—found in his shop near Constitution Square. For exquisite handwoven ladies' coats, capes, dresses, and slacks ensembles go to Levantis (3 Nikis Street). The prices on furs are low, so you may be tempted to buy them; don't—the quality is poor. If you want Greek gold jewelry, see Ilias Lalaounis at 6 Panepistimious Avenue or at the Athens Hilton. If you're into needlepoint, shop at Erghohiro, Voulis St. 18. Marvelous women's botiques are Kouros on Syntagma Square and Contessina at #12 Boukourestiou. The main shopping areas for clothing and Greek handicrafts in general are along the main streets right off Constitution (Syntagma) Square and around the Plaka district. To be specific for a moment, the best place for really good souvenirs of *any* price range is A. Martin's Attika Giftshops (6 Constitution Square). And while you're at the Square, buy the sponges from the vendor there—they're much cheaper than ones purchased in the States and are great for putting on make-up. For baby gifts, meander over to Vaghenas (Kanari and Merlin Streets). To find a gift for men, stroll over to the Bon Ton, Stadiou 4 and 25. Hand-embroidered slippers, shawls, and handbags have superior workmanship, but the designs are a bit Peoria circa 1952. If Rhodes is on your itinerary, save your shopping for there since prices are much lower due to a special tax deal. Don't buy *any* imports *anywhere* in Greece because of the very high tax.

HAITI: (PORT-AU-PRINCE) Best buys are the high-quality Haitian "primitive" art (painting and sculpture). Find it at the Centre D'Art, 17 Rue de la Révolution, or at Issa's on Avenue Chile. Good buys are Haitian rugs, German cameras, French perfumes and Swiss watches. Go to Jacqueline's or Hanotte for clothing. Brightly-colored Haitian-made clothes are best at Sue's Boutique on the way to Pétionville, and Carlos on Avenue Pie XII. For a department store loaded with Wedgewood Royal Worcester china. Omega watches and Georg Jensen silver at half of the stateside costs, go to La Belle Creole on Rue Bonne Foi. Bargain at the Iron Market for local items.

HONG KONG: Shops are open 9 AM to 10 PM every day. Hotel shops are only open until 6 PM. This is the grandmother of all shopping paradises, but it is not the place it used to be . . . but then what is?

Prices are bargain, but not outrageous ones like in the good old days sans inflation, Oriental prosperity, and rising wages. You can spend a whole day (at least) at the Ocean Terminal, Asia's largest shopping complex, in Kowloon. But before you go *anywhere*, pick up "Stop and Shop" by the Hong Kong Tourist Association for names of reliable stores; don't shop anywhere which doesn't display the HKTA sign. And if something isn't cricket with your dealings at those HKTA stores, report it to the Association, on the 35th floor of Connaught Center in Hong Kong. Since most women want to have at least something custom made, be aware that silk is a better buy than cotton since the former is woven in Hong Kong while the latter is imported. And wool is a good buy since it's easier to cut and thus your chances of getting a bad fit are reduced. Hong Kong brocades are a unique good buy but are very dressy, so get them only if you have someplace to wear them. If you want a whole area of fabrics, stroll through Cloth Lane (appropriately named) on Wing On Street. Fine accessories such as custom-made snakeskin shoes and hand-beaded evening bags are good values. Some good dress shops, in descending price order, where you can buy ready-made clothes are: the Dynasty Salon in the Peninsula, Sheraton and Hilton hotels; Things at 13 D'Aguilar Street; and for zingy clothes, the International Dress Shop in the Ocean Terminal. For custom-made clothes, go to the Joyce Boutique, Mandarin Hotel; the Thai Salon at 96 Nathan Road; Elegant Fashions (a great spot for tailor-made leather goods) at 12 D'Aguilar Street; and Sifal Ltd. in the Ocean Terminal for batiks. Only have shoes made for you if you wear a standard size at home. If you do, your best bets are King's Shoes and the Mandarin, Furama and Excelsior hotels, as well as Benny's Footwear Co., 15 Cameron Road., Kowloon. Allow as much time and as many fittings for shoes as for dresses. I once had so many fittings (they just couldn't seem to get them right—or maybe they were trying to bind my feet!) that the shoes had to be delivered to my *plane* since time had literally run out. It was certainly not worth the aggravation.

If you ever want to check the authenticity of your jewelry purchase, go to Sennet Frères, 5 Pedder Street, for a reasonably-

priced gem appraisal. Save further money on your jewelry purchases by carrying them back to the States unstrung—you'll save 3-
33% in duty charges. And you can save about 10% by bringing
back unset gems; have them design the setting and airmail it home
while you carry the gem with you. For watches, I would suggest
Lane Crawford Ltd., Des Voeux Rd., Hong Kong, or Manson House,
Nathan Rd., Kowloon. Again, as with jewels, Crawford's doesn't
offer the "bargains" that some of the other shops do, but they also
don't replace the mechanism of a name watch with a junk one. For
excellent optical goods at less than U.S. prices, go to the Hong Kong
Optical Co., 57 Queen's Rd., Hilton Hotel, Hong Kong, or the Ocean
Terminal in Kowloon. While the frames and lenses are superb, the
opticians are usually not as well trained as the home team, so bring
a written prescription from home or have the optician simply copy
the lenses you already have. Cameras and radios are also good buys
—and even better ones if you ask for the 10% discount which they
will probably grudgingly give you. Go to Central Camera on Pedder
Street and Asia Photo on Ice House Street in Hong Kong or Kowloon's Asia Photo on Humphrey's Avenue. And always buy from a
reputable dealer to be sure the parts aren't from Tangier! Watch
that watch sale! Other shopping notes of miscellany: that ever-
present phenomenon, the flea market, is on Hollywood Road; there
are herbalists' shops scattered about where you can buy cure-alls
from preserved eel to rhino-horn powder; and (from the ridiculous
to the sublime) Cat Street has antiques and bric-a-brac.

HUNGARY: Shops are open 10-6. Frankly, there's not much to buy if
the main recommendation is paprika. Really! It's their native spice
and is available in both sweet and hot types and is a perfect gift for
you or your gourmet friends. So are the local wines. Any half-way
decent-looking clothes are imported from somewhere else, so wait
until you get *there* to buy. Children will enjoy wooden toys and
small curios.

INDIA: Stores are open from 8:30 AM to 5:30 PM. For fixed and good
quality of regional crafts go to the state-run emporia. If you go to a
street pedlar, you must bargain or pay three times the going rate!
Buy ivory, embroidered slippers, Kashmiri paisley shawls, silk

hostess costumes and papier-mâché or clay toys for the kids. Warning: if shipping anything home, *watch* while they affix the stamps—people there are so poor that stealing stamps significantly improves their standard of living! This isn't chauvanistic Americana speaking; there used to be signs in the post offices warning you of this! Although I think women are usually sorry about saris, I'll give you some information about them if you're going to go ahead and buy one anyway. Though I still bet that if you wear it *once* back home, it will be once too often. If you do buy a sari, that is just the beginning. You'll also have to have a blouse (choli) and a long skirt petticoat, not to mention the skills of draping the whole thing and then moving like a graceful Indian woman. Different areas of India have different types of materials—the south favors heavy silks and vivid contrasting colors; Benares is big on brocades; Benga specializes in off-white shot with gold; Rajasthan opts for gay "tie and dye" patterns. The costliest fabrics are often the Jamdani muslins—it takes eight men one whole day to weave a single inch!

INDONESIA: Stores are open from 9 AM to 5 or 6 PM. Batik material is the pride of Indonesia and can be found in Djakarta at G.K.B.I. on Dj. H.A. Salim. Wood and stone carvings are also beautifully done here and the best bet is the Djalan Nusantara area. Or go to the arcade of the Hotel Indonesia. But if you can get away from Djakarta, do; it's really not worth visiting when you compare it to the charms of Bali, and if you do get to that enchanted island, you will find that the workmanship is finer and prices are lower. Go to the Bali Art Foundation in Denpasar for the finest and most reasonable Balinese arts and crafts.

IRAN: (TEHRAN) With the sudden spurt of oil money, prices have risen drastically, so bargains are few. I would recommend the Atosa Jewelry and Partieh Jewelry stores in Tehran. And for Persian handicrafts, the Government Handcraft Centers on Takhte Jamshied and 296 Villa Avenue are *the* places to go. You can also bargain in the bazaar in the southern section of the city—this is a great place for sheepskins and copper, but know *before* you go.

IRELAND: (DUBLIN) Before you buy anything in town, keep in mind that the largest duty-free shopping area in Europe is at the Shannon Airport. The best department stores (Brown Thomas and Switzer's) are on the best all-round shopping street, Grafton St. For jewelry, look for Market Ireland. Go to the Irish Cottage Industries at 18 Dawson Street for marvelous tweeds. I would buy the tweed material and have it designed there or at home, rather than buying anything ready-made, since their clothes are terribly dowdy at whatever price. Irish linens have been renowned for ages, and while they're beautiful and cool for summer, they also wrinkle like a rag unless you stand up the entire time you're wearing them! The only type of ready-made clothing I would recommend are Aran fisherman's sweaters. Waterford and Galway hand-cut crystal are beautiful and less expensive than you would pay stateside. Actually, Ireland is more of a place to load up on gifts for men than for yourself; please them with beautiful sports vests, sweaters and Peterson pipes. You can save the Value Added Tax (6.7%-19.5%) if you have items sent directly home or in bond to your plane or ship.

ISRAEL: Shops are open from 9 AM-1 PM, and 4-7 PM, except on Fridays, when they close at 2 PM. They close three hours for lunch and all day Saturdays. (However, they're open on Sundays.) Best buys are tax- and duty-free diamonds, Yemenite handiwork, olive-wood artifacts, bargain-priced furs, copper, leather goods, children's dolls and embroidered shirts. Check the "Tourist Shopping Guide" from the Ministry of Tourism and then check out the stores with the "Recommended for Tourist" sign.

ITALY: (ROME) Shops are open from 9 AM to 1 PM, and from 3:30 or 4:30 PM to 7 PM. They usually close for a couple of hours at lunch, and for half a day on any of the plentiful Feast Days. As you can see by the varied shopping hours, it's hard to pin them down—so check with a specific store before traipsing through that crazy Roman traffic! Good buys are antiques, silver, lingerie, silks, Venetian glass, lace, knits, mohair coats, and gold jewelry (weighed and numbered in Italy). Children will love you for bringing back statues of Pinocchio, toys, and dolls. For toys go to E. Guffanti (Via Due Macelli 59). The best department store in Rome is CIM. The toniest shopping area in Rome is now the Via Borgognona's pedestrian mall. At the other end of the price range is the bargain area, Via Cola Di Rienzo. If there's a man at the end of your trip you want to impress, bring him something from Brioni (Via Barberini 79)—but only go here if the relationship is worth a steep price tag! For glamourous lingerie to wear in that special Brioni relationship, go to Cesari (1 Via Barberini) or Trepiedi (Piazza Lucina 36); indeed, the latter is supposed to give an uplift to some of our better-known international stars. Pick up an absolutely unwrinkable silk jersey dress (which can fold up into the size of nothing) for the rest of your trip—it's at La Mendola (Piazza Trinita dei Monti 15); Laura Aponte (Via Gesu e Maria 10) is another place for lightweight, uncrushable and very packable knits. For jewelry fit for a queen (in the good old days) or a shah (in the not-so-good new days), you must go to Bulgari (Via Condotti 10); if you can't afford to buy, then go to look—missing it would be like missing the Louvre in Paris. For reasonable and superior quality gloves, go to Catello d'Auria (Via Due Macelli 55)—but only if you'll really wear the gloves at home; I purchased seven pairs of gloves in 1963 and haven't worn any of them since. If your nylon collection has run down (pun intended), this is a good place to stock up, since Italian pantyhose fit better and wear longer than ours. Pick them up at Eredi P. Caraffa (Via Lazio 10). Gucci (Via Condotti 21) is still the status leather with prices to match. Natch. If you're running low on drugs and/or toiletries, go to Lepetit Farmacia (Corso Umberto 417). What Chinese herbalists are to Hong Kong, so is the Officina Profumo Farmaceutica (16 Via della Scala) to Rome. Here you'll find a freckle remover (virgin milk), antihysterical water, sachets made from powdered iris root and so on through a myriad display of exotica. It's no flash in the pan, however, having been around since 1612! Being a good sport, you might wish to indulge. Buy antiques at one of the many antique shops on the Via de' Coronari. For a good cross-section of gifts for anyone on your list, go to Fendi (Via Borgognona 36 A/B); this is a bit of a pricey jet-set place. BEWARE: (1) the worst flea market (the Porta Portese) in the world; (2) the world center of purse-snatching; and (3) the world's worst postal service—get around it by registering anything you have to mail or lugging it with you and mailing it from another country.

JAMAICA: Go to the duty-free shops in Kingston, Montego Bay and Ocho Rios. For clothes boutiques go to the Sheraton Kingston Hotel area. In Kingston go to the Things Jamaican workshop and store for native handcrafts. Caribatik is the name for batik clothing and since it's been designated by the U.S. government as art, there's no duty on it. So pick it up at Caribatik stores in Montego Bay, Port Antonio, or Ocho Rios. The best shopping areas in Montego Bay are along Gloucester Avenue, the coast road, and the Beachview Arcade across from the Doctor's Cave Beach. In Ocho Rios go to the shopping complexes at Pineapple Place and Coconut Grove.

JAPAN: (TOKYO) Stores are open from 10 AM-7 PM, open Sundays but closed one other day of the week (it varies). This is the land where the department store has reached new heights—literally. They are cities within cities and have anything you want from food to kimonos to lacquerware to precious gems to rooftop zoos, kabuki performances, and art galleries. These mammoth department stores are in the Nihonbashi and Ginza areas. Most have an information desk for foreign patrons on the ground floor, although their English is not always as good as would be expected from people in that position; I once wanted the ladies' room, and drew a picture of a toilet after I saw they didn't understand spoken English, and they nodded and smiled and directed me to the antique chairs! At least it was something to sit on. These stores have all the good buys of Japan: pearls, damascene, fans, bambooware, lacquerware, woodblock prints, silk fabrics, fans, transistor tape recorders, radio and television sets, cameras. While the department stores do have electrical appliances, you'd be wiser to go to the Akihabara area for loads of electrical appliance *discount* stores. A good gift for that man on your list is the distinctive menuki jewelry obtainable at the Japan Sword Shop at B Avenue and 12th Street. Silver in Japan is about half of what it would cost stateside, but since it's a bit softer, it does tend to scratch easily. Japanese pottery has taken hold on the world market, with the best recognized being Noritake. It's cheap and good, as are Satsuma, Kutani, Bizen and Awaji. Satsuma can be rather garish, with a tendency towards a lot of gold decorations. Kutani specializes in elaborate and brightly colored pictures. Bizen is big on animal decorations and Awaji favors monochromatic designs. Department stores have the best selection of these. Lacquer has developed into a beautiful art in Japan over the last 600 years. Lacquer soup bowls are a hostess's delight and boxes can be used to hold everything from hair clips to cigarettes. If getting a box, make certain the top lifts off since anything with hinges seems to come unhinged rather shortly! The best lacquerware can be found at the Yamada Heiando, behind the Takashimaya department store. DON'TS: (1) Don't buy their shoes—they'll never have anything your size unless you have a tiny foot. (2) Don't buy their clothes—they simply won't fit us since we're built so differently. I think American women look ridiculous in kimonos—we're too busty, too hippy, and don't do the right things with the backs of our necks, which the Japanese consider *the* erogenous zone. But if you insist, at least just get a summer garment—it'll be cheaper, easier to get into, more comfortable once you're into it, and it doesn't need an obi (waist sash). This fair-weather item is called a yukata and makes a comfortable housecoat. If you do decide to get a yukata, kimono, or happi coat (a hip-length jacket), go where they can be had cheaply. Which is to say, go to the Kimon Mart at 10th Street and T Avenue. (3) Don't buy silk yardage. The best designs go for the kimono and obi materials which aren't the right size for western duds. (4) Don't bargain anywhere in Japan; it's considered bad form. All items are marked. You are entitled to eliminate the regular Japanese purchase tax (up to 20%) on certain items if you buy at a shop with a window sign saying "tax-free" sales. As you purchase any tax-exempt items, the shopkeeper will attach a "record of purchase of commodities tax-exempt" to your passport. When you leave Japan, customs will collect these "records" and confirm that you are taking the purchased items with you. You may also send purchases by mail, in which case the post office will give you a certificate to be attached to your passport. **MEXICO: (MEXICO CITY)** Shops are open from 9 AM-6 PM, with some closing from noon to 2 PM. The main shopping areas are the Pink Zone, off Reforma on Amberes, Génova, Hamburgo, Niza

Londrés. On Sunday go to the Flea Market at La Lagunilla. Look for silver in the good silver shops in the Génova-Niza area; genuine sterling must have a spreadeagle hallmark on it. Leather is a good buy if you can be sure that the whole item is leather and not just a thin strip of it glued over plastic; to be sure you're getting the real thing, go to the places along Calle Pino Suárez. Copper is beautiful and practically eternal if you find the good stuff and not something iron over which someone has sprayed copper paint! Don't get fleeced when buying serapes; they should be all wool. Make certain that those lovely straw baskets have handles which will hold on. I'll break the negative mood with a recommendation for beautiful glassware with no warnings; buy lovely, reasonable glass at the Avalos Brothers' glass factory at Carretones 5.

NETHERLANDS: (AMSTERDAM) Shops are open from 9 AM-6 PM, closed Monday mornings. Good buys are bulbs (they'll tell you what's best for your area), gold and silver items. Delft china, diamonds, ceramics, pewter and copper wares. Amsterdam's shopping district is in the area bordered by Kalverstraat, Heiligeweg and Leidsestraat. The best department stores are De Bijenkorf and Vroom en Dreesmann. Children will love you for bringing home dolls in the Dutch national costume. If you're going to buy a child wooden shoes, trace his/her foot back home and buy several sizes bigger. If you want to buy diamonds, you must go to the most respected place around. Makes sense. That has to be the house of Bonebakker (Rokin 88). They've only been around for 180 years and still have a superb reputation. Your diamonds will be sold tax-free if they're unset or total $450 and can be proved so by a reputable dealer. See why I told you to go to old Bonebakker? If you go to Focke & Meltzer (Kalverstraat 152 and P.C. Hooftstraat 65) you'll find a great selection of Delft china and European crystal. Marvelous antiques (lots of pewter) are tucked away at Frank Eweg Antiek (Klein Duimpje, Grimburgwal 6-8). Is there a cigar-smoking man in your present, but at home? Pick up a little something for him at P.G.C. Hajenius (Rokin 92-96). He'll love the Dutch cigars and cigarillos. The duty-free shop at the Amsterdam airport has savings up to 60%, making it one of the best in the world. But these bargains are only available to those traveling outside the Belgium-Netherlands-Luxembourg area. If you're not able to take advantage of the airport tax-saving situation, stay away from imported perfumes and wines since the tax could practically give you another trip back to Amsterdam.

NEW ZEALAND: (AUCKLAND) Shops are open from 9 PM-5:30 PM, Fridays until 9 PM, and closed Saturdays and Sundays. Just as there isn't much to see in Auckland, there isn't much to buy either. But look around if you must for sheepskin jackets; Maori jewelry, blankets and wood carvings; local greenstone jewelry. Look for these around the main hotels and Queen Street or Milne's and Smith & Caughey Ltd. department stores.

NORWAY: (OSLO) Shop hours are 9 AM-5 PM weekdays, 9 AM-1 PM Saturdays. *Nothing* is open the week before Easter. Good buys are Norwegian enameled silver and jewelry, regional furniture, textiles, handknit sweaters, woodwork (such as cheese boards and salad bowls). Karl Johansgate is the leading shopping street, with the Vika shopping center a new close second. Not to mention the charming collection of small shops, selling everything from jewelry to antiques, at the Bazaar. Don't buy furs here; they aren't properly worked, and the U.S. duty will cancel out any savings. As to shopping savings, you should realize that you can save 12% on your purchases if you buy more than 100 kroner worth of items and have the purchases sent directly to your point of departure. Since this does take a bit of time, don't wait until the last minute. For beautiful crafts go to the Forum (Rosenkrantzgate 7); it's a non-profit operation with beautiful handcrafted items made by Norway's best artists. And everything there is free of the 16⅔% purchase tax. For jewelry go to David-Andersen (Karl Johansgate 20). Go to William Schmidt & Co. (Karl Johansgate 41) for handmade wool sweaters, handbags, ski boots, and gloves made of sealskin. For that justly famous Norwegian copper, go to Bergfjerdingen (Damstredet 5).

PANAMA: Panama is not only a duty-free port, but it also has a good duty-free airport spilling out with transistor radios, tape recorders, electric shavers, cameras and other such gadgets of international appeal. Other good buys are liquor, Danish silver, English bone china, French perfumes and Swiss watches. Panama City's main shopping street is Avenida Central while Colón's is Front Street. Salsipudes off Avenida Central is a colorful waterfront market. Buy your "name" watches at Casa Fastlich, 22 Avenida 7 Central or Tahiti at 137 Avenue Central. Buy silver and gold jewelry at H. Stern's, Riviera or again, Fastlich. Find fine china at Shaw's, 14 Avenue of the Martyrs, Panama City and Front Street in Colón. To buy embroidered linen to go with your new china, stop in at Galeria Panamá, 17-85 Avenida Central or Nueva India at #115 Avenida Central. For perfume and liquor, the most reputable spots are at the El Panamá and El Continental lobby shops: heed this warning since these items are the easiest "fool the tourist" items, with any liquid being a passable substitute. The best bet for dresses is Felix B. Maduro, S.A. on Avenida Central as well as the Chambonet y Quinta Avenida department store. And don't forget to bring back a Panama hat from the American Bazaar.

PERU: (LIMA) Stores are open from 9 AM-1 PM and 3 PM-7:30 PM. Best buys are alpaca fluffy hats, slippers, mufflers, and stoles in natural brown and beige; handwoven wool fabrics; and heavy wool ponchos in oranges and red. Children will love toy llamas and native reed flutes ("quencas"). Don't buy or export their archaeological items—you'll get in big trouble with the law. The best markets in Lima are the Lima Market (Avenida de la Marina) and the Mercado Central (Huallega 650). Diron Union has many good tourist shops.

PHILIPPINES: (MANILA) Best buys are anything of wood, some brassware, pearl and coral products, bamboo items, antique Filipino jewelry, cigars, abaca, and buri palm products. For reputable goods go to the shops in the major hotels or look for luxuries in Manila's Ermita district. Or go to Tesoro's on A. Mabini which is the only place that carries the gay, durable Lepanto fabrics made by mountain weavers. Some top Western couturiers have franchises here, enabling you to pay less for "name" clothes—hop over to the Makati department store for these designers' deals. Berg's (421 Escolta, Manila) is another good department store and is a good place to pick up embroidered wash-and-wear ramie-tetoron dress fabrics. You don't haggle in the better shops but you do on Rizal Avenue. Since the superstitious shopkeepers believe that a good business day will be insured by a good first sale, go early and be that first good sale. It'll be cheaper for you than for the people who go later.

PORTUGAL: (LISBON) Shops are open from 9 AM-1 PM and from 3 PM-7 PM; from June through September they close at 1 PM. (They know how to live.) Save the 15% surtax on luxury goods by paying with a travelers' check or having your purchases delivered to your departure point. Fashionable stores are on the two main streets, Rua Garrett (the "Chiado") and Rua Augusta. The Ritz has marvelous but expensive shops. At the other end of the spending spectrum, there is a market held in Lisbon every Tuesday and Saturday on the Campo de Santa Clara. At this Thieves' Market (I'm not being disparaging—that's what *they* call it), you can find everything from worthless plastic objects to precious art treasures. A best buy in Lisbon is gold jewelry at W.A. Sarmento (Rua do Ouro 251). And go to Joalharia Correia (253-255 Rua Aurea) for filigree work and silver. Stop in at Sereira (Rua S. Bernardo 108) for home accessories, chic clothes, and fabrics. Remember, if you do buy those gorgeous fabrics, to find a good dressmaker in Portugal or at home —and if it's the former, be able to allow plenty of time for fittings in this mañana country. Hand-embroidered goodies lurk at Pavilhao do Madaira, 15 Avenida de Liberdada. Take home some Portugese folk music and Fado records (Valentim de Carvalho, 97 Rua Nova do Almada). Kids will love their painted wooden roosters, beanie hats, and miniature costumes. And cork is to Portugal what perfumes are to France, so buy cork-soled shoes, coasters, playing cards, and chessmen (I can't bring myself to call them chesspersons) at Casa da Corticas (Rua da Escola Politécnica 4).

PUERTO RICO: (SAN JUAN) Best buys are hand-embroidered clothing, hand-carved tortoise shell, Puerto Rican rum, woven mats, records of local music, cigars rolled to your order (wouldn't that be a surprise for *him*?), silk-screened fabrics, and their newly-noticed paintings and sculpture. Shop at the Craft Market at Hornos Militares for local products. Locally-designed women's clothes are best at Martha Sleeper's Shop, 106 Fortaleza in old San Juan. La Casa Del Arte at 152 Fortaleza Street has Puerto Rico's biggest art gallery. Pick out a pretty evening sweater trimmed in lace and ribbons (I like them better than Hong Kong's beaded variety) at The Everglades Shop. Go to Barbara Ann's on the Tourism Pier for original creations in women's and children's wear. Pick up home accessories at Cavanagh's place on the Santurce-Old San Juan road.

SINGAPORE: You'll get good deals at this free port. For the best but riskiest deal, haggle your way through the myriad of tiny shops in Change Alley. Or pay a little more but be sure of what you're getting at Robinsons (Specialist's Center, Orchard Rd.) or C.K. Tang (also on Orchard Rd. and also a department store). Shopping the major arcades (at big hotels or Fitzpatrick's and Cold Storage Supermarkets) ranks below the department stores in reliability, but above the Change Alley shops in that category. Buy jewelry at North Bridge & High Streets. Chinese Emporiums have things from the People's Republic of China—they're quite cheap (the labor there is not exactly union) and you'll find many bargains if you don't mind your money going back to China.

SPAIN: (MADRID) Hours are from 9 AM 1:30 PM and again from 4-8 PM with a virtual abandonment of stores during mid-afternoon for a civilized lunch. Best buys: Spanish handicrafts, home furnishings, fabrics, leather goods, rope-soled shoes, antiques, Toledo jewelry, Spanish tiles, and wrought-iron ware. For the younger set, bring back statues of bullfighters and Don Quixote, not to mention the painstakingly detailed handmade infants' wear. For exquisite hand-embroidered linens that put Jackie O's Porthult to shame, go to Casa Bonet at Zurbano 67 in Madrid. That should just get you started in the embroidery department—so then go to Srta. Emilia de Valeiras (apt. at Diego de León 39) for more fine craftsmanship on lingerie, silk blouses, and beautiful children's dresses. The best women's boutiques are Ungaro (Velázquez 19) and Ted Lapidus (Serrano 53). Haute couture is dreadfully expensive, but if you insist on knowing, the big names for the big prices are Pedro Rodriguez (Alcalá 54), Miguel Rueda (General Oráa 5), and Pertegaz (Generalísimo 12). If that totally depletes your shopping allowance, go to the El Rastro on Sunday morning in the Ribera de Curtidores for thousands of second-hand bargains. Go to Kreisler (Serrano 19) for Spanish handicrafts—he has the best from all Iberia. If you want to take home a special reminder, go to Artespana (Hermosilla 14, Avenida José Antonio 32) for souvenirs. Buy anything leather—from purses to coats to skirts to belts—at the House of Loewe (Avenida de José Antonio 8). Go to Rossy (Serrano 44) for a wild assortment of costume jewelry. For bargain-priced, non-bargain-category French perfume and cosmetics, pop in to Alexandré (Avendia José Antonio at San Luis). You won't believe there is a Sears Roebuck in Madrid, but there is—but it is only to be recommended for emergency replacements like pantyhose. Ditto for their Woolworth's. In general Madrid's best stores are on Avenida José Antonio, Alcalá, Carrera San Jerónimo, Serrano, Sevilla and Peligros. The best department stores (Sears doesn't count in this league) are Galerias Preciados and El Corte Ingles. Shoppers will appreciate the convenience and economy of Madrid's microbus—it's cheaper than a taxi but will take you anywhere along the shopping route. Look for a bus stop with a big "M" in front of the number of the regular bus line it serves. BEWARE of (1) the metal on cheap handbags, since it tarnishes; (2) highly taxed imported items; (3) purchases over $450, because you'll need an export license for anything in excess of that amount; and (4) anything "hawked" by sidewalk vendors.

SWEDEN: (STOCKHOLM) Stores are open from 9:30 AM-6 PM, and until 7 PM on Mondays and Fridays. On Saturdays they're open from 9 AM-2 PM. Best buys are cutlery, glass, silver, antiques, handicrafts, home furnishings, and ceramics. Find everything on the list at the biggest shopping center in northern Europe, Farsta. Or go to the main department stores—NK and Åhléns. Or traipse about the Old Town, the Västerlanggatan, which has charming narrow auto-less streets lined with shops and boutiques. Or go to the Downtown Shopping Center near the Haymarket area. For that gorgeous Swedish glass (especially Orrefors and Kosta) pay about half what you would stateside by shopping at Svenskt Glas (Birger Jarlsgatan 8). For silver and gold baubles in all price ranges, go to

Kurt Decker AB, Biblioteksgatan 12. Warm up your kitchen at home with the copperware you can bring back from Stockholm's A. Lindström (Själagårdsgatan 21). For the best in furs go to Ivan Petersson at Birger Jarlsgatan 6 or Svedberghs at Norrmalmstorg 4. The best women's boutiques are Match (Mäster Samuelsgatan) and La Donna (Kindstugatan 4). Have gold, silver, carpets, liquors and furs sent directly to your home or to your departure point and keep your sales slip to avoid paying the 20% luxury tax in addition to the 20% purchase tax.

SWITZERLAND: (GENEVA) Shop hours are so variable that I'm not going to risk my credibility by mentioning specifics. Since Switzerland is justly famous for its watches, I'll tackle that item first, but do read up on watches in the earlier section of this chapter. You can't go wrong with Bucherer or Gubelin watches, which are found in their branch stores in the major cities in Switzerland. While you can bring in an armload of assorted Swiss watches past our customs, you can only bring in so many of certain brand names. Check, before you write out your check, as to which brands are unrestricted. Besides watches, you'll go wild over Swiss chocolates, antiques, handicrafts, leather goods, and cameras. Geneva's best camera buys are at Photo Mont-Blanc (17 rue de Mont Blanc). If you need to pick up little gifts, go to L'Ile au Trésor (rue du Purgatoire 3). You must get a Swiss music box—they're not just for children (I still love mine); go to La Boîte à Musique (7 rue des Alpes) for these musical masterpieces. The largest drugstore in the world is the Pharmacie Principale at Rue du Marché 11; this potpourri has everything from an Elizabeth Arden salon to bikinis to turtle oil to mod-style clothes. Go to Bon Génie (rue du March 34) for anything that isn't still breathing—that is, clothes and accessories for both sexes and all ages. It ain't cheap though, since Gucci, Cardin, Dior, and others of that ilk lurk there. In general, the smart shops are on the Rue de la Confédération, Rue du Marché, Rue de la Croix and Rue de Rive. For cheaper fare, go to the Flea Market on the Plaine de Plainpalais (Wednesdays and Saturdays, 8 AM-4 PM). You'll hate me for telling you where you can get such good (but caloric) chocolate, but I feel it my duty to give you all the hints—even those that aren't good for you. The best chocolate in Switzerland is made by Lindt & Sprüngli and is available, *unfortunately*, throughout the country.

TAHITI: Shops are open from 7:30 AM to 5 PM with a three-hour lunch closing that varies with each establishment. Most stores are also open Saturday mornings when the mood hits them. Best buys are hand-blocked Polynesian prints, pareo cloth, mother-of-pearl items, brightly colored bikinis, carved wooden tikis, French perfumes and lingerie, paintings on black velvet, shell leis, and—for the kids—grass skirts, outrigger kits, and T-shirts. Buy the gay Tahitian frocks at Marie Ah You and Madame Chin Tin Sou, both in Papeete. Vanilla beans will impress your gourmet friends—and they're only a nickle apiece here! French perfumes and lingerie are about half the price they would be stateside—if you could even get them. Go to the municipal market in Papeete for some Sunday morning shopping.

TAIWAN: (TAIPEI) The best place to get the local crafts is at the Taiwan handicraft Promotion Center, 1 Hsuchow Rd., or any of the many such stores along Chungshan N. Rd. Shish Lin (a Taipei suburb) has a great assortment of bamboo items. For coral and jade jewelry go to Hengyang Road. Children will love the Taiwanese puppets you bought at Haggler's Alley. Buy delicate lacquerware at Mme. Chen (151 Changchun Rd.). Purchase small brass items for the home at George and Sydney Brassware (170-1 Chungshan N. Rd., Sec. 2). Since Taiwan has the only ramie fiber rugs, purchase one at E-E, 33 Changan W. Rd. Silks and damasks are spilling over at Hung Hsianh Department Store, 122 Po Ai Rd. Your packages will get home safely and quickly if you take them to the Central Post Office; come prepared with a waterproof magic marker and extra cushioning material.

THAILAND: (BANGKOK) Store hours are 9 AM-6 PM with the Thai Handicrafts Center open every single day of the week. Thai silks have been famous for years, but before you buy these shimmering, gorgeous colors, be forewarned that they wrinkle as soon as you sit down and stay wrinkled until ironed. The most famous (for color, not wrinkling!) are those at the Thai Silk Company at 9 Suriwong

Rd. Look for Shinawatra's soil-release, wash and wear, non-crease Thai silk—ditto with their Thai cotton; find these wonders at their shop at 302 Silom Road. If you can find anything handwoven from the northern Chiangmai area, buy it. I saw identical things at the exclusive Gump's in San Francisco for ten times what I paid in Chingmai. Star sapphires, star rubies, semi-precious stones, silver and gold are good buys at Alex & Company, 14 Oriental Avenue, and the Siam Intercontinental and Dusit Thani hotels. Many women buy princess rings, which are shaped like a crown and made of gold with nine different stones arranged in circular form. Thai Nielloware is a unique type of silver with inlaid designs which appear black when held at an angle but look white when seen straight. See H. Sena and Company, Oriental Avenue for this special kind of silver. Pick up beautiful lacquerware and carved wood at Thai Home Industries, Oriental Avenue. Unique to Thailand is celadon pottery which you can purchase at Celadon (naturally) House, Silom Road. Pick up gifts for men at John Fowler's Man's Shop (Plaenchi Center). For the kids on your list, bring back teak spirit houses, leather shadow puppets, and paper parasols.

TURKEY: (ISTANBUL) Oriental jewelry, leather goods, marble and alabaster articles, small carpets, mocha grinders and cups, and Turkish waterpipes are the things to take home from here. Recommended shops are along Istiklal Caddesi Street and the Grand Bazaar.

UNITED KINGDOM: (LONDON) Shop hours vary surprisingly for this otherwise orderly people. The general rule is open from 9 AM-5:30 PM, Saturdays open to either 1 PM or 5:30 PM. Big stores have one night open per week and it varies from store to store. On Sundays everything is blotto. Best buys are cashmeres, tartans, silver, china, leather goods, antiques, rare books, and English flower perfumes. Carnaby Street is about as "in" as white socks and ankle bracelets. The new way-out boutique center for trendy clothes is King's Road. For young styles that are less far out than King's Road, try the chic stores on Bond Street and in Chelsea. English attempts at *haute couture* are rather dismal—nothing against Queen Elizabeth personally, but just look at the way *she* dresses! Since the English version of high fashion is wearing dowdy, loose-fitting clothes, I suggest you forego high fashion ready-mades or tailoring. Another no-no: British nylons seem to last as long as it takes to get out the front door. For cashmeres and tartans go to W. Bill Ltd., 93 New Bond Street, London. The English should know about rainwear since they live in a perpetually damp climate—which may account for their marvelous Burberry raincoats. Check them out at the House of Burberry, 18 Haymarket. Many of you might be hooked on Sonia Rykiel or Missoni, since they've been massively exported to the U.S.; find them and other gorgeous (though not cheap) items at Brown's (27 South Molton Street). For smaller budgets, go to Laura Ashley (Harriet Street and Fulham Road). One of the few places outside of American shores to cater to that peculiar American "last" for shoes is Alan McAfee (38 Dover Street). One of the most famous department stores in the world is located right in London; it's Harrods on Brompton Road, and I defy you to come up with one thing they don't have! Marks and Spencer department store is less expensive and will allow you to return clothing after trying it on back in your hotel. Lillywhites is the Abercrombie and Fitch of Great Britain. The most famous flea-type market is Portobello Road on Saturday mornings. It does cost a few bucks to get there by cab, but it'll be worthwhile for the people-watching even if you don't buy a thing. That marvelous English flower perfume is wafting through the air at the House of Floris (89 Jermyn Street). Find unusual small gifts for that hard-to-please person waiting for you back home at Rally (11 Grosvenor Street). If there's a man anywhere in your life at present, you must go into Dunhill (30 Duke Street, St. Jame's S.W. 1)—other pipe and smoker's shops are always compared to this standard of the trade. If you're not going to get your man a smoking gift, go to James Lock & Co., Ltd. (6 St. James Street) for really fine men's accessories. If you're into needlework, thread your way to the Tapestry Bazaar (20 Beauchamp Place). For gag souvenirs (like canned London fog) try The Old Curiosity Shop (13/14 Portsmouth Street). Whether or not you have a fortune to spend on art, go over to the world-famous Sotheby's (34-35 New Bond Street); actually, it's much less imposing than publicity would indicate, since most of their items are less than $250. You just *hear* about the $1,000,000 ones! For classic English antiques and china, head for The General Trading Company (Mayfair) Ltd. (144 Sloane Street, Sloan Square). The duty-free shops at London's Heathrow airport are about the most expensive in Europe. So do your buying elsewhere. Always mention that you're a tourist (accents aren't always sure indicators) so you'll be saved the British Purchase Tax (5%-33⅓%).

U.S.S.R. (MOSCOW) Stores are open from 8 AM-8 PM, with some closing for lunch and most closing on Mondays. For a non-capitalistic country, I've found no country more eager for those American dollars! Prices are high and quality low. The clothes are twenty years behind what they're wearing in Dubuque and their perfume is less preferable than b.o. And don't buy those poorly worked furs or anything mechanical. (Just where are you going to have it serviced?) These aren't political judgements; they're objective consumer ones. The best buys are Russian vodka and phonograph records. Other good buys are black caviar, Ukranian hand-embroidered skirts or blouses, fur hats, and that traditional Russian wooden doll with smaller and smaller and smaller ones inside. (I still have one my grandmother brought over more than 80 years ago!) GUM is the name of the Moscow department store, but, alas, their souvenir department is filled with really junky tourist items. For better souvenirs than you'll find at GUM, go to the Russian Souvenir Shop (9 Kutuzovsky Prospekt). Hard currency stores are called Beriozka where, as I mentioned, they'll be only too happy to take your dollars. Such stores are found in large hotel lobbies. Small stores are best found on Gorky Street. Shops do not mail things abroad for you, so buy light little items you can tuck in your suitcase.

VENEZUELA: (CARACAS) Best buys are gold jewelry and pearls, leather goods, woven capes, and local arts and crafts. The best handicraft stores in Caracas are the Palacio de Las Industrias (Calle Real, Sabana Grande) and Arte Folklorico (Conde and Principal). Cacique coins can be made into great bracelets and other types of jewelry. You can get one that relates to your occupation or profession. Ask. Buy the pearls that come from the waters of Margarita Island. Buy the "at home" dresses which the Guajiro Indians make at very reasonable prices. Piñatas are large, hollow papier mâché figures filled with tiny gifts. Children love them for all the surprises they hold. The best buys are at the free port shopping area at Porlamar on Margarita Island—so if you're going there, don't buy in Caracas. If you stay on the island a minimum of three days and are not under 18 years old, you can purchase up to $200, duty free. To take advantage of this, you must buy (for a small fee) a card from the tourist office; then, when you buy at the numbered Duty Free Shops, they'll check off your purchases on the card.

U.S. VIRGIN ISLES: (CHARLOTTE AMALIE) Main Street is lined with stores selling cameras, watches, perfume, liquor, jewelry at free port prices. Tortoise-shell jewelry, rubies, sapphires and pearls are also good buys. The Wadsworth Boutique has interesting jewelry, scarves and other accessories. The Countrystore has a nice selection of needlepoint and crewel kits. The Stowaway Boutique has African beachwear, German cosmetics and English dresses. Bobbie's Island Dresses has custom-made clothes.

YUGOSLAVIA: (BELGRADE) Stores are open from 8 AM-noon, and 4 PM-8 PM. That four hours in-between is when everything is shuttered for lunch. Unfortunately for the devout shopper, the best clothes are expensive imports, so stick with native handicrafts (wooden carvings, ceramics, metal and copper hand-hammered souvenirs, handwoven textiles) from Fontane (Knez Mijailova 2-4). Children will like the embroidered peasant blouses, but they'll be a bit too much for *you* to wear. They're a bit overdone, but children will find them merely gay.

So return home without a sou or yen or franc or ruble, but with a reminder of your fabulous experience!

About
How to Get
About

BUS STOP

TAKING BUSES *within* a city is a time-consuming but good way to meet the people and save money. But try to avoid buses at rush hours or you'll be packed in like the proverbial sardines—and since lots of countries aren't very body-odor conscious, you'll be ready to keel over quickly.

21

If you do decide to take a bus, make certain you know their operating hours; most don't run around the clock. And some countries have too many unsavory characters hanging around lonely bus stops to make bus travel a good choice for a single woman.

Many bus drivers don't know English, so you'll save yourself a lot of grief if you have your destination written in the local language. Your hotel desk clerk can do this for you. Better also carry a pocket map or card from your hotel to show drivers. Sit up front where the driver can signal you when to get off. Actually, sitting up front is a good thing for a woman to do at all times; it protects her from the possible assailants who would only try the back of the bus, away from the burly driver.

How to be comfortable on a bus: Carry a sweater for air-conditioned comfort. Get out at rest stops and walk about a bit. Wear sunglasses if you sit up front. (The front windows have less of a tint than side ones, for safety purposes.) Carry a supply of local currency for toilet slots. You'll find yourself on less crowded buses if you travel on non-rush-hour weekdays, avoiding weekends and holidays.

See if you can get a one-ticket pass which allows you to go anywhere in the city within a certain amount of time for one low fare. Intra-city transportation may also include subways or monorails; check on them—sometimes they're better than the local bus system.

Look into the "culture buses" and "mini bus" services that for a very small fee provide an easy way to see high spots. Study the area and decide what's worth coming back to.

Longer-distance tour bus travel is a good way to see more of the countryside than the clouds you see from a 747. See if you can get a double-decker bus (much better view). Many long-distance tour buses have lavatories; make sure the bus you pick has one, but don't sit next to it. If you join a package trip (plane and bus, for example), you can save a lot of money. Ask about an all-inclusive ticket which different countries issue covering unlimited mileage throughout the country for a set rate during a specified time. These are real money-savers which your local travel agent should be able to tell you about.

UP YOUR METER!

IN SOME countries, you cannot get a taxi by hailing one on the street. So always check *before* you need one. Ask at the airport—sometimes it's cheaper to share a cab than to take the airport limo. Check with your concierge, or ask at an office complex or department store if you have to phone for a cab or go to a taxi stand. Check on how to recognize the legitimate ones—they are usually a special color or have a distinctive symbol on top.

Many taxi drivers do not understand English. Be sure to have your destination (and the phone number) written in the language of the land; your hotel desk clerk can do this for you.

Restaurants, stores, and nightclubs have cards and/or match boxes that come in handy when directing your taxi driver for a revisit to those places. And don't get out of the cab unless you're sure it's the right place.

CAB CASH

$ In general, avoid cabs if you're on a budget. Fares are low in only a few countries (Ireland, Spain, and Portugal, to name a few). But sometimes you will save money over other means of transportation if you find someone to share with you.

$ Some taxis raise their rates after certain hours, so find this out beforehand and travel accordingly. Learn approximate fares and tipping policies in advance. Some countries—like Japan—believe it or not, have "no tipping" policies.

$ Check prices of the taxis standing in front of your hotel. They may be special and may charge more than the going rate. Sometimes you can save money by trudging around the corner to a normal taxi stand.

$ Baggage is always charged extra, so again travel light.

$ Some cities have fabulous monorail systems which make taking taxis a waste of money. Tokyo's monorail system is so good and so cheap, you'd even be wise to take it to and from the airport. And it's faster than any taxi since it can't get caught in traffic.

PEDALING IT AROUND TOWN

PEOPLE BIKE more abroad than at home, so if you're interested in seeing the sights while you trim your thighs, read on. **23**

Look into taking your own bike with you, or consider rental bikes: the national tourist organization or your concierge should be able to help you. Check the airlines—one even offers a bonus of a new speed bike!

For safety's sake, keep at least one hand on the handle and both feet on the pedals whenever you're in motion. Don't carry anything (like packages) which might interfere with your control. Be watchful of pot holes, soft shoulders, drain grates, railroad tracks. Make certain your bike has good brakes, a warning bell or horn and a rear reflector. If you'll be riding at night, make certain there's a good light and that you're wearing light-colored clothing. (If not, use reflector strips.)

Learn the local rules of the road. What are their hand signals? On which side of the road do they ride?

With just a bit of knowledge and forethought, you can see the local terrain the way the locals do!

TRAIN TIPS

ALWAYS TRY to make reservations in advance. If a train takes them, use them, because everyone else does, and if you don't you'll end up with either bad accommodations or nothing at all. **24**

Have your departure time and the track number written in the local language, so you can get help in the crowds at the last minute. Carry a piece of paper with your destination on it so that you can show it to a porter on the train and he can tell you when to get off. And never throw away your ticket; they're often asked for several times.

You may get stuck *anywhere* at a provincial station if you've arbitrarily decided to "lay over" there for awhile at night—and you may be out in the cold (or heat) since some of those places close up completely. So don't just hop off trains anywhere, anytime without definite plans.

You'll often have a choice of smoking or non-smoking cars, so take whatever appeals to you. But whatever car you do pick, make certain it's the right one for your destination, since many cars are dropped en route. Make certain you're at the right station. Don't laugh; there may be several big stations in a town, only one of which has your departure.

Make sure you allow plenty of time before departure if checking your bags through—there may be mounds of forms and red tape along with customs declarations. And when you leave the train, make certain you're leaving with everything you came with— you'd be amazed at what people leave behind.

Never entrust your baggage to an out-of-uniform "porter" and remember your uniformed porter's number so you can track down your luggage if there's any problem. Porters are always hard to find; they diminish in proportion to the amount you're weighed down with! So travel light, have local coins handy for lockers, and carry collapsible travel wheels.

Different countries have different money-saving arrangements for train travelers. Check each country to find out specials such as honeymoon rates, family reduced rates, or bargain rates for certain times of the week or certain hours of the day. Since good deals vary so much from country to country, either ask your travel agent *here* for specifics, ask at the tourist offices when you get *there*, or go to the station. The best bargain usually involves paying a certain amount in advance for unlimited mileage within the country during a specific time period. You can get BritRail Passes or Finnrail Passes or whatever for travel in the specific country.

Since Eurailpasses are the most popular and the ones you'll be most likely to use, I'll go into detail on them. They'll give you unlimited first class rail travel in thirteen European countries for specified lengths of time: fifteen days, $145 U.S. dollars; twenty-one days, $180; one month $220; two months, $300; three months, $360. Actually, a Eurailpass is not really limited to train travel. It's valid on many European ferries, river and lake steamers, and hydrofoils, as well as some Europabus lines and other motor coaches. You must purchase your Eurailpass in America and begin your trip within six months of purchase.

The following will help you in other countries. A *wagon-lit* is like our Pullman compartments. *Couchettes* are really inexpensive sleeping arrangements—a bunk, pillow and blanket in a room for four (first class) or six (second class). It's a men-and-women-together sort of thing, so wear clothes that you can sleep in comfortably and wake up respectably unwrinkled. Abroad, use the language barrier to insure a private sleeping compartment without paying the full cost. If a non-English-speaking family employs verbal abuse to make you move to another compartment, pretend you just don't understand—even if you do. Improvise a "private" compartment: share it with one other person and then pull down the shades. People are less likely to enter and then you and your traveling companion will have room to stretch out on the two seats and sleep.

In most countries you can get accommodations ranging from deluxe to third class. Of course, first class is the most comfortable, but second class is the most sociable. Train travel is a way of life in other countries, so you'll meet non-tourists galore in this less regal travel category. Your choice of train classes should vary with the country; in some countries (like Switzerland and Sweden) their second class is like our first class—in others (like India and northern Africa) their first class ones are like our third—so you can imagine what their second class would be like!

Take a picnic lunch of more than you need on the train and offer to share a bit of cheese or wine with a fellow passenger. It's cheaper than eating in the dining room and a good way to meet people. Of course, you may be able to meet people in the dining room, but it could be an expensive gamble.

The prime prerequisite for the traveler on a limited budget is time. If you travel by bus or second-class train, you will be at the mercy of erratic scheduling and crowded bookings. So if time is as valuable to you as money, fly. Exceptions vary within countries—Japan's trains seem to be as fast as some countries' planes. Check, check, check.

If you want to combine train travel with other vehicles, some trains do carry cars, as do some ferries. And just as subways and buses are generally cheaper than cabs when going about in the city, trains and buses are cheaper than planes.

AUTO OUGHT TO'S

YOU CAN rent, lease, or buy a car, or have your own car shipped almost anywhere you'd want to go. The more advance planning, the better the deal in any car transaction.

25

First of all, consider what you already have: your own car. I would suggest enlisting the services of the American Automobile Association (AAA). You can join them for a minimal fee and they'll take care of all your car shipping arrangements. Most steamship lines will take on your car as accompanied baggage, but since space is limited for both cars and passengers, you should make reservations far in advance of the sailing date. Have your gas tank practically empty since the gasoline will be drained from your car for shipment.

Do you want to buy a car overseas? The price itself is no longer a great bargain, but you'll save on foreign transportation—you won't have to rent a car abroad or take trains, planes, taxis and buses. Your local authorized foreign car dealer (Fiat, Porsche etc.) can tell you what your new car will cost abroad, what safety and emissions standards it must have to get back into the U.S., customs requirements, how and where to pick up the car, how to have it shipped home, and how to arrange for insurance. And because the sale is arranged in his dealership, the dealer gets credit for the car and so will give your new car the same warranty and service as with a regular domestic sale. (You were afraid of that!)

If you're coming back from your trip with a car (your own or a new one), you must have it steam-sprayed and cleaned to meet the U.S. Department of Agriculture's regulations. The steamship company in charge of shipping your car back will do this.

There's a car purchase and repurchase plan whereby you buy a car abroad before leaving home and the manufacturer guarantees to repurchase it at an agreed-upon price (minus depreciation). The manufacturer will send you a refund check after the car is returned to the manufacturer for repurchase. The AAA is very experienced in handling this so you might want to leave the planning to them. This is more economical than renting a car if your trip will be over thirty days—though not a bigger savings than outright purchase.

Renting cars is an increasingly popular tourist choice. As with anything else, reserve far in advance, especially for popular places at peak season. Rent-a-car agencies are everywhere, but you'll get best choice of cars in major cities. They'll take anyone who's breathing who can also pay and has either a U.S. license or an International Driver's Permit—though some companies won't rent to anyone under a certain age, be it 25, 23, or 21. Either go through an international car rental agency here, through your airline, incorporate it into an air/drive package, or go directly to a rental agency abroad. See what maps, driving regulations, and other necessary facts you can obtain from them. You'll pay more at big name companies (Hertz, Avis, etc.) since you can use your credit card and can drop off the car, at no extra cost, someplace other than where you picked it up. Rent a small, gas-saving car; most countries (except Kuwait, Panama and Nicaragua) have much more expensive gas than we do. Those narrow little cars will also be great on narrow, hairpin turns. And try to rent a locally-produced car if at all possible; that way, if something goes amiss, you won't have to wait for parts.

Check out the hidden costs of renting a car before you set foot in it. Don't just consider the daily rate, cost per mile, and gas. There's also insurance: the coverage that comes with the car does not always include collision—for full coverage you'll have to pay an additional daily rate; and tax, which is figured after all the miles have been counted up and charged for. Some local firms add a surcharge if you're under a certain age (sometimes it's 25). And there may be a drop-fee if you plan to leave the car in a town other than where you picked it up. See if you can have your car delivered to your hotel. You should also be aware that you can usually get a driver as well as a car from these agencies. And do find out if there is a supplemental charge for only one person in the car.

Make sure the rental agency representative shows you how the car works. Slight differences can be annoying or hazardous: a Volvo I picked up in Sweden had a different way of dimming and brightening lights—a little terrifying the first time I tried to light up a dark, deserted Swedish country road.

Although your local driver's license is often valid, it's a wise precaution to have an International Driving Permit. AAA is officially authorized to issue an IDP to any person 18 or older who holds a valid U.S. driver's license. All it takes is the application, two signed passport-size photographs and a $3 check.

Keep in mind that you usually must have both a local U.S. driver's license *and* an IDP to get insurance. Don't drive one block without checking and if necessary taking out appropriate protection. Always make certain you have full coverage in the country you'll be driving in. U.S. automobile insurance coverage is not valid in all countries.

The safest places to leave your car overnight are garages affiliated with your own hotel. If the affiliated garage is not obvious, ask your doorman where to park and whether pick-up and delivery are included. Always empty and lock your car when garaging it for the night; indeed, don't leave anything in sight when parking during the day even for a short time. And since most garages and parking lots are not legally responsible for your articles, you might want to take out baggage insurance.

While gasoline is generally more expensive abroad than here, some countries (such as Italy and Yugoslavia) give you a break through discount coupons. Check at the borders to see if you qualify for these savings. Redeem unused coupons when you leave the country.

Gasoline is measured differently abroad. The British imperial gallon is larger than ours, as is the Irish version. And the octane rating may be lower than what you are accustomed to, so order super gas; it's a bit more expensive, but better.

Keep your tank as full as possible: some countries have holiday closings or infrequent stations in the countryside. Know how much gas your tank holds and how that translates into kilometers. (Just as gas is measured in liters, miles are measured by kilometers.) To convert from kilometers to miles, divide the number of kilometers by 8 and multiply the result by 5. For a fast reference, this chart should help:

Feet	1.00	3.00	5.00	10.00	20.00
Meters	.30	.91	1.52	3.04	6.09
Miles	1.0	5.00	10	62	100
Kilometers	1.6	8	16	100	161
Gallons	1	5	10	15	20
Liters	3.75	18.95	37.90	56.85	75.80

Make certain your car is in good repair by having it checked out before going on secondary roads or up mountain passes. Know ahead of time if you'll need anything special (tire chains, or radiator coolant). If you'll be going where gas stations are few and far between, have a hand-operated siphon for emergency purposes, rather than carrying potentially dangerous gas reserves. Have the oil changed, the transmission fluid checked, and the car lubricated frequently. And take along a first aid kit in case the worst should happen.

Tires are of great importance, especially for country roads which may be rutted and contain rugged stones. They should be as new and high-quality as possible. Make sure the tread marks aren't too worn. Four- or six-ply nylon cord, or one of the tough fiberglass, steel, and nylon combinations is most durable. Carry a flare, a spare tire, and an aerosal tire inflator or pump and tire gauge. And know how to change the tire!

If your car breaks down, a white cloth tied to the antenna or door handle is an international cry for help. If you're stranded in a desolate place, lock yourself in the car until someone trustworthy appears. If you're driving in America, a CB radio will keep you in touch with other travelers should you need help. It's also a good idea to give a friend or relative your license number and a description of your car. That way the state police can always find you if you're needed in an emergency.

On those scenic off-beat roads, remember to watch out for potholes and wandering cattle and donkeys. Don't race your motor going up hill, and keep it in first gear. (The vehicle going up has the right of way over the one coming down.) Wait until your boiling radiator cools down before taking the cap off. Beware of running into livestock. And protect your trunk luggage from dusty roads by covering it with a sheet of plastic or just a sheet.

Always check with your local auto clubs (your AAA card will get you into them); the local government tourist office; information counters of international airline offices; hotels and railway stations; or your concierge for directions, maps and road tips.

I've always found people to be kind and helpful when I've asked directions in a pleasant, clear, slow voice. Why do some people feel that if they shout, people will understand them better? Don't ever be embarrassed about asking directions. I've gone from gas station to gas station asking directions. Sometimes I've gotten no further than the very next gas station, but I've stopped again. I've noticed that so many men stubbornly refuse to ask for directions (it must be a macho thing) and stay lost for hours—let us not make the same mistake. Do be aware that if a peasant gives you the distance from place to place, you should translate it from donkey to car time.

Try to avoid driving in large cities—each country's citizens seem to vie for the title of worst driver, though I think it's narrowed down now to the Japanese, the Italians, and the French. If you must drive, try to avoid morning (7-9 AM) and evening (5-7 PM) rush hours as well as weekend throngs to and from the country. Try to be off the road by 4 PM, not only to avoid crowds, but also to assure yourself of a better selection of accommodations. If you plan your countryside excursions for weekdays and city visits for weekends, your contra-cyclical planning should pay off in fewer crowds.

Except for a few really super highways, you won't make the time abroad that you would here, so allot more time for fewer miles. Super-highways such as the Italian autostrada or German autobahn are great for making good time, but you won't see anything. Better to wend your way through small towns and picturesque countryside.

If you do want to make really good travel time, get on the road before dawn and then eat breakfast *during* the rush hour. If you can't get going without morning coffee or tea, carry a plug-in hot coil and packaged caffeine products.

While driving, stop frequently. You'll see more, break the monotony, and limber up. A box of Kleenex and moist towelettes may be the most important things you put in your car, since gas station restrooms are not always very clean. And carry a sweater and light top to change into if you'll be driving through temperature changes.

Carry some nourishment—water, of course, across a desert! A thermos is always a good idea since you can't be sure of the purity of the local water. You might want to add some local cheese and have picnics along the way, but no wine. Don't drink anything if you'll be driving abroad: you don't have to be drunk to get into trouble. In this as in other legal questions, *their* laws are the abiding ones, not yours. (Of course, it's a terrible idea to drink and drive anywhere—here as well as in foreign countries.)

Ask the local tourist bureau for information about local driving restrictions and speed limits. Now for some specifics about countries to which you might be going.

Now for some specifics about countries to which you might be going.

BELGIUM: Your U.S. license is valid. In case of real trouble, the Royal Automobile Club's Touring Secours Service will come to your rescue through their motorcycle-patrolled highways. In case of serious accidents, telephone 900. Gas is expensive.

BERMUDA: There are absolutely no rental cars allowed. If you must get about by auto, it'll have to be with driver included.

COLOMBIA: Rental agencies abound, but so do ruts on the highways. Streets are not well-marked. Best to rent a car and driver.

DENMARK: There are lots of dependable car rental agencies. (Minimum age is 20.) You can pick up a rental car at your railroad station through the Danish Railways. Parking disks are used (see "France"). The main driving problem here is watching out for the enormous numbers of bicycles. If you bring a car with you, you'll need your U.S. license plate. Gas is expensive. For a change, I have something good to say about the drivers—they're about the most courteous and law-abiding in the world, and it does take getting used to!

DOMINICAN REPUBLIC: Rent a jeep or Land Rover—you'll never make it over their impossibly impassable roads by regular auto. A U.S. driver's license is good for sixty days.

FINLAND: The Finns have a real thing about drivers who imbibe; so don't drive if you've had even one drop to drink, or you could end up in a Finnish slammer! Finnish speed limits vary with the road— the better the road, the higher the speed limit. If you bring your own car, you'll need your local driver's license, car registration, and an identification/international registration letter plate.

FRANCE: You'll need the car's registration certificate and your U.S. driver's license if you are bringing in your own car. The roads are good but crowded. Horn-blowing is not allowed in major cities.

Passing on the right is permitted on *autoroutes*. Parking disks are used and can be obtained from police stations, concierges, gasoline stations, post offices and banks. The driver puts these cardboard disks in her car window to show when she arrived; the disk is movable to any time and it's strictly the honor system—with a high fine if you're caught cheating! When the disk is set, the time at which the driver must vacate automatically shows up through a special opening on the face of the disk.

GREAT BRITAIN: Use your regular United States driving permit. Drive on the left-hand side of the road, pass on the right. You can't "feed" meters—one coin per parked vehicle is all that's allowed; when your time is up, move your car.

GREECE: You must have an international driver's license to drive either your own or a rented car. Rates for rented cars vary with the season. Make certain you have puncture-proof tires for secondary roads: horses and donkeys were probably there before you, leaving horseshoe nails on the road.

GUATEMALA: Let someone else do the driving. Most of the roads are dirt, and they wash out after rains (which are frequent).

HAITI: This new "in" place should be out for driving: the roads are unmarked and rutted.

HONG KONG: Rental cars are abundant, but streets are so congested and the sightseeing/shopping area so compact, you should try to get about by foot or via public transportation. Driving is on the left, if you insist.

IRELAND: If you bring your own car, you'll just need your American driver's license and the car's registration. While rental rates fluctuate according to season (they're cheapest in winter), they're always lower than ours. The roads are generally good. Driving is on the left, but the sparse traffic makes this an easy adjustment. There are speed limits only *within* cities. Not only are gas stations usually closed on Sundays, but they also have limited open hours other days, so gas up whenever possible. Irish and American miles are different; the former a bit longer.

ITALY: These otherwise friendly people become hostile maniacs behind the wheel, so don't drive if possible, especially in metropolitan areas. Most accidents occur in Rome on Sunday and Monday, so time your driving accordingly. Rent a Fiat so you'll be assured of good service and available parts. Buy gasoline discount coupons; you'll need them with their expensive gas! If you're stranded on the *autostrada*, call 116 (the emergency breakdown number).

JAPAN: Vehicles keep to the left, pedestrians to the right. Get road maps in English at bookstores in large cities. Tokyo is one of the most difficult places in which to drive, because streets aren't numbered and everyone drives like unemployed kamikaze pilots. They do bow after they've rammed your car, though. A special operator's license is required to drive here.

JAMAICA: While gas and car rentals are not cheap, the mileage charges at rental agencies do drop in summer. Drive on the left, though out in the country not everyone does. Use your horn with abandon.

MALAYSIA: Traffic keeps to the left. Rental cars are available. Roads are superb in West Malaysia, but East Malaysia has iffy roads made even iffier by the monsoons (October through January).

MEXICO: Mexicans have a real thing for one-way streets so watch for an arrow with one point. (Two-way streets have an arrow with two points.) Descend dangerous (winding or foggy) Mexican mountain roads slowly and in second gear. Car and fuel costs in Mexico are about twice those of the U.S. Double-check your auto insurance to be certain you have *Mexican* coverage. I urge you to be insured in every country, but it's especially important in Mexico, since uninsured drivers may be arrested, and involvement in any accident there is a very serious matter. Indeed, because of the legal hassles so many *gringos* have gotten involved in there (you are *not* presumed innocent until proven guilty), I strongly urge you to hire a reputable driver.

NETHERLANDS: Your valid U.S. driver's license is sufficient. Good, well-marked roads and good rental rates are the rule here. Priority is given to traffic from the right (except at road intersections). Fast traffic takes precedence over slower-moving conveyances such as motorcycles and bicycles. Streetcars always have priority. Membership in the Royal Netherlands Touring Club is cheap and worthwhile; it will enable you to get assistance if you're having car trouble.

NORWAY: You can pick up rental cars throughout the country. Only the main highways are paved. Gas stations can be pretty scarce, so never pass one up! The Norwegians share the Finnish attitude about drinking and driving, so don't drive if you've had a drop to drink. Always check as to snow conditions on the roads and passes ahead, except in summer months.

PANAMA: There are standard rates for standard rental cars. And the roads ar good, especially the Pan American Highway.

PORTUGAL: Your U.S. driving license is valid. If you shipped your car from the States, do yourself a favor and let the Portuguese AAA handle the enormous amount of paperwork. The roads are better than the drivers, but don't blow your horn at them (though you'll be sorely tempted) unless it's a real emergency. Depend on the Automóvel Club de Portugal for emergency motorist service. Gas stations are abundant but often closed on Sundays and holidays.

PUERTO RICO: U.S. driver's licenses are valid for 120 days. There are many rental agencies with average prices.

SINGAPORE: Traffic flows left. Self-drive cars are available, but an international license and a returnable deposit are required. It's hideously expensive and time-consuming to ship a car to or around southeast Asia. Better to arrange daily excursions via a hired car and driver.

SPAIN: Buy their all-risk Tourist Insurance Policy at a Spanish tourist office. If you bring your own car into Spain, you'll need your auto registration, U.S. license, and proof of insurance (the green card), which you receive from the AAA when you purchase overseas auto insurance. The Reale Automovil Club de España (10 Paseo del General Sanjurjo, Madrid) can answer any auto queries. Use your horn in a city only in an emergency. Signal your passing on a highway during the day by using your horn; at night you flash your lights. Repeat your signal when you return to the right lane. A truck will signal you by green flashes if it's okay to pass; red flashes tell you it's dangerous to pass.

SWEDEN: For your own car, you'll need registration papers and a

U.S. (or international) license. Speed limits vary, as do road conditions. Fines for parking violations are very high, so learn their rules and abide by them. Don't blow your horn except in emergencies. If you are in an auto accident you must be examined for alcohol in your blood stream, even if the accident is not your fault. And you could be thrown in the slammer if they do find any alcohol, so if you plan to drink, take a taxi.

SWITZERLAND: For your own car, you'll need registration papers and your U.S. driver's license. No horn-blowing in cities except for emergencies. Vehicles on the right *always* have the right of way. Check ahead of time to see if mountain passes are passable.

TRINIDAD: Drive on the left. Your American license is valid. Good roads.

U.S.S.R.: If you're bringing your car in from abroad, you must have a "certificate of obligation" to remove the car from Russia when you leave. Check with Intourist about insurance. Stick closely to your itinerary (which you had to have for a visa). Guard carefully the identification papers (the Motoring Tourist's Memo) you'll get at the border. Have your U.S. driver's license translated into Russian at the border Intourist office. (An international driver's license will save you the trouble since it already comes in Russian.) Gas is a bargain compared to what you've been used to at home.

VENEZUELA: Roads are good and rentals cars are available and reasonable—but not nearly the bargain that gas is (12-25¢ a gallon!).

VIRGIN ISLES: Left-hand driving. You can get a Virgin Isles driver's license with $1 and your domestic license! Good car rental agencies with good collision coverage.

YUGOSLAVIA: This is one of the easiest Eastern European countries in which to rent a car. Bring your auto registration papers and green card (for insurance coverage). Good major highways.

"With just a little bit of forethought, you can see the local terrain the way the locals do!"

No matter where you are and what you need, these phrases should help:

ENGLISH	GERMAN	FRENCH	SPANISH
Will you please . . .	*Würden sie bitte . . .*	*S'il vous plaît, voulez-vous . . .*	*Por Favor*
fill the radiator	Kühlwasser nachfüllen	remplir le radiateur	llene el radiador
check the spark plugs	die Zündkerzen prüfen	vérifier les bougis	cheque las bujias
check the oil	den Oelstand prüfen	vérifier l'huile	cheque el aceite
check the tire pressure	den Reifendruck prüfen	vérifier le gonflage	cheque el aire en las llantas
grease the car	den Wagen abschmieren	graisser la voiture	engrase el auto
wash the car	den Wagen waschen	laver la voiture	lave el auto
"Fill it up"	Ich möchte tanken	faites-le plein	llene el tanque
I want . . . liters	Ich möchte . . . Liter	Je voudrais . . . litres	Yo quiero . . . litros
check the battery	die Batterie prüfen	Vérifier les accumulateurs	cheque la bateria
clean the windshield	die Windschutzscheibe putzen	essuyer le pare-brise	Limpie el parabrisas

There is something wrong with . . .	*Es ist etwas nicht in ordnung mit . . .*	*Il y a quelque chose qui ne va pas dans . . .*	*Algo no funciona en . . .*
the engine	dem Motor	le moteur	el motor
the brakes	den Bremsen	les freins	los frenos
the steering	der Steureung	la direction	la dirección
the lights	den Scheinwerfen	l'éclairage	las luces
the clutch	der Kupplung	l'embrayage	el clutch
the transmission	der Schaltung	la transmission	la transmisión
the oil pressure	dem Oeldruck	la pression d'huile	la preción de aceite
the fuel system	der Benzineleitung	l'arrivée d'essence	el tanque de gasolina
Please fix this flat tire.	Würden Sie bitte diesen Reifen flicken.	Voulez-vous réparer cette crevaison.	Por favor arregle esta llanta ponchada

Is this the right way to the . . .	*Ist dies der richtige weg . . .*	*Est-ce la direction pour aller . . .*	*Por aquí se va . . .*
museum?	zum Museum?	au musée?	al museo?
cathedral?	zum Dom?	à la cathédrale?	a la catedral?
lake?	zum See?	au lac?	al lago?
castle?	zum Schloss?	au château?	al castillo?

Write how many kilometers it is to . . .	*Schreiben Sie auf wieviele Kilometer es ist nach . . .*	*Ecrivez combien kilometres pour aller . . .*	*¿Cuantos kilometros hacia . . .*
to the right	rechts	à droite	la derecha
to the left	links	à gauche	la izquierda
straight ahead	gerade aus	tout droit	hacia delante
turn	abbiegen	tour	virar
first	erster	premier	primera
second	sweiter	deuxième	segunda
third	dritter	troisième	tercera
traffic light	Verkehrsampel	le feu rouge	semaforo
river	der Fluss	la rivière	río
bridge	die Brücke	le pont	puente
street	Strasse	la rue	calle
road	Strasse	la route	calle
intersection	Kreuzung	le carrefour	intersección

Please where is . . .	*Bitte wo ist . . .*	*S'il vous plaît, ou est . . .*	Por favor donde está . . .
a service station?	eine Tankstelle?	une station-service?	la gasolinera?
a garage?	eine Garage?	un garage?	el garage?
a hotel?	ein Hotel?	un hotel?	el hotel?
a restaurant?	ein Restaurant?	un restaurant?	el restaurante?
a policeman?	ein poliezei?	un gendarme?	la policía?
a telephone?	ein Telefon?	une téléphone?	el teléfono?
a toilet?	eine Toilette?	une toilette?	un baño?
Where can I park?	Wo kann ich parken?	Où puis-je stationner?	¿Donde puedo parquear?

Business

Business
Business

HAVE YOU HEARD THE ONE ABOUT THE TRAVELING SALESWOMAN?

A WARNING! For a few moments, we're going to leave the light-hearted tone of this book and be business-wise and a bit stuffy. Sorry, but there is just no way to describe the government's Target Industry Program, Trade Opportunities Program, Export Mailing List service and the like with a jaunty air. Don't grin, but do bear it and read on if you plan to do business overseas.

26

If you *don't* have business plans in your travel plans, you may want to skip this chapter. And when an author actually gives the reader permission to skip something, said reader had better take her at her word.

MAKING ARRANGEMENTS First you have to get to your business destination—and your means of transportation can provide your first help. Different airlines offer different business services. Some (like Japan Airlines) can arrange interpreters and bilingual business cards, others (like British Airways) can provide you with a communications center and secretarial service. Still others (like Eastern) provide an airletter especially for businesswomen. Since the various airlines' services change periodically, I won't attempt to list them. But it would behoove *you* to check which airlines going your way have which services.

Planes aren't the only know-while-you-go carriers. Some trains (from your own Amtrak to the German Federated Railroad) offer on-board secretarial service. Check ahead if this is what you need—they aren't listed since so few businesspeople actually use them.

If you're going to be doing business in a major city, you can usually obtain secretarial assistance on short notice through a local agency. You can also check with the local labor exchange as well as your personal business contacts.

Telephone answering services, including wake-up service, are also available in those areas in which there is sufficient demand. This service generally includes answering calls for subscribers, accepting and forwarding brief messages, and handling orders to a limited extent.

The big international hotel chains are much better to stay at for business reasons than the quaint little 300-year-old inns. For example, Hilton has a list of bilingual on-call secretaries, translation equipment, interpreters, typewriters, and telex facilities. In addition, many have photostatic services. Sheratons can arrange simultaneous translators for big meetings, and bilingual secretaries for you alone—plus telex facilities, rental typewriters, and adding machines. Some of their facilities have yachts you can charter for a day of business meetings or business entertainment. Most hotels will give complimentary rooms per so many reservations for a convention; this is all arranged through the sales department.

Before leaving your home city, arrange for letters of introduction to the executives of the firms you wish to see. Ask at the consulate of your destination about doing this since polite forms do vary from country to country.

You'll also want to have business cards made up before you go. These should be in English on one side, the local language on the other. Three to five hundred are considred average for a business trip of a couple of weeks—you'll find they come in handy at hotels, restaurants, and stores as well as with business associates.

Many countries have a directory of foreign residents published in English. You will find it invaluable even for a short business stay. It usually lists the names, home and office addresses, and phone numbers of foreign residents and firms as well as airlines, hotels, business firms, and diplomatic offices.

Keep in touch with the business world by buying international newspapers, local English language periodicals, and financial digests.

However you travel, plan to get to your destination well ahead of your scheduled convention or meeting so you won't be making important decisions when your biological clock is still back in Omaha! Do plan on spending longer than "a few days." Even if negotiations have been carefully made in advance, there can be unforseen delays, and a rush trip may be worse than no trip at all.

Doing business in developing countries is more difficult and time-consuming than in the developed countries because of a slower pace, telephone problems, heavy traffic during business hours, and the difficulty of making appointments more than a day in advance. Since it is hard to keep more than three or four appointments during a working day, the length of your visit should be a number of days even for an initial survey of the market.

Interpreters are usually available for hire on an hourly or daily basis in larger cities. Names of reputable organizations can be obtained from the American Embassy or Consulate, if all else (your hotel, business contacts, etc.) fails.

Once you're there, you'll have to know how to cable back. You can send cables from your hotel or from the cable offices located in all major cities. Remember, names and addresses count as words. Most firms doing business in foreign countries register a one-word cable address; your cable address should not be longer than ten letters, nor less than three. When not cabling, always use airmail.

Clothing considerations are easy. If you're going to different offices, by all means take just enough changes of office attire to appear at one office—you can repeat everything at each different office. They'll never know. For example, if you'll be spending five working days in Europe, each one in a different office, just take enough for one day—and wear it every day. And if it isn't drip dry, you should bring along arm shields.

Chances are you will hear and read a lot about how "different" customs are everywhere. This may be quite true, but it is also true that you will not be wrong, or give offense, by doing what is thoughtful and courteous by your own standards. But you will feel more at home in business meetings abroad if you are somewhat acquainted with some of the local manners and customs, so do a bit of background reading. If you live in a large city with a business library, that should prove invaluable. And many airline publications, like JAL's "Understanding the Japanese—If That's Possible," can help you bridge the cultural gap. You will find your stay more pleasant if you are familiar with some of the history, customs, and culture.

Notice what others do. Sometimes there's a great deal of hand-shaking, other times slight bowing. Do what they do unless you feel dreadfully uncomfortable—then don't because you'll look like the ass you feel like!

The custom of gift-giving among business acquaintances is far more common in many countries than you may be used to. You should let your good manners be your guide in receiving and presenting gifts. You may wish to take a few things with you to have when the occasion arises. For instance, if your company has "give-aways" such as pens, paperweights, rulers, or the like, you may find a supply handy for much-appreciated little tokens. For more elaborate gifts, bottles of good liquor such as scotch or cognac are appropriate to present to colleagues. Don't be surprised, though, if the recipient of your gift is reluctant to open it in your presence. It is not always customary. However, he or she will probably not be offended if you urge him/her to do so.

Be prompt for appointments and business meetings; it's considered very important in most places (particularly in Japan and Northern Europe). If you do hit a country like Italy or Mexico, where people always "run late," it's still better for you to arrive early and wait for them than vice-versa.

If you must take business associates out for drinks or meals, you can avoid the awkward moment of fumbling for the check by stating clearly at the outset that you'd like them to be your guests. It's also a good idea to either phone ahead or take the waiter aside beforehand and tell him you want the check.

You can arrange to have a European charge account, enabling you to sign for hotel and restaurant bills, car rentals and the like. You only pay the resulting total once—like a monthly bill. This is great for women on a business trip (expense account) where you'll want records for your income tax. Travel credit organizations such as American Express handle this service. Or see if you can use your employer's credit card, if only for emergencies. It's hardly giving you carte blanche—they'll know who charged what in London on March 7th!

"Sometimes there's a great deal of handshaking, other times slight bowing."

Also, it's a good idea to travel with your own credit cards even if it's a business trip. They should be packed or carried separately from business credit cards so that if one is lost or stolen, you still have the other.

You can avoid embarrassing situations by asking male business associates to meet you in the hotel lobby, rather than in your room. If a business trip involves traveling around the city and you don't know your business associates, you might prefer to rent a car so you can come and go as you please and not be dependent upon strangers.

Once abroad, go on a busman's holiday and visit facilities similar to your home ones. Foreign visitors are welcome at many factories, plants and institutions if they go through proper channels. Either write on letterhead stationery before leaving home, requesting an inspection, or go through your host country's chamber of commerce or tourist organization.

If you are a representative of a business concern and are going abroad in fulfillment of a contract with an agency of the U.S. government, submit with your passport application a letter from the concern by which you are employed. The letter should show your position, destination, purpose of travel, intended length of stay, expiration date of the contract, and, when pertinent, the contract number and the branch of the armed forces which is sponsoring the travel. Such letters are required because it is necessary to endorse the passports to show the destination of contract personnel who are proceeding to certain countries.

Don't forget to bring samples of your merchandise or have them sent to you. A commercial visa allows you to bring in samples up to a certain value, duty-free. The foreign country's consulate can provide you with further information since different countries have different visa requirements. If you intend to send samples of merchandise back to Europe, investigate air cargo service and rates as well as the slower but cheaper sea mail. If you're doing the latter, be sure to find out in advance whether freight charges are only to the port of entry, or to the delivery address.

The following is a country-by-country guide for the traveling businesswoman. You will note throughout this list of countries that some holidays will be listed without specific dates; that's simply because these dates vary from year to year.

ARGENTINA

Customs: Look and be conservative. *Always* make an appointment in advance for a business call. Use business cards with English on one side, Spanish on the other. Have patience, that un-American virtue. Don't rush into business discussions—socialize first with *impersonal* amenities. Much business is done during lunch, and espresso coffee is often served during afternoon business appointments. If an Argentine entertains you with dinner at home, bring flowers or send them the day after dinner.

Language and Culture: Spanish is the official language but English is spoken by many professional people, particularly in the larger cities. Italian, German, and French are heard frequently. The best months for business travel in Argentina are April through November. Argentine businesspeople usually vacation in January and February (it's their summer) and some firms close for a time during this period. The prominent Argentine is usually a frequent traveler. Thus, another reason for a prior appointment well in advance—at least you'll know he/she will be in town! Try to avoid business travel in Argentina during the two weeks before and after Christmas and during the week before and after Carnival and Easter.

National Holidays: May 1, Labor Day; May 25, Revolution (1810) Day; June 20, Flag Day; July 9, Independence (1816) Day; August 17, Death of General José de San Martin; October 12, Discovery of America (Columbus Day); and December 25, Christmas. On a number of "nonwork days," government offices, banks, insurance companies, and courts are closed, but closing is optional for business and commerce. These include: January 1, New Year's Day; January 6, Eiphany; and several days with moveable dates—Carnival Monday and Tuesday before Ash Wednesday, Holy Thursday and Good Friday before Easter, and Corpus Christi; August 15, Assumption of the Virgin Mary; November 1, All Saint's

Day; and December 8, Feast of the Immaculate Conception. In addition, there are a number of local patriotic or religious holidays, especially feasts of patron saints (e.g., November 11, St. Martin of Tours, in the capital) which may be observed by part or all of the community in various cities or provinces.

Business Hours: Business hours for commercial operations vary but are generally 9 AM to 7 PM Monday through Friday. Government office hours are 12 noon to 7 PM Monday through Friday, closed on Saturdays and holidays. Although closing time may vary slightly among provinces, banking hours are 12 noon to 4 PM Monday through Friday, but closed on Saturdays, holidays, November 6 (Bank Employees' Day), and December 30. However, appointments with bank officials outside regular banking hours can often be arranged.

AUSTRALIA

Customs: Be punctual. While Aussies are more informal than Americans socially, they're more formal in business attire and manner. When addressing Australians, use personal titles.

Business Hours: 9 AM-5:30 PM, Monday through Friday. Closed Saturday. Hours vary among states and occupations.

Commercial Holidays: The principal holiday season is in December and January, so it's usually best to schedule business visits at other times of the year. Major holidays are New Years Day (Jan. 1), Australia Day (last Monday in January), Good Friday, Easter Sunday, Easter Monday, Anzac Australia Day (April 25), the Queen's Birthday (except in Western Australia, where it's usually on a Monday in June), Christmas Day, and Boxing Day (December 26).

Commercial Language: English.

AUSTRIA

Customs: Correspondence and visiting are quite important in the conduct of business here. Prompt handling of correspondence (via airmail and telegrams) is expected even if the answer is negative. Personal visits are warmly welcomed and generally regarded as the best way of establishing new trade contacts. Appointments for such visits should be made well in advance of the intended date. Marketing and sales policies should aim at achieving durable business relations rather than immediate sales. In this regard, it should be noted that the economic tempo in Austria is generally slower than in the United States. Hard selling is usually just not accepted. In most cases, Austrian firms prefer to deal directly with the U.S. company rather than with one of its European representatives in another country.

Commercial Language: German. The importance of German-language trade literature, catalogs, and instructions for the use and servicing of products cannot be overemphasized. The agent who has such material is in a much better competitive position than one who can only show prospective customers trade literature in English. Most large commercial and industrial enterprises can, however, correspond in English and French as well as German.

Business Hours: The customary hours of business are Monday through Friday, from 8 or 9 AM to 5 or 6 PM. Shops and business firms usually close during lunchtime. Some commercial offices and most banks remain open continuously during the day but close at an earlier hour. Unless previous appointments have been made, public officials and private businesspersons aren't available for Saturday interviews.

Commercial Holidays: January 1, New Years Day; January 6, Epiphany; Easter Monday; May 1, Labor Day; Ascension Day; Whit Monday; Corpus Christi Day; August 15, Assumption; October 26, National Holiday; November 1, All Saint's Day; December 8, Immaculate Conception; December 25, Christmas; December 26, St. Stephen's Day. Along with the above national holidays, the following local holidays are also observed in the provinces: March 19, St. Joseph's Day, in Carinthia, Styria, Tyrol, and Vorarlberg; September 24, St. Rupert's Day, in Salzburg; October 10, Plebiscite-Anniversary, in Carinthia; November 11, St. Martin's Day, in Burgenland; November 15, St. Leopold's Day, in Lower Austria, Upper Austria and Vienna. December 24 and December 31 are bank holidays.

BELGIUM

Customs: Although individuals vary (of course), the Belgian businessperson is usually more conservative than his American counterpart. Don't start off on a first-name basis. Wear conservative clothing, and use business cards with only your name and business title; leave advertising messages for promotional brochures. Don't talk about politics, religion, or local language differences.

Prior appointments are necessary for making both business and government calls in Belgium. Traditionally on Bourse Day (Wednesday in Brussels and Monday in Antwerp), most Belgian businesspeople meet by trades at particular restaurants for lunch to discuss and conduct business, so appointments may be more difficult to make these days. Appointments are best scheduled after 10 AM and before 5 PM. Although some firms are open on Saturday morning, the time is usually devoted to staff conferences or sales meetings rather than to business appointments. Belgians like business lunch invitations, usually running from 1 to 3 PM, with a customary one drink before and wine with the meal. They don't have the American after-work drink custom.

Commercial Language: Belgium is a bilingual country. In the north and west, the common language is Flemish. In the south and east, French is spoken. German is the language in the Eupen-Malmedy region. Brussels is bilingual, with signs in both French and Flemish. English is widely understood in business circles.

Business Hours: The customary hours in Brussels for business are: offices, 8:30 AM to noon, and 2 to 6 PM Monday through Friday; banks, 9 AM to 1 PM and 2:30 to 3:30 PM Monday through Friday; most retail stores, 9 AM to noon and 2 to 6 PM Monday through Saturday. In Antwerp, the hours vary somewhat: offices, 9 AM to noon and 1 to 5 or 5:30 PM, or 2 to 6 PM Monday through Friday; banks, 9 AM to 1 PM and 2:30 to 3 PM; retail stores, same hours as offices, Monday through Saturday. Some business firms are open on Saturday mornings. A number of stores also have later hours than the traditional ones, to permit evening shopping.

Commercial Holidays: Belgium has ten national holidays: January 1 (New Years Day), Easter Monday, May 1 (Labor Day), Ascension Day (sixth Thursday after Easter), Whitmonday, July 21 (National Holiday), August 15 (Assumption Day), November 1 (All Saints Day), November 11 (Armistice Day), and December 25

(Christmas). If a national holiday falls on a Sunday, it is celebrated on Monday. Certain other days are celebrated as holidays either traditionally or within local jurisdictions.

BRAZIL

Customs: The pace of negotiation is slower than it is in the United States, and is based much more on personal contact, with important business deals rarely concluded by telephone or letter. Many Brazilian businesspersons don't react favorably to quick and infrequent visits by foreign sales representatives. They prefer a more continuous working relationship implying a long-term commitment in Brazil. Also, the Brazilian buyer is concerned with the after-sales services provided by the manufacturer/exporter.

The slower pace of business negotiation in Brazil does not mean that the Brazilian businessperson is less knowledgeable about industrial technology or modern business practices than his/her U.S. counterpart. In fact, one should be as prepared technically in making a call on a São Paulo firm as on a Chicago company. In addition, the American should learn as much as possible about the Brazilian economic and commercial environment.

Office Hours: While office hours in Brazil are generally 8-8:30 AM to 5:30-6 PM, the decision-makers begin work later in the morning and stay later in the evening. It's sometimes difficult to arrange a call on a Brazilian executive outside of the hours 10 AM to noon and 3 to 5 PM, although this is less true in São Paulo. Lunch usually lasts two hours. It's the custom in Brazil to drink coffee during a business appointment.

Commercial Language: Many Brazilian businesspersons speak English, but not enough to do so to conduct business in that language except in special circumstances. The non-Portuguese-speaking U.S. businessperson may find that he or she needs an interpreter on more than fifty percent of his business calls. Correspondence as well as product literature should be in Portuguese, with English as a substitute being preferable to Spanish. Specifications and other technical data should be in the metric system.

Holidays: New Year's Day (Jan. 1), Carnival (four nights and three days preceding Ash Wednesday), Good Friday, Easter Sunday, Tiradentes Day (April 21), Labor Day (May 1), Independence Day (Sept. 7), All Souls Day (Nov. 2), Proclamation of the Republic (Nov. 15) and Christmas Day (Dec. 25).

CANADA

Customs: Generally similar to those at home, with a bit more formality.

Commercial Holidays: New Year's Day, Good Friday, Easter Monday, the Queen's Birthday, Victoria Day (Monday preceding May 25), Dominion Day (July 1), Labor Day (the first Monday in September), Thanksgiving Day (second Monday in October), Remembrance Day (November 11), and Christmas Day. In addition, each province has its own holidays. In Quebec, the additional holidays are the Epiphany (January 6), Ash Wednesday (the seventh Wednesday before Easter), Ascension Day (forty days after Easter), St. John the Baptist's Day (June 24), All Saints Day (November 1), and Conception Day (December 8). In every province except Quebec, Boxing Day, December 26, is celebrated as a holiday. Civic Holiday (the first Monday in August) is celebrated in Ontario and Manitoba. Holidays can also be established by municipalities.

Business Hours: The Canadian work week and business hours are essentially the same as ours.

DENMARK

Business Hours: Times vary, but the opening hour is usually 8-9 AM, closing at 4-4:30 PM. Businesses are closed on Saturday.

Commercial Holidays: New Year's Day, Maundy Thursday, Good Friday, Easter Monday, Prayer Day (fourth Friday after Easter), Ascension Day (forty days after Easter), Whit Monday, Danish Constitution Day (June 5), and Christmas (December 25-26). In addition, many firms are closed during July and August.

Official Language: Danish. However, most business Danes know English. German will help.

FINLAND

Customs: The most important characteristic of Finnish business etiquette is punctuality. Delivery terms as well as appointment schedules are expected to be kept. Titles, when known, should be used in business correspondence in the inside address of the letter; however, the envelope should be addressed to the firm.

Commercial Language: Finland has two official languages, Finnish and Swedish, and most business houses can correspond in either. In addition, most businesses can respond in English or German. Catalogs, brochures, price lists, and specifications are accepted in English and usually German. Use the metric system.

Business Hours: Banking hours vary slightly with different banks, being generally 9:15 AM to 3:30 or 4 PM in the summer, 9 AM to 5 PM in the winter. Most offices close on Saturday. Because of the prevalence of vacations in July and August, most Finnish businesspeople are not available during those months except by advance appointment.

Commercial Holidays: The following holidays are observed by all Finnish banks and businesses: New Year's Day, Epiphany (Jan. 6), Good Friday, Easter Monday, May Day (May 1), Ascension Day, Whit Monday, Midsummer's Day, All Saints Day, Finnish Independence Day (Dec. 6), Christmas, and Second Christmas Day (Dec. 26). In addition to this, most businesses close at 1 PM on the workday immediately preceding a holiday.

FRANCE

Trade Customs: The great majority of French businesspeople either do not speak English or pretend they don't! However, some, especially top executives of large firms, are fluent in it and like using it. So while conversations with French businesspeople can sometimes be held in English, correspondence should be in French. Catalogs, promotional literature, and instructions should be translated into French, and as a general rule, metric weights and measures should be used. Prices should be quoted c.i.f. (cost, insurance, and freight) at French port.

Commercial Holiday: New Years Day, Easter Monday, Labor Day (May 1), Ascension Day, Whit Monday, Bastille Day (July 14), Assumption Day (August 15), All Saints Day (November 1), Armistice Day (November 11) and Christmas Day. Summer, in general, is a poor period for doing business in France. Most Frenchmen take extended vacations, mainly in August and a considerable number of business firms close during August.

GERMANY

Customs: In both dress and manner, Germans are somewhat more formal than Americans. When addressing Germans, personal titles are important and should be used whenever possible. Germans don't use first names until a friendship has developed, usually over a period of years. A promotional gift (Zugabe), directly associated with a single transaction or sales effort, is distinguished from a business gift, which is presented in order to maintain a good business contact. Business gifts are generally considred in good taste if they do not exceed $40 in value, a figure rooted in German income tax law. A business or advertising gift is considered to be in bad taste and contrary to law if it results in a sense of obligation on the part of the recipient.

Language: German is the language preferred by most business firms, but almost all companies engaged in foreign trade are also able to correspond in English and one or more other foreign languages. Due to the importance of German at the retail level and among end-users, promotional literature and manuals should be printed in German. Fast handling of correspondence is important; use airmail and postal routing codes.

Business Hours: German wage and salary earners generally work forty-two to forty-three hours per week. A five-day week of appointments for business discussions can usually be arranged during the hours of 9 AM to noon and 2:30 to 5 PM on weekdays, except during trade fairs and other peak business periods. Punctuality is an important feature of German business relations and should be kept in mind when scheduling and keeping appointments.

Commercial Holidays: New Year's Day (Jan. 1), Good Friday, Easter Monday, Labor Day (May 1), Ascension Day (forty days after Easter), Pentecost or Whit Monday, Day of German Unity (June 17), Repentance Day (in November), Christmas (December 25) and December 26. Epiphany is celebrated as a legal holiday only in Baden-Württemberg and Bavaria (January 6). Corpus Christi is a holiday in Baden-Württemberg, Hesse, North Rhine-Westphalia, Rhine-

Palatinate, and the Catholic areas of Bavaria; All Saints Day (November 1) is celebrated in all of the foregoing, except Hesse, and Assumption Day (August 15) is a legal holiday in the Bavarian Catholic communities. Business firms in cities with large pre-Lenten festivals are generally closed on Shrove Monday. July and August are the most popular vacation months, during which time it is often impossible to reach many of the key, decision-making executives.

GREECE

Customs: Greek businesspeople are astute bargainers. Success in business dealings here depends on a combination of patience and quick judgment. Greeks are warm and cordial in their personal relationships, and business is usually conducted over a cup of coffee, if not actually in a coffeehouse or taverna. The wealth of good restaurants and places of entertainment makes it easy for a visiting businessperson to reciprocate the courtesies shown him/her.

Commercial Language: Greek is spoken by 96% of the people and is used for all business and official purposes. Language is not a major barrier for the foreign businessperson, however, as a relatively high percentage of local officials and businesspersons are acquainted with either English or French.

Business Hours: From May to October, 8 AM to 1:30 PM and from 5 PM to 8 PM; from October to May, 8 AM to 1:30 PM and from 4:30 PM to 7:30 PM.

Commercial Holidays: New Year's Day; Epiphany; Kathara Deftera; March 25, Independence Day; Holy Saturday (half-holiday for government, banks and business enterprises); Easter Monday; May Day; Whit Monday; Assumption Day; Holy Cross Day (half-holiday for shops only); OXI Day Eve (half-holiday for government services only); OXI Day; Christmas Eve (half-holiday, only shops open all day long); December 25, Christmas Day; Boxing Day; New Year's Eve (half-holiday—only shops open all day long).

HONG KONG

Commercial Language: English and Cantonese are the languages of government and commerce. English is understood throughout the Colony. Most business firms are able to correspond in English. Although catalogs, promotional literature, and instructions are acceptable in English, as a general practice instructions for handling a given product should also be in Chinese characters or self-explanatory symbols.

Business Hours: Most large business offices are open from 9 AM to 5 PM with lunch between 1 and 2 PM. On Saturdays, the hours are 9 AM to 1 PM. Some Chinese business houses open at 10 AM and close around 8 PM. Banking hours are from 10 AM to 3 PM on weekdays and 9:30 AM to 10 PM in other areas. For offices, Sunday closing is general.

Commercial Holidays: Every Sunday, the first weekday in January, Lunar New Year's Day, the second and third days of Lunar New Year, Good Friday, the day following Good Friday, Eastern Monday, Ching Ming Festival, the Queen's birthday, Tuen Ng (Dragon Boat Festival), the first weekday in July, the first Monday in August, Liberation Day, the second day of Mid-Autumn Festival, Chung Yeung Festival, Christmas Day, and the first weekday after Christmas.

INDIA

Customs: Business is usually conducted at a much more leisurely pace than we Americans are used to. An exchange of pleasantries and extensive hospitality on the part of Indian businesspeople can both charm and exasperate the visiting American. But a tactful response can steer business negotiations to an acceptable middle course.

Languages: Almost all Indians in government and business circles can speak and write English. While Hindi is the official language, government publications are printed in English as well, so the use of English is not a problem, although there may be some differences in choice of vocabulary or expression, since the Indians tend to follow an adaptation of British usage.

Commercial Holidays and Business Hours: Indians celebrate New Year's Day, Republic Day (January 26), Independence Day (August 15), Mahatma Ghandi's Birthday (October 2) and Christmas Day. In addition, there are thirty-two other religious or special occasions which are celebrated either nationally or regionally. Government offices are normally closed on these days. Since many of these holidays fall on different days of the year, businesspeople are advised to check with the Indian Embassy or Consulates in the United States prior to leaving for India. The working hours for most Indian government offices are 10 AM to 1 PM and 2 PM until 5 PM, Monday through Saturday, except the second Saturday of each month. The typical business office is open from Monday through Friday 9:30 AM to 1 PM and 2 PM to 5 PM. Business executives and officials prefer business appointments late in the morning or afternoon.

INDONESIA

Customs: Personal contact is extremely important in selling in Indonesia, since almost no sales are made without initial face-to-face negotiations between the customer and the foreign firm or its Indonesian agent.

Languages: The national language is Indonesian (or Bahasa Indonesia, a form of Malay). Since Indonesia became independent in 1945, Indonesian has been used increasingly throughout the archipelago. It is now not only the "lingua franca" between ethnic subgroups but also the language of all written communication, education, government, and business. English is the most widely spoken foreign language and is taught in the schools. It also is used in business circles and in most business communications.

Commercial Holidays and Business Hours: The main holidays in Indonesia are: New Year's Day, January 1; Good Friday; Hari Maulud Nabi (Muslim festival), March 13; Ascension Day; Waicak Day (celebrating Buddha's birth); Galunggan in Bali (a New Year feast lasting ten days), June 9; Sekaten (birth of Mohammed); Independence Day, August 17; Idul Fitri (Muslim festival), September 25-26; and Christmas Day, December 25. As you'll notice by the lack of specific dates on certain holidays, these change with the lunar calendar. The American Embassy and Consulates will be open on Mohammed's Birthday as well as Good Friday, but will be closed on the other holidays as well as on U.S. national holidays. In addition to the holidays listed, business visitors should note the Islamic month of fasting, Ramadan. During the following lunar month twenty-eight days) Indonesian government offices and many business establishments work a shorter business day, generally 8 AM to 12 noon. The month of Ramadan is concluded by the holiday of Idul Fitri. Business activities should be started no later than 7:30 AM.

IRAN

Business Hours: Banks are open as follows: winter from 8 AM to 12:30 PM and from 3 PM to 6 PM; summer from 7:30 AM to 12:30 PM and from 5 PM to 7 PM; Thursdays, closed in the afternoon. Fridays, closed all day. Government offices are generally open from 8 AM to 4:30 PM, Saturday through Wednesday. Private firms and shops are generally closed on Fridays (the Moslem Sabbath) and open the other six days of the week.

Commercial Holidays: Business firms and banks are closed on the following official holidays: March 21 and 22, New Year (Now Ruz); April 2, Thirteenth Day of the New Year (Sizdah); August 5, Constitution Day; October 26, the Shah's Birthday. In addition, there are eleven religious holidays, the dates of which vary from year to year, during which most offices are closed; and the U.S. Embassy is officially closed on these days as well as on official American holidays. Business visitors are advised to avoid the Iranian New Year holiday period: Iranian executives frequently are out of town during a two- or three-week period following that date.

IRELAND

Customs: The most important characteristics of Irish business etiquette are punctuality and courtesy. Delivery terms as well as appointment schedules are expected to be kept. Address mail to the firm rather than to individuals, using employee's titles only on the inside letter address. Do not get into discussions about Ireland's economic/political/religious differences—you'll end up alienating someone.

Commercial Language: Two languages are spoken in Ireland —Irish and English. Irish is the first official language. While English is normally used in business contracts and is the language of correspondence, some expressions and words have different meanings from those accepted in the United States; for clarity of meaning you had better define unfamiliar terms. Prompt acknowledgement of communications from Irish firms is always appreciated. Specifications may be according to U.S. or English measurement standards. The government of Ireland, however, will change over from these present standards to the metric system in the near future.

Business Hours: Banking hours are generally 9:30 to 12:30 and from 1:30 to 3 PM. Banks are usually opened until 5 PM on Fridays. Offices are opened from 9:30 AM to 5 PM while stores are opened from 9:30 AM to 5:30 PM. Because of the prevalence of vacations in July and August, most Irish businesspeople are not available during these months except by advance appointment.

Commercial Holidays: New Year's Day (banks only); St. Patrick's Day (March 17); Good Friday; Easter Monday; First Monday in June (bank holiday) First Monday in August (bank holiday); Christmas (December 25); and St. Stephen's Day (December 28).

ISRAEL

Customs: Business in Israel tends to be conducted in a very informal atmosphere and there is no "business etiquette" as such. The Israeli will not hesitate to express his opinion and he welcomes an open discussion. He is almost always well informed on international business developments and is well aware of competitive factors.

Trade Customs: Hebrew and Arabic are the official languages of Israel, but English is widely used in the business community and predominates in specialized fields such as electronics. All correspondence and documentation in foreign trade may be conducted in English. The government also requires that prepackaged goods be clearly labelled as to contents and weight; English can be used to satisfy this requirement.

Hours and Business Holidays: Business establishments are generally open from 8 AM until 4 PM in winter, and from about 7:30 AM to 2 PM during the summer. Most offices close early on Friday to prepare for Sabbath, which lasts from sundown Friday until sundown Saturday. Banks are usually open from 8:30 AM to 12:30 AM and from 3:30 PM until 5 PM, Sunday through Thursday. On Fridays and on the days preceding holidays, they are open from 8:30 AM until noon. Government offices are generally open to visitors between 9 AM and 1 PM. Sunday through Thursday. Working hours usually extend before and after visitors' hours and if the matter is urgent, most departments will be accommodating. All business activity ceases on Saturdays and religious holidays, the dates of which vary from year to year: Passover, first day; Passover, last day; Israel Independence Day; Pentecost; Rosh Hashana (New Year); Yom Kippur (Day of Atonement); First Day of Tabernacles; Last Day of Tabernacles; Hanukkah.

ITALY

Customs: By and large, what is considered good business practice in this country also applies when doing business in Italy. Businesspeople there also appreciate prompt replies to their inquiries, and they expect all correspondence to be acknowledged. In the north of Italy, promotional literature and correspondence is short and factual. In the south, where customs are different, Italians place much more value on personal contacts than on correspondence.

Commercial Language: Italian is the official language, and it is spoken in all parts of Italy, although minorities in the Alto Adige and Aosta regions speak German and French, respectively. Correspondence with Italian firms, especially if the letter is the first ever sent, should be in Italian. If a reply comes in English, then the subsequent correspondence with the Italian firm can be in English. The use of Italian is not only regarded as a courtesy, but assures prompt attention, and prevents inaccuracies which might arise in translation. Most large commercial firms, however, are able to correspond in English and French in addition to Italian. It's important to have trade literature, catalogs, and instructions for the use of servicing of products printed in Italian.

Business Hours: The usual Italian business hours are from 8 or 9 AM to noon or 1 PM and from 3 to 6 or 7 PM. Working hours for the various ministries of government are normally from 8 AM to 2 PM without intermission. Bank hours are from 8:30 AM to 1:30 PM.

Holidays: New Year's Day (January 1); Epiphany (January 6); Feast of St. Joseph (March 19); Easter Monday; Liberation Day (April 25); Labor Day (May 1); Ascension Day; Republic Day (June 2); Corpus Christi; St. Peter's and St. Paul's Day; Assumption Day (August 15); St. Gennaro Day (September 19), celebrated in Naples only; All Saints Day (November 1); St. Giusto Day (November 3), celebrated in Trieste only; National Unity Day (November 4); St. Ambrose Day (December 7), celebrated in Milan only; Immaculate Conception (December 8); Christmas and St. Stephen's Day (December 25 and 26). Generally, August is a poor month for conducting business in Italy, since most business firms are closed for vacations.

JAPAN

Customs: In Japan, you won't pay for any business entertaining. Nor will your associate pay directly. He'll sign for the tab and his company will be billed later. Expense accounts are a way of life in Japan and they *expect* to entertain you.

Commercial Holidays: January 1, New Year's Day; Jan. 2, 3, 4, Bank Holidays (all commercial firms are closed); Jan. 15, Adult's Day; Feb. 11, National Foundation Day; Vernal Equinox Day (variable date); April 29, the Emperor's birthday; May 1 (May Day), most manufacturers closed, service firms open; May 3, Constitution Memorial Day; May 5, Children's Day; September 15, Respect of the Aged Day; Autumnal Equinox Day (variable date); October 10, Physical Culture Day; November 3, Culture Day; November 23, Labour Thanksgiving Day; December 28, New Year's holiday begins (lasts about five to ten days). There is also a time period in late spring called "Golden Week," when some firms remain closed the entire week. Some manufacturers close for a week during the summer.

Business Hours: 9 AM to 5 PM, Monday through Friday; 9 AM to 12 noon, Saturdays. Closed Sunday.

KENYA

Customs: Business dress is comparable to that in the U.S. Personal visits are warmly welcomed and generally regarded as the most efficient method of establishing new trade contracts. Punctuality is important to Kenyan businesspersons and the business visitor should be on time for appointments. As a general rule, appointments should be made in advance of a business call. Prompt handling of correspondence is both expected and appreciated.

Official Language: Although Swahili is the official language of Kenya, English is widely used in business and commerce. Business correspondence, catalogs, and advertising material prepared in English are readily understood by most potential buyers. Business cards are widely used; they are usually imprinted in black and white, although there is no objection to the colored American styles.

Business Hours: Business establishments and government offices are open Monday through Friday from 8:15 AM to 12:30 PM and from 2 PM to 4:30 PM. Most offices are also open on Saturday from 8:15 AM to noon.

Holidays: January 1 (New Year's Day); Good Friday*; Easter Monday*; May 1 (Labor Day); June 1 (Mandaraka Day), Id ul-Fitr*; October 20 (Kenyatta Day); Id ul-Azhi*; December 12 (Independence Day); December 25 (Christmas Day); December 26 (Boxing Day). Those dates marked with an asterisk (*) vary from year to year.

KUWAIT

Commercial Language: Arabic is the official language, but English is widely spoken and is generally acceptable in business and government circles. Catalogs and promotional literature in English are acceptable. Use of Arabic by foreign firms in corresponding with Kuwaitis is greatly valued and can be a competitive advantage to the foreign firm.

Holidays: Religious holidays vary from year to year; the Department of Commerce's last issue each year of *Commerce Today* lists the Kuwaiti holidays for the upcoming year. The only fixed holidays in Kuwait are New Year's Day and Kuwait National Day (February 25). October through May or June is generally considered the best period for foreign business visitors to Kuwait. Because of the intense heat, many local businesspersons are absent from the country in the summer.

Business Hours: Friday is the Muslim sabbath, and all government and business offices are closed. Government hours generally are 7:30 AM to 1:30 PM in winter, 6:30 AM to 12:30 PM in spring and autumn, and 6 AM to noon in summer. Larger private industries generally work 7:30 AM to 2:30 PM, Saturday through Wednesday. Business offices and retail trades generally are open from 7 AM to 1 PM, close for the afternoon, and reopen from 5-8 PM; many, however, do not reopen on Thursday evening.

MALAYSIA

Language: The population of Malaysia is a racial mélange of Malaysian, Chinese, Indian, and Eurasian; the mix of languages and dialects rivals the racial mix. Malay is the official language. English is understood and spoken in most business circles. In addition, Tamil, Hindi, Mandarin, and several Southern Chinese dialects are spoken.

Business Hours: Most business establishments have office hours from 8:30 or 9 AM to 1 PM, and from 2:30 to 4:30 or 5 PM on Mondays through Fridays. Most offices are open on Saturday from 9 AM to 1 PM. The hours observed by the government offices are 9 AM to 4:30 PM on weekdays and 9 AM to 1 PM on Saturdays.

Holidays: Not all holidays are on fixed calendar dates, since many are variable in accordance with Muslim or lunar calendars. A businessperson should check with the Malaysian Embassy before departure to avoid any conflicts. The national religion of Malaysia is Islam.

NETHERLANDS

Customs: Dutch businessmen are unusually courteous, earnest and honest. Most do not use first names until a firm friendship has been formed. Friendships are highly valued, however, and once an American businessperson has gained her partner's confidence, she can count upon the latter's full and cheerful cooperation.

Commercial Holidays: New Year's Day, Good Friday, Easter Monday, the Queen's birthday (April 30), Ascension Day, Whit Monday, Christmas Day and Day after Christmas.

Business Hours: A 45-hour, five-day work week for offices and factories, which are usually closed weekends.

Commercial Language: Dutch, but English is understood.

NEW ZEALAND

Commercial Language: English is the official language of New Zealand.

Holidays: New Year's Day, New Zealand Day (February 6), Good Friday, Easter Monday, Anzac Day (April 25), Queen's birthday (although actually on April 21, the holiday is generally observed early in June), Labour Day (in October), Christmas and Boxing Day (December 26). In addition to the public holidays mentioned above, there is in each provincial district a holiday for the provincial anniversary. These dates are as follows: Auckland (January 29). Canterbury (December 16), Hawk's Bay (November 1), Marlborough (November 1), Nelson (February 1), Northland (February 6), Otago (March 23), Southland (March 23), Taranaki (March 31), Wellington (January 22).

NORWAY

Language: Many Norwegian businesspeople, especially those dealing in import and export, are fluent in English, the preferred commercial language. Norwegian businesspeople often travel in the United States and in Europe, generally read English-language trade and technical magazines and books, and are thus very well acquainted with trade and business practices in the United States. However, as you travel from the main centers such as Oslo, Bergen and Stavanger, you will find fewer English-speaking businesspeople.

Business Hours: Business hours throughout Norway are generally from 9 AM to 4 PM.

Holidays: New Year's Day, Holy Thursday, Good Friday, Easter Monday, Labor Day (May 1), Norwegian Constitution Day (May 17), Whit Monday, Christmas Day, and the day following Christmas.

PERU

Language: Spanish and Quechua are the official languages in Peru, but Spanish is the language of commerce. Many businesspeople in Peru have a thorough command of the English language, but naturally, prefer to use their native tongue. U.S. business firms should present their quotations, catalogs, illustrations, price lists, and other trade information material in Spanish. Bilingual businesspeople should speak Spanish to their Peruvian counterparts with a view to generating friendly feelings and confidence. If unable to speak Spanish, the visitor should avoid the use of English colloquial expressions or phrases.

Office Hours: Office hours in Peru are (1) the straight time shift (Horario Corrido), from Monday through Friday, with a total of 40 working hours; and (2) the two-shift office (Horario de 2 Jornadas), from Monday through Friday and half-day on Saturday, with two or three hours for lunch and 44 to 48 working hours a week. In addition, the year's working time is divided into winter office hours (April through December) and summer office hours (January through March). In summer time, private and governmental banks, ministries and other public entities work only 5 hours per day (8 AM to 1 PM) instead of the normal eight-hour workday. Other private businesses, including department and retail stores, work eight hours daily from 10:45 AM to 7:50 PM (for sales personnel) and from 8 AM to 5 PM (for administrative personnel). The work day of eight hours generally begins at the following times each morning:

	Winter	Summer
Private company offices	8 to 9 AM	7:45 to 8:15 AM
Government offices	7:45 to 8 AM	7:45 to 8 AM
Factories	6 to 8 AM	6 to 8 AM
Government banks	8:30 AM	8 AM
Private banks	8:55 AM	8 AM

Holidays: January 1, New Year's Day; Holy Thursday (half day only); Good Friday; May 1, Labor Day; June 29, St. Peter and St. Paul; July 28, Independence Day; July 29, Independence Day, August 30, Santa Rosa de Lima; October 9, Peruvian National Day; November 1, All Saints Day; December 8, Immaculate Conception; December 25, Christmas.

THE PHILIPPINES

Commercial Language: There are three official languages in the Philippines: English, Spanish and Pilipino. However, English is widely spoken and is the major medium of instruction in the Philippine school system, as well as the usual language of commercial correspondence. In an attempt to develop a common language other than English, the Philippine Government has supported the creation of Pilipino, based on Tagalog, as a national language, and requires that it be taught in the schools. Relatively few Filipinos any longer speak or use Spanish.

Business Hours/Holidays: Office hours for business firms and the Philippine Government normally are from 8 or 8:30 AM to 5 PM with two hours for lunch. Since the mid-day siesta break remains a rather firm custom in the Philippine business world, the afternoon's business may not start before 2:30 or 3:30 PM. It is best, therefore, to attempt to accomplish business objectives in the morning or late afternoon. Offices are generally closed on Saturdays and Sundays and on the following public holidays: January 1, New Year's Day; Easter holidays, which include Holy Thursday and Good Friday; May 1, Labor Day; June 12, Independence Day; July 4, Philippine-American Day; November 30, National Heroes' Day; December 25, Christmas; December 30, Rizal Day. In addition, special holidays such as Bataan Day and General Elections Day may be called by the President of the Republic.

SAUDI ARABIA

Customs: Personal contact is the key to doing business in Saudi Arabia. While written correspondence is important as an initial introduction, several visits are normally necessary before a foreign firm finally wins a significant contract. Saudi custom does not stress promptness, so business visitors should not be affronted by tardiness in keeping appointments. Business discussions are often prefaced by long conversations on unrelated topics. Following this warm-up, which usually includes coffee or tea, Saudis appreciate a straightforward presentation without a "hard sell." Seldom will any commitments be made as the result of one visit. Foreign businesspersons should be careful to follow up a meeting with correspondence providing any added information requested and arranging for future discussions to reach a definitive agreement. Women, beware! You have your work cut out for you. It could be the biggest challenge on earth to succeed in being taken seriously as a businesswoman.

Commercial Language: The official language of Saudi Arabia is Arabic. However, English is widely spoken in both the Government and the private business community.

Holidays: Because the Islamic Calendar is based on the Hijri year of 12 lunar months with 354 days, the dates of holidays vary from year to year. During the month of Ramadan (in the fall), all Muslims refrain from eating, drinking, and smoking from sunrise to sunset. Non-Muslims must also observe the fast while in public, and business hours are shortened. To check precise holiday dates for the upcoming year consult the Department of Commerce's last issue each year of *Commerce Today.*

Business Hours: Saudi Government hours are Saturday through Wednesday, 8 AM-4 PM during the winter (September 23-May 21), and 7 AM to 3 PM during the summer, with one hour at noon for lunch prayer. During Ramadan the schedule is 8 AM to 2 PM. Government offices are open to the public in the morning only. Businesses are normally open from 8:30 AM to 1:30 PM and from 4:30 PM to 8 PM six days a week. Bank hours are 8:30 AM to noon Saturday through Thursday. All business and offices are closed on Friday, the Muslim Sabbath.

SINGAPORE

Languages: While the official language is Malay, the language of business in Singapore is English. Local traders will usually know at least two languages. Various dialects of Chinese, and, to some extent, Malay, are used by the local businesspeople when dealing with each other and their customers. Japanese, Thai, and Indian are also used locally. Because of the international character of Singapore, almost every language is used, but most people in business speak and understand English.

Business Hours: Businesses operate on a five-and-one-half-day week, Monday through Saturday. Office hours are generally from 8:30 or 9 AM to 1 PM, and from 2:30 to 4:40 or 5 PM. Most offices are open for a half-day on Saturday, closing at 1 PM. The hours observed by the government offices are 9 AM to 4:30 PM during the week and 9 AM to 1 PM on Saturday.

Holidays: New Year's Day, January 1; Labor Day, May 1; Vesak Day, May 17; National Day, August 9; Hari Raya Punsa, October 29; Christmas Day, December 25. Holidays with dates subject to annual change are Hari Raya Haji, Chinese New Year, Good Friday, and Deepavali. When a holiday falls on a Sunday, the next day is taken as a public holiday.

SOUTH AFRICA

Customs: Business customs in South Africa are generally similar to those in the United States and Western Europe. South African businesspeople dress conservatively; women should wear suits or dresses. Business cards should be simple, including only the basics such as name, address, and business title. Punctuality is important to the South African businessperson, who generally makes every effort to be on time. Make appointments in advance of a business call.

Commercial Language: Although English and Afrikaans are South Africa's two official languages, English is most frequently used commercially. However, there is some language sensitivity in South Africa, particularly among the Afrikaner population. Consequently, many firms print much of their literature, including annual statements, in both languages.

Holidays: New Year's Day, Good Friday, Easter Monday, Ascension Day, Republic Day (May 31), Settlers Day (first Monday in September), Kruger Day (October 10), Day of the Covenant (December 16, Christmas Day, and Boxing Day (December 26).

Business Hours: Office hours are generally from 8:30 AM to 5 PM Monday through Friday and from 8:30 AM to noon on Saturdays; however, many firms are now adopting the 5-day work week. Lunch is generally from 1-2 PM, with many businesses closed during this period.

SOUTH KOREA

Commercial Language: While Korean is the universal language of the country, many Koreans speak and understand English to a greater or lesser extent. Many business firms are able to correspond in English. Knowledge of Japanese is also fairly wide-spread. Catalogs, promotional literature, and instructions are acceptable in English.

Business Hours: Most offices, government and private, are open from 9 AM to 5 PM on weekdays with one hour at noon for lunch, but close at 1 PM on Saturday. Banks close at 4 PM daily and at 1 PM on Saturday. Meanwhile, department stores, shops, restaurants, hospitals, barber shops, and other service establishments remain open as late as 10 PM and are open over weekends and even on public holidays. Except for Cheju Island and Chungchongbukdo province, a curfew is in effect from 11 PM to 4 AM.

Holidays: Public and business offices close on the following statutory holidays: January 1-3, New Year Celebration; March 1, Independence Movement Day; March 10, Labor Day; April 5, Arbor Day; June 5, Memorial Day; July 17, Constitution Day; August 15, Liberation Day; Korean Thanksgiving Day (variable date); October 3, National Foundation Day; October 9, Korean Alphabet Day; October 24, United Nations Day; December 25, Christmas Day.

SPAIN

Customs: Spain's traditional courtesy and hospitality apply to business relations. While it is customary to entertain only intimate friends in the home, many public places of entertainment are located in the larger cities and business visitors should be prepared to reciprocate the courtesies accorded to them there.

Commercial Language: Spanish is the commercial language, although Catalan is used extensively in the Barcelona area. It is important to have trade literature, catalogs, and instructions for the use and servicing of products printed in Spanish. Business cards should be printed in both English and Spanish. Many large commercial houses, however, conduct correspondence in English or French in addition to Spanish.

Holidays: January 1 (New Year); January 6 (Epiphany); March 19 (St. Joseph's Day); Maundy Thursday, after 2 PM; Good Friday; May 1 (Labor Day); Ascension (forty days after Easter); Corpus Christi (three weeks after Ascension); July 18 (National Day); July 25 (St. James Day); August 15 (Assumption); October 1 (Day of the Caudillo), only government offices close; October 12 (Columbus Day); November 1 (All Saints Day); December 8 (Immaculate Conception); December 25 (Christmas). Local holidays include May 15 (San Isidro), celebrated in Madrid only; the following holidays celebrated in Barcelona only: Easter Monday; June 24 (St. John the Baptist); September 24 (Our Lady of Mercy); and December 26 (St. Stephen's Day); and June 19 (Liberation Day) and July 31 (St. Ignatius Day), holidays in Bilbabo. Besides the Spanish legal holidays, many businesses observe other local holidays and feast days.

Business Hours: The legal national work week is 48 hours and constitutes six eight-hour days. The trend is toward a reduction of the work week which now averages about 44 hours. Business hours are generally from 9 or 10 AM to 7 or 8 PM with a two-hour lunchbreak from 2 PM to 4 PM. Businesses are closed on Sunday.

SWEDEN

Commercial Language: Swedish businesspeople generally are serious, articulate, and well informed on a wide range of international economic, political and social questions. Many Swedish businesspeople, particularly those dealing in export and import, in Stockholm, Gothenberg and Malmo are fluent in English, the preferred commercial language. A knowledge of German often is useful, particularly with older, non-English-speaking Swedes. Like their Norwegian counterparts, Swedish businesspeople travel in the United States and in Europe, and are usually familiar with American business practices.

Business Hours: Offices generally open at 8:30 or 9 AM and close at 5 PM on weekdays (sometimes at 3 or 4 PM in summer). Most business offices are closed on Saturdays. Banks are open weekdays usually from 9:30 AM to 3 PM and closed Saturdays throughout the year. On Monday to Friday, many banks, especially in large towns, are open one or more evenings from 4:30 to 6 PM.

Holidays: Sweden has eleven national holidays: New Year's Day; Good Friday; Easter Sunday; Easter Monday; Labor Day (May 1); Ascension Day (sixth Thursday after Easter); Whit Monday; National Holiday (June 6); Mid-summer Day (the Saturday between June 19 and 26); All Saints Day (first Saturday in November); and Christmas (December 25 and 26).

SWITZERLAND

Languages: German is spoken in Bern, Zurich and Basle, French in Geneva and Lausanne, and Italian in Lugano. For Swiss companies, the general practice is to prepare financial statements in the language that is used at their headquarters, but English is widely understood and spoken by businesspeople.

Holidays: Businesses are closed on the following federal holidays: January 1 (New Year's Day), January 2 (Barzelisday), Good Friday, Easter Monday, Ascension Day, Whit Monday, August 1 (Swiss National Day), December 24 afternoon (Christmas Eve), December 25 (Christmas Day), and December 26 (St. Stephen's Day). In addition, the afternoon of May 1 is observed in all major cities as Labor Day. Thirty other holidays are celebrated locally: in Zurich the next to the last Monday in April (Sechselauten) and the second Monday in September (Knabeschiessen); in Basel carnival days during the first week in Lent, and in Geneva the second Thursday in September (Thanksgiving), and December 31 (Reformation Day).

Business Hours: In general, daily business hours run from 8 AM to 5 PM with a one or two hour lunch break Monday through Friday. Banks open a quarter- or half-hour later and close a half-hour earlier, and are closed on Saturdays. Stores are usually closed on Monday mornings.

THAILAND

Language: English is an accepted language for business and is widely spoken in Bangkok's commercial and government circles. However, in dealings pertaining to consumer goods (which must be retailed by Thai nationals in accordance with the Alien Occupations Law), a local agent or representative will be necessary to reach the non-English-speaking population.

Holidays: New Year's Day, January 1; The Songkran Festival (Buddhist New Year), April 13; Coronation Day Anniversary, May 5; Visakhja Puja (Buddhist Festival), May; Buddhist Lent begins, June/July; Queen's Birthday, August 12; Chulalongkorn Day, October 23; King's Birthday, December 5; New Year's Eve, December 31.

TURKEY

Languages: Turkish is spoken by 90 percent of the population, but business contacts can be made in English, French, or German.

Holidays: Turkey observes both civil and religious holidays. The latter are based on the old Arabic Calendar, resulting in different days each year. There are seven official holidays: National Sovereignty and Children's Day, from April 22 PM to April 23; Spring Day, May 1; Youth and Sports Day, May 19; Freedom and Constitution Day, from May 26 PM to March 28; Victory Day, August 30; Anniversary of the Declaration of the Republic, from October 28 PM to October 30. Religious holidays are: The Feast of Sugar, in Fall; and The Feast of Sacrifice, in Winter.

Business Hours: Offices are closed Saturday afternoons and a day or two before and after the holidays. Stores are open on Saturday afternoons and are closed only on the first day of religious holidays.

YUGOSLAVIA

Languages: The principal language in Yugoslavia is Serbo-Croatian, spoken by about two-thirds of the population. English is the most prevalent foreign language in Yugoslavia. While most larger enterprises and those engaged in foreign trade can correspond in English, sales can be enhanced by having trade literature as well as instructions and service manuals translated into Serbo-Croatian.

Holidays: January 1 and 2 (New Year's Day), May 1 and 2 (International Labor Day), July 4 (Fighter's Day), Nov. 29 and 30 (Day of the Republic).

Business Hours: Offices are restricted to a five-day week. Government offices are open from 7 AM to 3 PM and on Wednesday to 5 PM. Commercial offices are open from 7 AM to 2:30 PM and banks from 7:30 AM to 3 PM. Stores are closed from noon to 5 PM and on Saturdays after 1 PM.

GOVERNMENTAL AGENCIES AND SERVICES   There is a wealth of help and information available to traveling businesspeople, through various government agencies. What follows is a summary of some of these services.

The Superintendent of Documents, U.S. Government Printing Office, Washington, D.C. 20402 will send you, for 35¢, its listing of "Key Officers of Foreign Service Posts—Guide for Businesspersons," with names of economic, commercial, scientific, and agricultural attachés you can contact on the spot (or preferably in advance). The Office of Commercial Affairs in the Bureau of Economic and Business Affairs in the State Department's Washington offices can help you on all matters of international trade, and State's Agency for International Development will encourage your export efforts in many practical ways. Here in the U.S., the Department of Commerce serves as distributor of State's data from overseas on foreign competition and marketing opportunities, and your nearest Commerce field office can give you a great deal of material of this sort. You can get on the State Department's mailing list for free publications simply by writing General Publications Division, Office of Media Services, Room 4827A, Department of State, Washington, D.C. 20520. Specifically, here's what they can do for you:

ASSISTANCE TO BUSINESS TRAVELERS OVERSEAS: Businesswomen planning to travel overseas to find agents or distributors for their product lines, or to gain first-hand knowledge of a country's business conditions, should visit embassies and consulates for advice and assistance from commercial officers and their local professional staffs. The Commerce Department sponsors a "Business Travel Announcement Service" to alert Foreign Service posts regarding projected itineraries and visitation objectives when such planning is submitted sufficiently in advance. Applications for this targeted special service should be filed with the nearest District Office at least two weeks before travelers leave the United States.

PUBLICATIONS: In addition to a variety of direct counseling services by Commerce, there is a broad range of publications. These include "Overseas Business Reports," which examine individual countries in terms of marketing factors and trade regulations; the "Foreign Economic Trends" series, which covers over one hundred countries' economies; "Foreign Market Reports" monthly indexes, Commerce research studies, and Foreign Service-prepared economic-commercial reports. "Global Market Surveys" and "Country Market Surveys," summarizing Commerce's market research findings, give a detailed marketing picture for specific high-export-potential products in individual overseas markets. The International Commerce section of the biweekly magazine "Commerce Today" also gives useful foreign commerce data. In addition to being available on an individual basis, many publications can be subscribed to.

WORLD TRADERS DATA REPORTS: Prepared by the U.S. Foreign Service at overseas posts and transmitted telegraphically, WTDRs provide background and commercial information on individual foreign firms. They include specifics such as product lines handled, trade connections, sales areas, and financial references. Available at $15 each. Request forms (DIB-431) are obtainable at any Commerce District Office or from U.S. Department of Commerce, Export Information Division, Room 1033, Washington, D.C. 20230.

AGENT/DISTRIBUTOR SERVICE: The Agent/Distributor Service (ADS) provided by the U.S. Foreign Service, on thirty days of receipt, identifies up to three potential foreign agents or distributors interested in a business relationship. The fee is $25 per ADS. For details, contact any of the Commerce Department's District Offices.

TRADE OPPORTUNITIES PROGRAM (TOP): A U.S. company, as a subscriber to TOP, specifies the products and the countries for which it wants trade opportunities, and that information is put into the TOP computer. Trade opportunities telexed to Commerce from Foreign Service posts are matched by the computer against the subscriber's information specifications. When a match occurs, a printout notice of the opportunity is mailed to the subscriber. Cost of each notice is 50¢, chargeable against the company's subscription. Information about TOP is available at Commerce District Offices.

TARGET INDUSTRY PROGRAM: Relying upon extensive government-sponsored market research, fifteen U.S. industries with the greatest export growth potential are each matched with the top fifteen to twenty most promising markets around the world for that industry. Key market information and associated promotion for each targeted industry is published in a Global Market Survey available through the District Offices.

COMMERCIAL NEWSLETTERS: Many of the larger U.S. embassies and consulates publish a newsletter which is distributed to the business community in the country or region they serve. At no cost, it is possible for U.S. firms to have certain new products described in this publication so that if a local businessperson is interested, she

"The chambermaid can literally
put you back together.
She'll sew what needs to be sewn,
get you extra hangers,
draw your bath, clean your room,
remove clothing spots, zip you up—
you'll wish you could find
a lover like that!"

may write to the American firm. Contact the nearest District Office for assistance.

BUSINESS COUNSELING: In-depth international business counseling services are provided to U.S. firms by the Departments of Commerce and State in Washington, and by the Commerce Department's forty-two District Offices. Commerce's Business Counseling Section in Washington offers guidance, and schedules needed appointments with appropriate federal officials. District Offices counsel businesspersons and point out foreign markets, possible agents or distributors, and financial information for export assistance. State Department country desk officers can brief businesspersons on the political climate in their country of responsibility. The Business Relations Division of the State Department can offer guidance on contacting appropriate offices in the State Department.

INTERNATIONAL EXHIBITIONS: The Department of Commerce sponsors participation by groups of American firms in U.S. pavilions at selected international exhibitions. Commerce also sponsors solo exhibitions of American products when there are no suitable trade fairs available. To assist U.S. businesspersons, "Commerce Today" periodically publishes a schedule of future international fairs. These exhibitions range from the general type, which promote sales in numerous product categories, to the highly specialized fair, designed to attract buyers of specific products. Events are listed by country, city, date, name, and fair management address, and are generally open to participation by any U.S. company in the related industry. Each firm may make arrangements for its own exhibit, including rental of space and utilities, transportation of products, and setting up and staffing the booth. For information on international trade fairs, contact the foreign fair management at the listed address or write the Office of International Marketing, Bureau of International Commerce, U.S. Department of Commerce, Washington, D.C. 20230.

TRADE MISSIONS: The Department of Commerce sponsors two types of overseas trade missions. The first is the specialized trade mission which is planned and led by the Department, where the best product theme and itinerary are determined on the basis of government research. The second type is the Industry Organized/Government Approved (IOGA) trade mission which is sponsored and recruited by state or private industry organizations; commerce provides overall guidance and supervision, plus the services of an experienced advance officer.

EXPORT MAILING LIST SERVICE: This aid provides up-to-date, individually targeted contact lists of overseas firms with export potential, coded by type of business, product, and country, and available on gummed labels or in standard printout. Charge is $15 for up to three hundred names, plus 5¢ for each additional name.

FOREIGN TRADERS INDEX DATA TAPE SERVICE: This provides data on magnetic tape on some 133,000 firms in 122 countries, by country. This service makes it possible for users to utilize their data processing equipment for their own information retrieval. For more information contact the nearest U.S. Department of Commerce District Office or write the Director, Bureau of International Commerce, Domestic and International Business Administration, U.S. Department of Commerce 262, Washington, D.C. 20230.

ASSISTANCE TO EXPORTERS: The Foreign Service of the Department of State cooperates with the Department of Commerce in providing the American business community with many of the following services:

U.S. Trade Centers: The Department of Commerce, with the assistance of the Foreign Service, operates U.S. Trade Centers in Beirut, Buenos Aires, Frankfurt, London, Mexico City, Milan, Paris, Seoul, Singapore, Stockholm, Sydney, Taipei, Tehran, Tokyo, and Vienna. These outlets, through scheduled promotions, can help U.S. firms test interest in their products, make direct sales, establish agencies, and make other business arrangements.

Joint Export Establishment Promotions: The Joint Export Establishment Promotion (JEEP) is a type of between-show promotion involving tailored promotions undertaken on a shared cost basis, especially designed to help individual firms or small groups of U.S. manufacturers of related products penetrate new markets under a cooperative arrangement with Commerce.

The Fine Art of Staying Out of the Slammer

CUSTOMS

27

ALL ARTICLES acquired abroad and in your possession at the time of your return must be declared. This includes:

* Gifts presented to you while abroad, such as wedding or birthday presents.
* Repairs or alterations made to any articles taken abroad and returned, whether or not repairs or alterations were free of charge
* Items you have been requested to bring home for someone else.
* Any articles you intend to sell or use in your business.

The price actually paid for each article must be stated on your declaration. If the article was not purchased, obtain its fair retail value in the country in which it was acquired. Even if you've used or worn the article, you must pay duty on it at the price you paid for it. The customs officer will make an appropriate reduction in its value for wear and use.

Customs declaration forms are distributed on ships and planes and should be prepared in advance of arrival for presentation to the immigration and customs inspectors. Fill out the identification portion of the declaration form. You may declare orally to the customs inspector the articles you acquired abroad, if you have not exceeded the duty-free exemption allowed. A customs officer may, however, ask you to prepare a written list if he thinks it is necessary.

A written declaration will be necessary when:

1. *The total fair retail value of articles acquired abroad exceeds $100; or*
2. *More than one quart of alcoholic beverages or more than 100 cigars are included; or*
3. *Some of the items are not intended for your personal or household use, such as commercial samples, items for sale or use in your business, or articles you are bringing home for another person; or*

4. *A customs duty or internal revenue tax is collectible on any article in your possession.*

The head of a family may make a joint declaration for all members residing in the same household and returning with her to the United States. Example: a family of four may bring in articles free of duty and valued up to $400 retail value on one declaration, even if the articles acquired by one member of the family exceeds his $100 exemption.

They will be helpful in making out your declaration. Also, pack your baggage in a manner that will make inspection easy. Do your best to pack separately the articles you have acquired.

WARNING! If you understate the value of an article you declare, or if you otherwise misrepresent an article in your declaration, the article may be liable to seizure and forfeiture—and you will be liable for a personal penalty and sometimes criminal prosecution.

Customs inspectors handle tourist items day after day and become well acquainted with the normal foreign values. Moreover, current commercial prices of foreign items are available at all times and on-the-spot comparisons of these values can be made. It is well known that some merchants abroad offer travelers invoices or bills of sale showing false or understated values. This practice not only delays your customs examination, but can prove very costly.

Don't rely on advice given by persons outside the Customs Service. It may be bad advice which could lead you to violate the customs laws and incur costly penalties. If you are in doubt about the value of an article or whether it should be declared, always declare it first and then ask the customs inspector.

Do not carry messages, money or packages of any kind into or out of any country for any other person, unless authorities of that country have confirmed that by so doing you will not be breaking your regulation.

YOUR EXEMPTIONS In clearing U.S. Customs, a traveler is considered either a "returning resident of the United States" or a "nonresident."

Generally speaking, if you leave the United States for purposes of traveling, working, or studying abroad and return to resume residency in the United States, you are considered a returning resident. Articles acquired abroad and brought into the United States are subject to applicable duty and internal revenue tax, but as a returning resident you are allowed certain exemptions from paying duty on items obtained while abroad.

Articles totaling $100 (based on the fair retail value of each item in the country where acquired) may be entered free of duty, subject to the limitations on liquors and cigars, if:

1. *You are returning from a stay abroad of at least 48 hours.*
2. *Articles were acquired as an incident of your trip for your personal or household use.*
3. *You bring the articles with you at the time of your return to the United States and they are properly declared. (Articles purchased and left for alterations or other reasons cannot be applied to your $100 exemption when shipped to follow at a later date.)*
4. *You have not used this $100 exemption, or any part of it, within the preceding 30-day period. Your exemption is not cumulative. If you use a portion of your exemption on entering the United States, then you must wait for 30 days before you are entitled to another exemption other than a $10 exemption.*
5. *Articles are not prohibited or restricted.*

CIGARS AND CIGARETTES: Not more than 100 cigars may be included in your exemption. There is no limitation on the number of cigarettes that may be imported for your personal use. This exemption is available to each person regardless of age. Your cigarettes, however, may be subject to a tax imposed by state and local authorities.

LIQUOR: One quart of alcoholic beverages may be included in this exemption if you are 21 years of age or older. Alcoholic beverages in excess of the one quart limitation are subject to a duty and internal revenue tax. Since state laws vary, information about such restrictions and taxes should be obtained from the state government. United States postal laws prohibit the shipment of alcoholic beverages by mail.

Articles imported in excess of your customs exemption will be subject to a duty calculated by the customs inspector, unless the items are entitled to free entry or are prohibited. The inspector will place the items having the highest rate of duty under your exemption, and any duty due will be assessed on the lower rated items. Except for custom-made articles, duty assessed will be based on the wholesale value of the articles.

Automobiles, boats, planes, or other vehicles taken abroad for non-commercial use may be returned duty-free if you can prove to the customs officer that they were taken out of the United States.

Foreign-made personal articles taken abroad, such as watches, cameras, or other articles which may be readily identified by serial number or other markings, should be registered with U.S. Customs before departure. Articles such as jewelry, clothing, etc. may also be registered if the customs officer thinks that they may be readily identified upon reentry into the U.S. All foreign-made articles are dutiable each time they are brought into the county unless you have acceptable proof of prior possession.

When registration of such articles cannot be accomplished, documents which fully describe the articles, such as bills of sale, insurance policies, or receipts for purchase or repair may be considered reasonable proof of prior possession.

Gifts valued at not more than $10 in fair retail value where shipped, can be received by friends and relations in the U.S. free of duty and tax, if the same person does not receive more than $10 in gift shipments in one day. The "day" in reference is the day in which the parcel is received for customs processing. If any article imported is subject to duty and tax, or if the total value of all articles exceeds $10, no article may be exempt from duty or tax.

Write "Unsolicited Gift—Value Under $10" in large letters on the outside of the package. Alcoholic beverages and tobacco products are not included in this privilege, nor are alcoholic perfumes valued at more than $1. Gifts mailed to friends and relatives are not declared by you on your return to the States. A "gift" parcel sent by a traveler to herself or anyone traveling with her will be subject to applicable duty and tax.

Gifts accompanying you are considered to be for your personal use and may be included within your exemption. This includes gifts given to you by others while abroad and those you intend to give to others after you return. Gifts intended for business or promotional purposes may not be included.

Household effects and tools of trade or occupation which you take out of the U.S. are duty-free at the time you return if properly declared and entered. All furniture, carpets, paintings, tableware, linens, and similar household furnishings acquired abroad may be imported free of duty if (1) they are not imported for another person or for sale, and (2) they have been used abroad by you for not less than one year (minus shipping time) or were available for use in a household in which you were a resident member for one year. This privilege does not include articles placed in storage outside the home.

Items such as wearing apparel, jewelry, photographic equipment, tape recorders, stereo components, vehicles, and consumable articles cannot be passed free of duty as household effects.

Personal belongings of United States origin are entitled to entry free of duty. Personal belongings taken abroad, such as worn clothing, etc., may be sent home by mail before you return and receive free entry provided they have not been altered or repaired while abroad. These packages should be marked "American Goods Returned." When a claim of U.S. origin is made, marking on the article to so indicate facilitates customs proceedings.

PROHIBITED AND RESTRICTED ARTICLES Certain articles considered injurious or detrimental to the general welfare of U.S. citizens are prohibited entry by law. Among these are absinthe, lottery tickets, narcotics and dangerous drugs, obscene articles and publications, seditious and treasonable materials, hazardous articles (e.g., fireworks, dangerous toys, toxic or poisonous substances) and switchblade knives. What would you be doing with those things anyway?

TRAVELING BACK AND FORTH ACROSS THE BORDER After you have crossed the U.S. boundary at one point, if you swing back into the U.S. to travel to another point in the foreign country, you run the risk of losing your customs exemption unless you meet certain requirements. If you make a "swing back," don't risk your exemptions—ask the nearest customs official about these requirements.

DUTY-FREE SHOPS Articles bought in "duty-free" shops in foreign countries are subject to U.S. Customs exemptions and restrictions.

Articles purchased in U.S. "duty-free" shops are subject to U.S. Customs duty if reentered into the U.S.

PHOTOGRAPHIC FILM All imported photographic films which accompany a traveler, if they are not for commercial purposes, may be released without examination by Customs unless there is reason to believe they contain objectionable matter.

Films prohibited from entry are those that contain obscene matter, advocate treason or insurrection against the U.S., advocate forcible resistance to any law of the U.S., or threaten the life of or infliction of bodily harm upon any person in the U.S.

Developed or undeveloped U.S. film exposed abroad (except motion-picture film to be used for commercial purposes) may enter free of duty and need not be included in your customs exemption.

Foreign film purchased abroad and prints made abroad are dutiable but may be included in your customs exemption.

Film manufactured in the U.S. and exposed abroad may be mailed home. Use the mailing device or prepaid mailer provided by the manufacturer or processing laboratory for this purpose. Mark the outside wrapper "Undeveloped photographic film of U.S. manufacture—Examine with care."

Delivery can be expedited if the package is addressed to your dealer or a processing laboratory for finishing. If the package is a prepaid processing mailer, no customs arrangements need be made. If not, arrange before you leave for the laboratory or dealer to accept and enter the film. If delivery is refused, the film must be sent to a warehouse and becomes subject to a storage fee.

If none of the above suggestions can be used, address the package to yourself.

"You are subject to local laws, no matter how different they are from ours."

SHIPPING HINTS Merchandise acquired abroad may be sent home by you or by the store where purchased. As these items do not accompany you on your return, they cannot be included in your customs exemption, and are subject to duty when received in the U.S. Duty cannot be prepaid.

All incoming shipments must be cleared through U.S. Customs. Customs employees cannot, by law, perform entry tasks for the importing public, but they will advise and give information to importers about customs requirements.

Customs officers collect no fee except the customs duty (if any) as provided for in the tariff schedules. Any other charges paid on import shipments are for handling by freight forwarders, commercial brokers, or other delivery services. Because of the difficulties and excessive expense often incurred by tourists shipping items home, the best advice is to take the item with you or send it by parcel post prepaid.

MAIL SHIPMENTS Mail shipments (including parcel post) have proven to be more convenient and less costly for travelers. Parcels must meet the mail requirements of the exporting country as to weight, size, or measurement.

The U.S. Postal Service sends all incoming foreign mail shipments to Customs for examination. Packages free of customs duty are returned to the Postal Service for delivery to you by your home post office without additional postage, handling costs, or other fees.

For packages containing dutiable articles, the customs officer will attach a mail entry showing the amount of duty to be paid and return the parcel to the Postal Service. Your postman will collect the duty and a postal handling fee when he delivers the package. If for any reason duty is later refunded, the postal handling fee will also be refunded. If an adjustment is made with a partial refund of duty, the postal handling fee will not be refunded.

EXPRESS SHIPMENTS Express shipments may be sent to the U.S. from Canada and Mexico and by air freight from other countries. The express company or its representative, when properly licensed, usually acts as the customhouse broker for you and clears the merchandise through Customs. A fee is charged for this service.

STORAGE CHARGES Freight and express packages delivered before you return (without prior arrangements for acceptance) will be placed in storage by Customs after five days, at the expense and risk of the owner. If not claimed within one year, the items will be sold. Mail parcels not claimed within thirty days will be returned to the sender.

If you have any questions and there is no customs office where you live, contact the nearest office of the District Director of Customs.

CUSTOMS DISTRICTS

STATION	ADDRESS	TELEPHONE
Anchorage, Alaska 99501	204 East Fifth Avenue	(907) 279-2543
Baltimore, Maryland 21202	103 South Gay Street	(301) 962-2666
Boston, Massachusetts 02109	2 India Street	(617) 223-6598
Bridgeport, Connecticut 06609	120 Middle Street	(203) 366-7851
Buffalo, New York, 14203	111 West Huron Street	(716) 843-5901
Charleston, South Carolina 29401	200 East Bay Street	(803) 577-4312
Chicago, Illinois 60607	55 East Monroe Street	(312) 353-4731
Cleveland, Ohio 44199	1240 East Ninth Street	(216) 522-4284
Detroit, Michigan 48226	243 West Congress Street	(313) 226-3177
Duluth, Minnesota 55802	515 West First Street	(218) 727-6692
El Paso, Texas 79985	Post Office Box 9516	(915) 533-9351
Galveston, Texas 77550	17th and Strand Street	(713) 763-1211
Great Falls, Montana 59401	215 First Avenue, North	(406) 453-7840
Honolulu, Hawaii 96806	335 Merchant Street	(808) 546-3115
Houston, Texas 77052	701 San Jacinto	(713) 226-4316
Laredo, Texas 78040	Post Office Box 758	(512) 723-5564
Los Angeles, California 90731	300 South Ferry Street	(213) 831-9281
Miami, Florida 33132	100 N.E. Seventh Street	(305 350-5791
Milwaukee, Wisconsin 53202	628 East Michigan Street	(414) 224-3924
Minneapolis, Minnesota 55401	110 South Fourth Street	(612) 725-2317
Mobile, Alabama 36602	Water and State Streets	(205) 438-4683
New Orleans, Louisiana 70130	423Canal Street	(504) 527-6353
Nogales, Arizona 85621	International & Terrace Sts.	(602) 287-3132
Norfolk, Virginia 23510	101 East Main Street	(703) 441-6546
Ogdensburg, New York 13669	127 North Water Street	(315) 393-0660
Pembina, North Dakota 58271	Post Office Building	(701) 825-6201
Philadelphia, Pennsylvania 19106	Second & Chestnut Streets	(215) 597-4605
Port Arthur, Texas 77640	Fifth & Austin Avenue	(713) 982-2831
Portland, Maine 04111	312 Fore Street	(207) 775-3131
Portland, Oregon 97209	N.W. Broadway & Glisan	(503) 221-2865
Providence, Rhode Island 02903	24 Weybosset Street	(401) 528-4383
San Diego, California 92101	2262 Columbia Street	(714) 293-5360
San Francisco, California 94126	555 Battery Street	(415) 556-4340
San Juan, Puerto Rico 00903	Post Office Box 2112	(809) 723-2091
Savannah, Georgia 31401	1-3 East Bay Street	(912) 232-4256
Seattle, Washington 98104	First and Marion Streets	(206) 442-5491
St. Albans, Vermont 05478	Main and Stebbins Streets	(802) 524-6527
St. Louis, Missouri 63101	1114 Market Street	(314) 622-4491
St. Thomas, Virgin Islands 00801	P.O. Box 518	(809) 774-2530
Tampa, Florida 33601	301 S. Ashley Drive	(813) 228-2381
Washington, D.C. 20018	3180 Bladensburg Rd. N.E.	(202) 964-8511
Wilmington, North Carolina 28401	2094 Polk Street	(919) 763-9417

A SHOULDER TO CRY ON (SOMETIMES)— YOUR AMERICAN CONSUL

IT'S A GOOD idea to register your name and local address as well as home address with the American consulate as soon as you arrive, if you are traveling sans group to a troubled area (like Belfast) or a communist country. Also bear in mind that long-term visitors or temporary residents in a country are often required to register with that country's Aliens Bureau.

28

American consuls will advise or help you if you are in *serious* difficulty or distress. However, they cannot do the work of travel agencies, information bureaus, banks and the police; nor can they help you find work or get residence or driving permits; and it is not a part of their duties to act as travel couriers or interpreters, to search for missing luggage, or to settle disputes with hotel managers. They cannot provide a free round-the-clock travel agency service, and above all cannot spare time to deal with casual inquiries. Especially during the tourist season, consuls are likely to be working under heavy pressure and must give priority to cases of grave emergency or distress.

NOW FOR WHAT THEY CAN DO. . . . If you find yourself in a dispute which could lead to legal or police action, it is wise to consult the consul. Consuls cannot give you legal advice, but if necessary they can provide a list of attorneys and tell you what local arrangements there are for free legal aid. They will also do whatever they can to protect your legitimate interests and to ensure that you receive just treatment according to local law. And they'll notify family and friends for you. Remember, be aware of the laws of the land—you are subject to local laws, no matter how different they are from ours.

If you are detained by the police or other authorities in a foreign country, you should ask at once to be allowed to communicate with the consul. He can attempt to obtain relief should you be subject to inhumane or unhealthful conditions of detention or be accorded treatment less favorable than are others in the same situation. In those countries where travel is organized by the government, the state travel agency may be better able to help and, if you find yourself in difficulties, you should make every effort to contact that agency or its local office; but then contact the consul if your problem cannot be resolved. If you urgently need the consul's help in a country where travel and communications present problems, it is usually better to telephone or telegraph rather than to send a letter.

Do not have on your person the smallest amount of any kind of illegal drug. Most countries have much stiffer drug laws than the U.S. Add that to the facts that you aren't covered by U.S. laws and constitutional rights, that foreign drug laws frequently make no distinction between soft and hard drugs, that bail is not granted in most countries in drug-trafficking cases, that you are "guilty until proven innocent," that few countries provide a jury trial, that you need not even be present at your trial, and that the average jail sentence in drug cases worldwide is about seven years.

If you run out of money abroad, the consul may be able to assist you to make inquiries of your family, friends, bankers and employers, or anyone else you may designate, to see if there is any way of getting you out of your difficulties. American consuls are not provided with funds to disburse to American citizens who find themselves in financial difficulties while abroad; nor can they cash or guarantee checks for you.

If you are injured or become seriously ill, the consul may be able to assist you to locate appropriate medical services and inform your next of kin. Note in your passport the name and address of anyone—relative, friend or legal representative—who should be informed of such an emergency.

If the city you're in has a civil disturbance or natural disaster, consult your consular office immediately. But if you can't get through the choked telephone wires, listen to the English-speaking news to keep abreast of things. If it's a natural disaster, call the largest hospital in the area and ask if there are any special precautions to take.

AMERICAN CONSULATES

COUNTRY	ADDRESS	TEL.
SOUTH PACIFIC, ASIA		
Australia	Moonah Pl., Yarralumia, A.C.T., Canberra	731351
Burma	581 Merchant St., Rangoon	18055
Cambodia-Khmer Rep.	Blvd. Preh Norodom & Samdeck Sutharot Rd., Phnom Penh	24511
Ceylon-Sri Lanka	44 Galle Rd., Colpetty, Colombo	26211
Fiji Islands	Jogia-Mistry Bldg., Cumming St., Suva	2-5304
Hong Kong	26 Garden Rd., Hong Kong	239011
India	Shanti Path, Chanakyapuri 21, New Delhi	70351
Indonesia	Medon Merdeka Selaton 5, Jakarta	40001-9
Japan	10-5 Akasaka 1-Chome Minato-Ku, Tokyo	583-7141
Malaysia	A.I.A. Bldg. Jalan Ampang, Kuala Lumpur	26321
Nepal	King's Way (Kanti Path), Katmandu	11199
New Zealand	IBM Center, 155-157, The Terrace, Wellington	41074
Philippines	1201 Roxas Blvd., Manila	58011
Singapore	30 Hill St., Singapore	30251
South Korea	82 Sejong-Ro, Seoul	722601
South Vietnam	39 Blvd. Ham-Nghi, Saigon	25251
Taiwan	2 Chung Hsiao West Rd., Second Section, Taipei	333551
Thailand	95 Wirless Rd., Bangkok	59800
EUROPE, AFRICA		
Austria	9 Boltzmanngasse 16, Vienna	346611
Belgium	27 Boulevard du Regent, Brussels	133830
Bulgaria	1 Alexander Stamboliski Boulevard, Sofia	884801
Czechoslovakia	Trziste 15, 12548 Prague	536641
Denmark	Dag Hammarskjolds Alle 24, Copenhagen	123144
Finland	Itainen Kaivopuisto 21, Helsinki	11931
France	2 Avenue Gabriel 75382, Paris	2657460
Germany	Mehlemer Avenue, Bad Godesberg, Bonn	1955
Great Britain	24 Grosvenor Square, W.1., London	4999000
Greece	91 Vasilissis Sophias Boulevard, Athens	712951
Hungary	V. Szabadsag Ter. 12, Budapest	329375
Ireland	42 Elgin Road, Ballsbridge, Dublin	64061
Israel	71 Hayarkon Street, Tel Aviv	56171
Italy	Via Veneto 119, Rome	4674
Lebanon	Corniche at Rue Ain Mreisseh, Beirut	240800
Luxembourg	22 Boulevard Emmanuel Servais, Luxemberg	40123
Morocco	2 Avenue de Marrakech, Rabat	30361
Netherlands	Museumplein 19, Amsterdam	790321
Norway	Drammensveien 18, Oslo	566880
Poland	Aleje Ujazdowskie 29/31, Warsaw	283041
Portugal	Avenue Duque de Loule 39, Lisbon	555141
Romania	Str. Tudor Argezhi 9, Bucharest	124040

Russia	Ulitsa Chaykovskogo 19/21/23, Moscow	2520011
South Africa	521 South African Mutual Building, Johannesburg	8343051
Spain	Serrano 75, Madrid	2763400
Sweden	Strandvagen 101, Stockholm	630520
Switzerland	93 Juvilaumsstrasse, Bern	430011
Turkey	110 Ataturk Boulevard, Ankara	186200
Yugoslavia	Kneza Milosa 50, Belgrade	645655

MEXICO

Mexico	Paseo de la Reforma 305, Colonia Cuauhtemoc	525-9100

CARIBBEAN

Aruba, Bonair, Curacao	St. Anna Blvd. 19, P.O. 158 Vice John B. Gorsiawea 1, Curacao	13606
Bahamas	Adderly Bldg., Nassau	322-1181
Barbados	P.O. Box 320, Bridgetown	63574
Bermuda	Vallis Bldg., Front St., Hamilton	1-2908
Dominican Rep.	Corner of Colle Cesar Nicholas Pensen and Calle Leopoldo Navarro, Santo Domingo	682-2171
Grenada, Grenadines, Haiti	Harry Truman Blvd., Port-au-Prince	2-0751
Jamaica	43 Duke St., Kingston	932-6340
Martinque (F. West Indies)	10 Rue Schoelcher, Fort-de-France	71-93-03
Trinidad & Tobago	15 Queen's Park West, Port-of-Spain	26371

CENTRAL AMERICA

Belise (Br. Honduras)	Gabourel Lane and Hutson St., Belise	3261
Costa Rica	Avenida 3 and Calle 1, San José	22-55-66
El Salvador	1230, 25 Avenida Norte, San Salvador	25-7100
Guatemala	8 Avenida 11-65, Zone 1, Guatemala	23201
Honduras	141 Avenida La Paz, Tegucigalpa	2-3121
Nicaragua	Blvd. Somoza Managua	26771
Panama	Avenida Balboa at 38th St., Panama	25-3600

SOUTH AMERICA

Argentina	Sarmiento 663, Buenos Aires	46-32-11
Bolivia	Banco Popular del Peru Bldg. (Corner of Calles Mercado y Colon), La Paz	50251
Brazil	Avenida Presidente Wilson 147, Rio de Janeiro	252-8055
Chile	Codina Bldg., 1343 Agustinas, Santiago	82801
Colombia	Edificio Bavaria Carrera, 10 No. 28-49, Bogotá	329-100
Ecuador	120 Avenida Patria, Quito	2-30020
Guyana	31 Main St., Georgetown	62686
Paraguay	1776 Mariscal Lopez Ave., Asuncion	21041
Peru	S.W. Corner Avenidas Wilson and España, Lima	286000
Surinam	Dr. Sophie Redmondstaat 13, Paramaribo	73024
Uruguay	Calle Lauro Muller 1776, Montevideo	40-90-51
Venezuela	Avenida Francisco de Miranda and Avenida Principal de la Floresta, Caracas	33-86-61

COMRADES ARE NOT ALWAYS COMRADES

COMMUNIST COUNTRY travel is a whole subject unto itself. A good general introductory rule is to always assume something is forbidden unless otherwise stated. **29** Specifics are next:

* Don't ever discuss politics.
* Don't wear provocative clothing in town anywhere. And avoid sexual entanglements; the government has been known to claim there's more politics than passion behind it.
* Don't bring in any religious articles or magazines, knives or guns, or anything even slightly pornographic (that means anything with nude pictures in it).
* Don't photograph military objects (including men in uniform), harbors or airports, hydro-electrical establishments, communications stations, scientific institutions, bridges, factories, or government offices. Don't take pictures of anything from moving planes or trains. (That seems to leave nothing but the babushka section of the GUM department store.)
* Don't sell anything (money or blue jeans or cigarettes—anything!).
* Don't engage in black-market money deals. Keep receipts of every money transaction you're involved in, including changing money and shopping. Occasionally there is something special— a duty on certain outgoing purchases over a specified amount of money, or prohibitions against making foreign currency money gifts to nationals or exchanging currency with private individuals. Since different countries have different monetary restrictions, always check upon *entering*. It's too late when you're leaving.
* Don't carry messages, money or packages of any kind into or out of any country for any other person, unless authorities of that country have confirmed that by so doing you will not be breaking their regulations.

★ Do keep track of your passport: it'll be out of your hands when you register at a hotel since they must record your presence with the police. But get it back the next day. And carry it with you *everywhere!*

★ Do pre-plan absolutely everything—not only for safety's sake, but also so you can be certain that you'll be able to do the things you want to do.

★ Do stick with your pre-arranged itinerary.

MsCellaneous

MAKING MOMENTS LAST

THE SIMPLEST camera is best unless you're really into **30** photography. I have had better luck with my cheap little Kodak Instamatic than most people have had with cameras four times as expensive (and complicated). Bring along an adjustable camera only if you know how to operate it. But stick to a simple or automatic one if you don't want to calculate exposures and set the lens.

Take a camera you already know how to use. Whether you use a camera you've had for a long time or one you've just bought for the trip, be sure to expose at least one trial roll of film and look at the results before you leave home. Check the operation of your flash as well as other photo equipment. And have a roll of film processed occasionally on your trip to be sure everything is *always* in working order.

How much film will you use? This varies, depending on your picture-taking habits and the length of your trip. You'll certainly take a lot more pictures on a trip than you would at home. Perhaps one or two twenty-exposure rolls of 135 or 126 film (or the equivalent number of exposures on other film sizes) or two or three rolls of movie film a day would be adequate if you're carrying your total supply. At least take enough film with you to get started so that you don't have to rush out to buy some at your first destination. But don't purchase foreign-made film unless you plan to have it developed there. Instamatic film cartridges, 620, 127, 35 mm, Super 8 movie film and flash bulbs/cubes are available almost anywhere you'll go. So try to take along a camera using one of those. This way you won't have to waste packing space on extra film and bulbs.

In general, it's a good idea to avoid repeated exposure of your film to x-rays. In spite of very convincing-looking signs at American airports, airport security x-rays can ruin all types of film. The best way to protect film is by using Film Shield protective leaded pouches manufactured by Sima Products Corporation of Skokie, Illinois. Or try to insist on hand inspection of your films—and be sure that the inspector doesn't then put it through a security machine! If you plan to use American mailers (like Kodak), you can send your exposed film to a Kodak processing lab instead of carrying it with you and risking exposure to x-rays.

Send your undeveloped pictures by airmail or air parcel post. Surface mail is a no-no; it increases the possibility of loss in picture quality due to delay in getting processed.

Don't postpone taking a picture because of less than ideal weather conditions. You won't have a second chance to recapture that moment, that scene.

When taking scenic pictures, remember to include people in the foreground for color and interest. If possible, have them wear bright clothing. Ask them to do something natural so that they won't stand stiffly in front of the camera. But never take pictures of people without asking them first.

Titles help you remember what you shot where. Photograph natural titles such as signposts, historical markers and familiar landmarks.

Love a scene but just ran out of film, or it's pouring, or you left your camera back at the hotel? Buy picture postcards.

When you take pictures from a moving vehicle, choose scenes that aren't too far away and photograph subjects that you are approaching or have already passed, holding your camera as close to the window as possible without touching it. Take pictures from the shaded side of the vehicle so that the sun will be behind you. If you have an adjustable still camera, use a shutter speed of 1/250 second or faster, if possible, to stop movement. With a camera that accepts interchangeable lenses, using a wide-angle lens will minimize blue in pictures made from a moving vehicle. If you're taking movies, follow these same tips and if possible film at thirty-two frames per second. The scenery will zip by quite fast in your movies if you film at the normal eighteen frames per second. If your exposure control isn't automatic, be sure to adjust the lens opening for the faster filming speed.

Now for my usual words of warning. Don't store your camera and film in sunlight or in a hot place, such as the glove compartment, dashboard, or rear-window shelf of your car. Heat can harm the camera and film. When storing your equipment in a car, put it on the floor behind the front seat, on the side opposite the exhaust pipe. To help get sharp pictures, keep the camera lens clean. Blow away any dust, or sweep it away with a small camel-hair brush; then gently wipe the lens with a clean, soft lintless cloth or special lens-cleaning paper.

On a short visit to a tropical region you should take a few precautions to protect your film from heat and humidity. When you finish exposing a roll, put it back in its plastic can if it was supplied in one. Replace the lid tightly. When it's impossible to protect the film from prolonged high heat and humidity, try to have it processed right away.

Also, protect your camera at all times by keeping it in your camera case. Make sure both your camera and case have good identification. And either bring receipts or insurance documents with you, or register the camera with customs before leaving the country, so you won't be charged import duties on it when you bring it back.

"See?
You *can* take it with you."

ELECTRICITY:
THE RIGHT CONNECTIONS

A CONVERTER is the gismo that converts 220-volt current into 110-volt current or vice-versa. An adaptor allows you to plug your appliance into different outlets. **31** Most countries don't use the two-pronged American plug. The Continental plug has two round, thin pins and will fit into most outlets around the world. There are three-pronged plugs and sockets abroad, and in some places there are even three or four kinds of plugs.

Adaptors do *not* convert voltage. They merely allow you to plug into the different types of wall receptacles around the world. You won't be able to figure out the current by looking at the outlet. Ask the hotel clerk. You can use an adaptor alone only with dual-voltage electrical devices. But with all 110V devices, you must add a converter before plugging into any 220V outlet. You can buy converters and adaptors in department or hardware stores, and sometimes you can borrow them from hotels.

Try to travel without electrical gadgets; then you won't be at the mercy of power failures (common occurrences in many countries). You have enough power struggles in life. But if you feel you *must* travel with an appliance, do have a lightweight all-purpose transformer.

Don't be foolhardy. If a foreign hotel asks you not to use electrical appliances, don't. It will be in *your* best interests to comply; a burnt out motor will render your appliance useless. (My electric Braun hairdryer blew out in Taiwan.) Since American products are designed to run on AC (alternating current), they'll burn out on DC (direct current).

Current in America is 60 cycles. On less than 60 cycles, your product may run slower but won't burn out. Actually, little differences don't really matter. 115 volts won't do anything differently than 110 would. But never take any appliances with you that will take 1,000 watts to operate. Most places just can't cope with them.

You'll notice as you travel that some hotels have 110V outlets, often marked "For Shavers Only." They'll quite safely handle 15-20 watt devices (manicure sets, electric toothbrushes), but don't use domestic appliances requiring wattage higher than the limit indicated.

See, you can take it with you.

CURRENT INFORMATION: COUNTRY-BY-COUNTRY

References to 110V apply to the range from 100V to 160V. 220V applies to the range from 200V to 260V. Where 110/220V is mentioned, voltage varies within the country.

Aden	220V	Costa Rica	110/220V
Afghanistan	220V	Cuba	110V
Algeria	110/220V	Cyprus**	220V
Angola	220V	Czechoslovakia	110/220V
Anguilla	220V	Denmark	220V
Antigua	110/220V	Dominican Rep.	110/220V
Argentina*	220V	Ecuador	110/220V
Aruba	110V	Egypt	110/220V
Australia*	220V	El Salvador	110V
Austria	220V	Fiji	220V
Azores	110/220V	Finland	220V
Bahamas	110/220V	France	110/220V
Bahrain	220V	Germany	110/220V
Bangladesh	220V	Great Britain**	220V
Barbados	110V/220V	Greece*	110/220V
Belgium	110/220V	Greenland	220V
Bermuda	110/220V	Guatemala	110/220V
Bhutan	220V	Haiti	110/220V
Bolivia	110/220V	Honduras	110/220V
Bonaire	110/220V	Hong Kong**	220V
Brazil*	110/220V	Hungary	220V
Brit. Honduras	110/220V	Iceland	220V
Brit. Virgin I.	110/220V	India	220V*
Bulgaria	110/220V	Indonesia	110/220V
Burma	220V	Iran	220V
Cambodia	110/220V	Iraq	220V
Canada	110/220V	Ireland	220V
Canal Zone	110/220V	Israel	220V
Chile	220V*	Italy	110/220V
China	220V	Ivory Coast	220V
Colombia	110V	Jamaica	110/220V

Japan	110V	Poland	110/220V
Jordan	220V	Portugal	110/220V
Kenya	220V	Puerto Rico	110V
Kuwait	220V	Rhodesia**	220V
Lebanon	110/220V	Romania	110/220V
Libya	110/220V	Saudi Arabia	110/220V
Liechtenstein	220V	Scotland	220V
Luxembourg	110/220V	Seychelles	220V
Macao	110/220V	Singapore**	110/220V
Majorca	110V	South Africa	220V
Malaysia	220V	South Korea	220V
Martinique	110/220V	Spain	110/220V
Mexico	110/220V	Sri Lanka (Ceylon)	220V
Monaco	110/220V	Sudan	220V
Morocco	110/220V	Sweden*	110/220V
Nepal	220V	Switzerland	110/220V
Netherlands	110/220V	Syria	110/220V
New Guinea	220V	Taiwan	110/220V
New Guinea	220V	Tonga	220V
New Zealand	220V	Trinidad	110/220V
Nicaragua	110/220V	Tunisia	110/220V
Nigeria**	220V	Turkey	110/220V
Northern Ireland	220V	Uruguay	220V
Norway	220V	USA	110V
Okinawa	110V	USSR	110/220V
Pakistan	220V	U.S. Virgin I.	110V
Panama	110V	Venezuela	110/220V
Paraguay*	220V	Vietnam	110/220V
Peru	220V	Wales	220V
Philippines	110/220V	Yugoslavia	220V

*Countries using DC in certain areas
**Countries in which plugs with 3 square pins are used (in whole or part)

KEEPING IN TOUCH

TYPE YOUR friends' addresses on self-adhesive labels **32** to stick on postcards. And mail early in your trip so you won't beat your cards home! Use the local stamps or cut-rate aerogrammes, but don't use stickers on the aerogrammes. If you aren't using my sticker idea, be sure you've recorded your friends' addresses. (So often we just carry around their phone numbers.) If you want to hear from your friends (and it does feel good to get mail from home), leave them your hotel addresses. If you don't have a set itinerary, have mail sent to you *Poste Restante* (general delivery) plus the name of the foreign city, plus your own name, of course. Always leave a forwarding address when you leave a hotel. Following are some useful phrases to help you keep in touch.

ENGLISH
COMMUNICATIONS

Air Mail
Letter (registered)
Post Office
Postage stamp
Telegram (cable)
Telephone
Telex

FRENCH
COMMUNICATIONS

Par avion
Lettre (recommandée)
Bureau de poste
Timbre-poste
Télégramme
Téléphone
Télex

GERMAN
KOMMUNIKATION

Luftpost
Einschreibebrief
Postamt
Briefmarke
Telegramm
Telefon
Fernschreiber

SPANISH
COMUNICACIONES

Vía aérea
Carta (certificada)
Oficina de Correos
Sello de correo
Telegrama (cable)
Teléfono
Télex

ITALIAN
COMUNICAZIONI

Posta aerea
Raccomandata
Ufficio postale
Francobollo
Telegramma
Telefono
Telex

And since phone rates fluctuate (let's face it—they don't usually go down!), this is just a general guide to give you an idea.

INTERNATIONAL TELEPHONE RATES

TO:		STATION RATES		PERSON-TO-PERSON	
		Day	Night/ Sunday	Day	Night/ Sunday
a,c,g	Argentina	$ 8.00	$ 6.50	$12.00	$ 9.00
a,c,g	Australia	9.00	6.75	12.00	9.00
a,c,d	Austria	6.75	5.10	12.00	12.00
a,c,d	Belgium	6.75	5.10	12.00	9.00
a,c,d	Brazil	9.00	6.75	12.00	9.00
a,c	Chile	8.00	6.50	12.00	9.00
a,c,d	Denmark	6.75	5.10	12.00	9.00
a,c,d	France	6.75	6.75	12.00	12.00
b,d,f	Germany	6.75	5.10	12.00	9.00
a,c,d	Greece	6.75	6.75	12.00	12.00
a,c,d	Hong Kong	8.00	8.00	12.00	12.00
a,c	Iceland	12.00	12.00	12.00	12.00
a,c,d	Ireland	5.40	4.05	9.60	7.20
a,c,d,g,i	Israel	9.00	6.75	12.00	9.00
a,c,d	Italy	6.75	5.10	12.00	9.00
a,c,d,g	Japan	9.00	6.75	12.00	9.00
c,g	Lebanon	9.00	6.75	12.00	9.00
a,c,d	Luxembourg	6.75	5.10	12.00	9.00
a,c,d	Netherlands	6.75	5.10	12.00	9.00
a,c	New Zealand	6.75	5.10	12.00	9.00
a,c,d	Norway	6.75	5.10	12.00	9.00
a,c,d	Peru	8.00	6.50	12.00	9.00
a,c,g	Philippines	9.00	6.75	12.00	9.00
c,d	Portugal	6.75	5.10	12.00	9.00
a,c,d	South Africa	9.00	9.00	12.00	12.00
a,c,d	Spain	6.75	5.10	12.00	9.00
a,c,d	Sweden	6.75	5.10	12.00	9.00
a,c,d	Switzerland	6.75	6.75	12.00	12.00
a,c,d	United Kingdom	5.40*	4.05*	9.60	7.20

a—telephone company credit cards honored for calls to U.S.
b—collect calls accepted to U.S.
c—collect calls accepted to and from U.S.
d—collect calls accepted only at person-to-person rate
e—no collect calls accepted to or from U.S.
f—reduced rates apply nights only
g—reduced rates apply Sunday only
h—evening rates for station-to-station calls also available
j—Night/Sunday rates also apply on Saturday
*—dial rate $3.60 daily

The rates quoted are for three-minute calls from the U.S. For each additional minute the charge is one-third the station-to-station rate. When a call is billed in the U.S., an excise tax is added. Collect calls and credit card calls are accepted in both directions except where noted. Collect calls are billed at the person-to-person rate unless otherwise indicated. Rates to the U.S. from abroad are in terms of the local currency and can vary from the rates shown above. Hotels outside the U.S. may add a surcharge on international calls, and these surcharges can be astronomical—as much as 100% or more! Always check before you call. In addition, there are some other things you can do to protect yourself from excessive hotel surcharges. Use a telephone credit card if possible; the surcharge on credit card calls is usually fairly reasonable. If you don't have a credit card, or if the country (like Germany) won't allow credit calls, make it a collect call, since those also have smaller surcharges. In many areas you can call from post offices or special telephone centers at the official rate. Or dial directly to the U.S. from your hotel room, dial your party and give the hotel phone number and your room number. Then ask for a call back. In Europe, you pay only for the actual length of the call. So your charge could be less than a minute.

ONCE IS NOT ENOUGH

WELL, YOU'RE back home. But you're hooked. Boston has the blahs, Dubuque is duller than ever. If only you could see one sari or have some really good won ton again or stalk a wild rhino or, or, or.... But the end doesn't have to be the end. It can be just the beginning of a lifetime of galavanting about this fascinating globe.

33

Travel should be more of a sometime thing than a one-time thing. Usually one trip inspires another. And for the next trip, you'll have learned from the first one—what you took along that you didn't need, what you left out that you shouldn't have, whether you prefer sunny Mediterranean pleasures to skiing through the snowy Alps. You'll also (probably) have finally garnered your courage to go it alone—if you haven't already. If not, you'll at least be better able to pick the exact kind of traveling companion(s) to jaunt about with.

If you have unlimited funds (and there must be *some* of you lurking about out there, Louis Vuitton luggage in hand), you can just go whenever, wherever the mood hits you. But if you're not independently wealthy, there are ways of seeing the world without blowing two months' salary on an annual two-week vacation.

You can work for the U.S. government overseas. Go to your local Civil Service Commission and register for the type of overseas job you desire—the list ranges from doctors to teachers to social workers to engineers to secretaries to economists. Most of these positions require competitive tests. If you are already working at a government agency, you can apply for an overseas transfer. Or try to work for the State Department, since you'll almost certainly be sent overseas if you pass their difficult entrance exam.

In the private sector, you can find out which American corporations have overseas branches. Write to the World Trade Academy Press, Inc., 50 E. 42nd St., New York, N.Y. 10017 for a list of U.S. companies' foreign branches. Such foreign jobs are usually only available if you have a talent another country needs and can't get from its own nationals. Don't just go abroad hoping for work,

---

"Traveling seems to become
an incurable disease, with
the symptoms eased only by
that incomparable feeling
of standing in the midst of
a totally foreign throng,
sniffing the strange smells,
hearing the different language,
seeing the various costumes. . . ."

---

however. There is unemployment almost everywhere—not to mention resident requirements; work restrictions, and other such pernicious things bureaucrats invent to keep others from fulfilling their fantasies!

Or work for an airline. You'll get terrific travel benefits even if you're not a stewardess; other often-forgotten positions with great travel advantages are in such airline jobs as reservation, ticket, and passenger agents. Or just get a job doing with them what you do for another corporation—public relations, secretarial or administrative work.

And don't forget travel agencies. Although they prefer it if you have had experience (usually from the airlines), they're worth looking into. Maybe you can get a training position with them for a start. As a travel agent you'll get lots of free trips and first class treatment; although you may find it frustrating to plan other people's treks through Kenya, world cruises, and winter jaunts to Marbella while you're in a "black out" in the Big Apple.

You could also become a free-lance travel writer. Start small. Go for a week-end trip near you, but don't tell the resort you're writing about them, or you'll never get "normal" treatment. Then send your article to your local paper. Not much of an investment—you can even do it while you're holding onto your old, more secure (?) job.

Or open a foreign clothes boutique. You'll have to go abroad to buy stock. You must get those French chemises or Italian sandles or Japanese silks *somewhere!*

Traveling seems to become an incurable disease, with the symptoms eased only by that incomparable feeling of standing in the midst of a totally foreign throng, sniffing the strange smells, hearing the different language, seeing the various costumes—all of it enveloping you in that exciting feeling of having been transported to another time and place. Which you have been. So don't get "well"—keep that obsessive travel bug for a lifetime. You can travel as long as you can literally get about. I've seen vacationing American women in their 80s sprinting past pack-on-their-back youth hostellers in Malaysia! I've also seen people not in such good physical shape (but still with a love of what's out there), taking an easier form of getting about (ships) or going to places where the going is easier (Naples, not Nepal).

So what are you waiting for? Re-read this book and get going—again!